MARYKNOLL'S FIRST LADY

MARYKNOLL'S
FIRST LADY

by Sister Jeanne Marie

Illustrated with photographs

DODD, MEAD & COMPANY

NEW YORK

Library of Congress Catalog Card Number: 64-12763

Printed in the United States of America
by The Cornwall Press, Inc., Cornwall, N.Y.

CONTENTS

CONTENTS

PART IV

All That Comes

ILLUSTRATIONS

Following page 152

PART I

The Time of the Star

—◦◦◦

" 'The Magi, seeing the star, said to each other:
This is the sign of the great King: let us go
and seek him . . .'

"This star Bossuet calls 'inspiration of the
heart' and to St. Leo it is 'the sign of grace.' "
—Mother Mary Joseph

CHAPTER 1

MOLLIE

I T WAS A LOVELY June evening in Northampton. On the campus of Smith College the scent of flowers hung in the warm still air. Among the black masses of the trees, lights shone from the college buildings and made golden rectangles on the darkening lawns. From the open windows came the chime of girls' voices and away in the distance the sound of a song and a mandolin.

The tall girl on her way to the Students Building walked lightly along, not hurrying. Now that she was away from the end-of-semester hubbub in her residence hall, she was full of long, long thoughts. On such a night as this, the past seems but a beautiful extension of a meaningful present and the mystery of tomorrow hints that it may be about to reveal itself. Life is a ripe fruit in the hand—ready and sweet. Mollie was asking herself what she was going to do with it.

She was a junior now, her evolution from freshman days mirrored in the Gibson girl pompadour and styling which had replaced the long copper-colored braid and girlish dresses of her first year at Smith. This time next year she would be a senior. She would wear a long white dress and walk in a procession with some two hundred graduates of the class of 1905. They would be flanked by pretty juniors carrying long ropes of laurel and eager to take from their seniors' hands the relinquished lines of leadership.

For a week everything would be "the graduates." They would plant ivy. They would be feted by their friends. They would be addressed by President Seelye in a final effort to fashion them into intelligent gentlewomen and socially responsible Christians. They would be congratulated discreetly by those members of the faculty who deemed congratulations their due. They would all be sung to without discrimination by the Glee Club. Finally, in a climactic ceremony of stateliness and sentiment, they would be handed their diplomas. And after that, then what?

There was one thing that Mollie knew that she would not be. When still at West Roxbury High School, she had let her handsome father know that she wanted to become a trained nurse. Usually she could win him to see things her way. This time she failed. Florence Nightingale and Sarah Barton notwithstanding, Mr. Rogers thought nursing entirely unsuitable for any young lady, including Mollie. He could not and would not consider it. Always sure that a man who loved his children as much as he did must know what is best for them, he told her to put that idea right out of her head.

Mollie was disappointed but by no means inconsolable. To love people in a practical as well as a personal fashion was her first inclination. She already knew all sorts of ways to do that and, nurse or no nurse, she could learn more.

Recently Mrs. O'Donnell, a friend of the Rogers family who lived in Northampton and had several grown stepsons, had spoken to Mollie about her future, concluding by saying, "At your age a young woman should be thinking about marrying and raising a family. You don't seem to have anybody in mind."

With the stepsons standing in the wings, as it were, of this little conversation, Mollie may have been amused, but she said only, "No, I'm not interested in anybody in particular, but I do think that I'll have a family someday."

She certainly seemed suited to have a family. People were her first interest, her main occupation, her favorite pastime. Even when she was in grade school she was referred to as motherly; at home she played a supportive second to her mother's gentle first; and here at Smith, classmates who knew her best early nicknamed her "Mother in Israel."

Although she could not read her own future at this point, Mollie could guess what some of these classmates were going to do. Elsie Mason? So full of life and fun, so solidly good, she had doubtless already made up her mind to marry that grave good-looking young man who had turned up to squire her to the Prom. Meta too would probably marry. Wherever she was, Sara Lauter would be the center of a whirlwind of activity. Joe Webster and Ruth Cook? They would find ways to share their gifts and goodness—through teaching, perhaps.

And what of Harriet Shadd? Would she go from hurt to hurt, blocked from personal fulfillment by barriers not of her own making? Mollie had thought about Harriet a great deal lately. Although not as closely associated with this refined and vivacious young girl as with those in her own residence, Mollie had a special love for her.

For one thing, they had met their first day at Smith at the Registrar's office, where both had gone for the academic fine-tooth-combing for which the Registrar was well known. Harriet, lonely and fearful, had responded with a full heart to Mollie's warm smile. They waited for each other and walked home together and so began a lasting friendship.

For another thing, Mollie had recently had a revelation of what life was like for Harriet, who looked Italian or perhaps Jewish, with fine features and olive skin, but was neither. She was a Washingtonian of both white and Negro blood. What this meant to one of her gifts and means and opportunities had been partially disclosed just a few weeks ago at the time of the Junior Prom.

The Junior Prom was the one social affair at Smith in the early nineteen hundreds to which young men were bidden. At other times, they might call under carefully specified conditions, but for a Smith girl to go out riding unchaperoned with one of these scarcely tolerated creatures merited expulsion. Appeal to Miss Eastman, the registrar, who was also a sort of dean of discipline, was usually fruitless, but it was tried.

"Miss Eastman, a young man, a friend of the family, would like to take me driving."

"Alone?"

"Yes. It is his idea, of course."

"Am I to understand from this that you are engaged to this young man?"

"No, I'm not, but I think if you let me go, I will be."

As a result of restricted visiting privileges and ubiquitous chaperonage, the Junior Prom had overweighted importance. Not to have an escort for the Prom was unthinkable. To have one both tall and handsome was very heaven. With delicate determination, the girls shopped around for the best specimens obtainable. In general, escorts were not difficult to secure. In addition to standing with a pretty girl in the blossoming apple orchard and being serenaded by scores of others playing mandolins and guitars, the dance at night and the following day's outing, the fact that an invitation was a kind of accolade to one's manly beauty, all had persuasive force. Apollos, of course, were not flooding the market.

One of the young Rogers who fulfilled specifications was to accompany Harriet, but at very nearly the last minute Harriet came to beg off. A collegian from Washington who *knew* had been to her to say, "How can you? You mean to say they don't *know?* What an awful thing for you to do! If you don't tell them, I will."

Anne Rogers, now a senior and Mollie's attractive cousin, saw no reason why they should change their plans. Mollie would not let Harriet off. The whole party closed ranks around her both at the dance and on the next day's outing on which about a dozen of them went together. Always well dressed, Harriet looked charming and seemed especially gay when picnicking at Whately Glen. However, when it came time to take pictures and Mollie tucked Harriet's hand through her arm and drew her to her side, Harriet shrank behind her out of sight. Those who *knew,* whether on one side of the barrier or the other, were to have no record of her in that group.

The kind of handicaps which Harriet faced, both within herself and without, Mollie had never known. Fourth in a family of eight children, she had been surrounded with love and regard from the time she was born. She was hardly in the world when her father, with three boys already showing him how challenging even young sons can be, was out among his neighbors passing around cigars because now, on October 27, 1882, he had a daughter.

Here was a girl who, he hoped, would be a mirror of her mother, whose even disposition, common sense, and gentleness were a perfect foil for his own quick intelligence and instantaneous reactions. A father deserving of the title had to be a demanding and dramatic head of the house. Just the same, it was a relief for him as well as for his children to have a wife, and now perhaps a daughter too, who would win him to sacrifice some order and proper discipline to affection and tranquillity.

Because she grew up as the beloved eldest daughter in a closely knit family with a wide circle of friends and relatives all in communication and sympathy with one another; because this small world fitted easily into a larger community in which the Rogers were not only accepted but exercised some leadership; because she herself was a child brimming with happiness and affection, more conscious of others' needs and wants than her own, Mollie had never experienced the radical uncertainty, the sharpened sensitivity, the disguised anguish and recurring rebelliousness which rejection brings.

Since her recent insight into the revelation of Harriet's world, both inner and outer, Mollie felt not only compassion for her but a new admiration—for her courage, the integrity that had survived so many corroding experiences, the enduring impulse toward the best in life.

Mollie admired many other girls whom she knew at Smith. Almost all Protestant, they were upright and principled Christians. More than once they had led her to re-examine the treasure of her Catholicity and to question her dedication to her own faith.

One morning, returning from early Mass, she ran up the steps of her residence feeling pleasantly hungry and thinking of the good breakfast that she was going to have. Another interesting day lay ahead and her spirits rose to meet it.

Coming in out of the light, she almost ran into one of the girls standing silently in the hallway watching her.

"Where have you been?" asked the girl. "Where do you go in the mornings?"

"To St. Mary's," said Mollie, smiling, "to Mass."

"Every day?"

"Just about every day, yes."

"You receive?"

"Yes."

"And you really believe that God comes to you—like that—every morning?"

Out of the fullness of her certainty, Mollie answered softly, "Of course I do."

Even in the subdued light of the hallway she could see the sudden tears rise in the eyes of the other.

"Oh, if I believed that!" said the girl, and turned away.

Mollie stood there for a moment. And I who do believe it had my mind on my breakfast, she thought.

That was the point of her probing now. I who believe, I who have the fullness of faith, I who have received so much, what am I doing with what God has given me? What have I actually done here at Smith and what will I do when I have graduated? I once had such dreams.

So she had. They had begun early. As a little girl she had dreamed, among other things, of being a missionary. Moved by many influences, from her doll collection of different nations to the stories read and told to her by her father about unhappy, neglected children like Oliver Twist to the accounts later spelled out in the *Annals* of the Holy Childhood and of the Propagation of the Faith, she had had reveries of a heroic career in which she would be a great help to the world. Xavier-like but even more successful, she would convert whole cities in faraway Oriental places.

However, she had also had less exalted dreams of growing up and owning a soda fountain to which she and all her friends could resort at will and without cost. And, when actually faced with a single Oriental, she had manifested anything but an apostolic disposition.

Visiting Great-Uncle George Plummer, a retired Salem sea captain, when she was still in the pre-school set, she was so frightened by his Chinese houseboy that she could scarcely eat when he appeared to wait at table. When he undertook to reassure her by grinning at her like a cheerful jack-o'-lantern, she was terrified. Time to go home could not come soon enough. She was so anxious to get away that she hurried out like an escaping Red Ridinghood, leaving behind a little red cape which was both new and much prized.

Now, some fifteen years later, as she walked along, a self-possessed and self-questioning young woman, a quaint childhood prayer that she had once made up came back to her together with the circumstances that had evoked it.

When quite small, she had overheard the grownups talking about someone who had died suddenly and who had "certainly been no credit to the Church."

From this conversation, Mollie, the little pitcher with big ears, had gleaned two massive ideas—death and scandal. Dying meant going to heaven, as her mother had told her, but it also meant leaving behind everybody who wasn't dying, too. That would never do for her family. It was unthinkable that any one of them—father or mother or Bill or Leo or Ned or herself— would go anywhere all alone, whether to Uncle Joe's or Uncle Frank's or Aunt Annie's or even to heaven. It just couldn't be.

From the attitude of the grownups she gathered that not being a credit to the Church meant something equally bad if not as hurting.

That night, saying her bedtime prayers aloud as usual, she laid both these new and ponderous problems in the lap of God in one short trustful petition, "Dear Jesus, let us all drop down dead together and please let me be a credit to the Church. Amen."

She repeated the petition now, amused at herself, yet experiencing again the faith and need of the child who had first made it.

Walking slowly, her mind flooded with thoughts of the future and memories of the past, Mollie had almost reached the Students Building. She noticed that it was well lighted and from the sound of voices and the sight of moving figures within the windows, concluded that at least one gathering was being held. Something was always going on there, club and society meetings, dances and dramatics, lectures and informal groups planning for all kinds of college activities. Tonight was apparently no exception.

Then suddenly the heavy doors were thrown open and excited girls poured out of the building and down the steps and over the paths and lawn. Among them, Mollie saw some officers of the Smith College Association for Christian Work and a number of girls whom she knew to be active in the college Missionary Society.

About five or six girls seemed to be the focus of the excitement. The others gathered around them exclaiming, laughing, talking.

"What's going on?" Mollie asked a little knot of nearly breathless girls who passed near her, all talking at once.

She was drenched in a little cloudburst of replies.

"Student volunteers!"

"They've just pledged themselves."

"Signed up."

"They're going to be missionaries."

"Leaving in September—for all sorts of places."

"For seven years."

"Or even longer maybe."

The girls detached themselves from her and hurried over to join the circle now forming around the volunteers.

Mollie looked. She saw Ethel, one of the idols of the college, sweet and kind as well as beautiful, talented, and well-to-do. Near her stood Marian, hardly less popular and less blessed. The others, too, were fine types of young American womanhood. Outlined in the light of the open doorway, in their light dresses, with piled-up hair accenting the delicate line of their throats, they looked particularly young, fragile, and feminine. Their very appearance seemed to accent their sacrifice.

The circle around them joined hands, spread out, and began to sing, "Onward, Christian Soldiers!"

As Mollie turned away, their young voices filled the night with exultation. She felt overcome. She forgot that she was going to the Students Building and what she had intended to do there. There was only one place where she wanted to go, one Presence in which she wanted to be. She took the shortest route there.

The door of St. Mary's Church was open. Mollie went inside, slid into a pew and knelt down. There she reached something that was part realization, part decision, part prayer: she would do something for the missionary work of the Church, even if for the present she could not see when or how or where she would do it.

She had been moving toward this turning point for some time. Her first year at Smith, before she had settled in at 17 Belmont Avenue, where she shared a room with Anne Rogers, a group of girls came knocking at her door. Mollie was still unpacking.

"We've come to sign you up," they said.

"You have? What for?" asked Mollie, drawing them into the room with her smile.

"One of the mission study classes," said the girls. "Which one would you like to join?"

"Well," said Mollie, "I'm a Catholic. So I'll have to join the Catholic group." She looked from one to the other in her frank and friendly way.

Presbyterian glanced at Methodist and Unitarian at Congregationalist. The Catholic mission study club?

Someone said, "There isn't any."

Someone added quickly, "But you would be welcome at any of the others, if you would like to join one."

Mollie thanked them warmly and declined. Certainly, she thought, Anne and I aren't the only Catholics at Smith. Why isn't there a Catholic mission group like the others?

She doubted that the college administration would discourage it. Everything that she had learned from Anne, from her teachers at West Roxbury High, made her feel that there was little, if any, prejudice against Catholics at Smith. She knew that President Seelye, himself a Congregationalist minister who had chosen an academic career in preference to pastoral living, insisted on Christian virtue and religious worship but showed no bias in regard to any particular group. Every girl had to attend services on Sunday. Where she went was her own affair. She also attended what was called "chapel" daily, a twenty-minute assembly period preceding the day's classes held in College Hall. A passage from Scripture was read, a hymn was sung or one of the psalms was chanted antiphonally, a short talk was given by one of the faculty or by some visiting celebrity. Weekly President Seelye appeared to conduct these exercises. From his extemporaneous prayers, students who had not kept up on current affairs could glean some information about events.

Among the predominantly Protestant student body, although there was no evidence of prejudice against their Catholic fellow students, there was some curiosity about them. The Protestant girls took it for granted that they themselves were the normal variety of Christian and the Catholics, the exotic. They had an impulse to probe, to question them, but good principles and good manners both prevented their interest from becoming either obnoxious or oppressive. Mollie never minded their inquiries and answered them as well as she could. When she felt that she was out of her depth, she had recourse both to the fine library which the pastor, Father Kenny, had inherited at St. Mary's rectory and to Father Michael Welch, his curate and Mollie's confessor.

What of the Catholics themselves? Comparatively few in number, they might be, as minorities are apt to be (and in this case, for evident historical reasons), too timid, too suspicious or too individually aggressive for successful group action. Whatever the tolerant climate at Smith, there still hung over Massachusetts some of the heavy atmosphere created by the all-too-recent A.P.A. movement, the protracted legal struggle over the Catholic parochial schools, and the long history of conflict and animosity between early arriving Yankee and late-comer Irish. The former felt economically and politically threatened by the mounting flood of Irish immigrants who fled to the United States to escape starvation in the old country. As the established

Yankee saw it, New England was in danger of becoming New Ireland. The Irish, for their part, bitterly resented being faced in their adopted homeland with opposition and discrimination from people of the same heritage—transplanted Englishmen—who had helped to make life in Ireland unlivable for them and theirs.

Grandfather Rogers had known what Irish-Yankee tension meant. Arriving in the new world just ahead of the cresting flood of his countrymen who fled the climatic disaster of the potato famine of 1845, he took his place in the vanguard of the ascending Irish. Young Yankees might snowball him because he was that almost unheard-of phenomenon—a northern Democrat—but he was on his quiet way upward economically and politically, early to become a builder and a member of the Common Council, an investor in real estate, and an outstanding taxpayer. Over six feet tall, slender, with fine features and quiet ways, he may have advanced so fast partly because Grandmother Rogers had a figurative finger in the middle of his back urging him ahead.

When they were both new immigrants in Canada, he a young carpenter, she a striking-looking eighteen, with her mother just dead and three younger sisters on her hands, he had asked her the momentous question, "Will you marry me, Mary Dunn?"

And she had answered, "I will—when you take me and my sisters to Boston."

It was the first hurdle that she set for him. He took it successfully.

In Boston, Patrick and Mary Rogers felt, as did all the Irish of their day, the external pressure exerted against them in business, politics, and social life. For able, intelligent, and determined people, this could prove more challenging than obstructive.

In Grandfather Plummer's house, on the other hand, the tension came not from without but from within. The dialectic between new Catholic Irish and old Puritan Yankee played itself out inside the home. Grandmother Plummer had been Bridget Josephine Kennedy, a lovely young woman who had charmed William Gardner Plummer right off his Calvinistic foundations. He not only married her, but did so in a Catholic ceremony to boot. He was an eighth-generation Yankee, whose chief religion was apparently more anti-Catholicism than Congregationalism. His people were Salem folk, but he lived in Charlestown, where in 1834 the bigots of the town distinguished themselves by burning down the Ursuline convent. He loved his wife—as did everyone who knew her—and as he grew older his natural goodness overcame much of his earlier prejudice, so that his grandchildren were both unafraid and affectionate with him. But when his own children were growing up, he gave in only reluctantly, and with sudden outbursts of anger and frightening scenes, to his wife's gentle but unrelenting insistence that their children be allowed to practice their Catholic faith. Mollie's mother never forgot some of these family impasses and how it felt to be obliged to go to a neighbor's house to get dressed in the white dress and veil that she would wear to her First Communion.

The sons of Patrick and Mary Dunn Rogers—Joseph, Francis, and Abraham—walked in their father's shadow, protected by his stature from the cold winds that he had had to face. A change was taking place, yet they too knew the meaning of anti-Catholic and anti-Irish sentiment. They felt it sometimes at school, met it in the shops and stores which hung out employment notices with a harsh postscript, "No Irish need apply." They ran into it occasionally even in those places especially beloved by boys—the firehouses, the livery stables, the waterfront.

Nevertheless, that they belonged any place else than in New England, that they were anything else but Americans, that they were going to do anything else but make a success of whatever they decided to undertake did not enter their heads. They stuck together, backed each other up, and fought each other's battles

as did other brothers who were not Catholics and second-genera-
tion Irish-Americans.

Even when the brothers married and established their own
homes, they did not lose their sense of partnership and to some
extent at least looked upon their fortunes and misfortunes, their
political thinking and acting, the raising and education of
their families, as joint projects.

Among their families, and their sister's as well, there was
much visiting back and forth. In the summer they all forgath-
ered with Frank at Rochdale, Rhode Island, for at least one full
convocation of the clan. They had carefully arranged and elabo-
rately engineered outings together to Revere Beach and to
Haughton's Pond, where the grownups relaxed under the evergreens and the children exhausted themselves running in and
out of the water, playing games, and eating the good things
which their mothers had packed into hampers and brought
along in the carriages.

When they were all together, Abraham could not help remarking that although he was the youngest, he had the largest
family. He was immensely pleased with his children and proud
both of what they were and of what they were on the way to
becoming. His hopes metamorphosed into plans which, as the
children grew up, became more and more definite. There were
enough boys for each one of the professions and an extra one to
be a priest, should God grant him that grace.

With his wife, he was completely content. He did not want
her modified in the slightest degree. He could think of nothing
that would improve her. He would bring an unexpected guest
home to dinner and introduce him to his wife, going on to demand proudly, "Isn't she wonderful? Would you ever think to
look at her that she could be the mother of those great strapping
boys?"

This might be a little opportune flattery at the moment, but
it was also his confirmed conviction that she was a wonderful

woman, ever young, ever satisfying to the eye as well as the heart. Even Grandmother Rogers found little that could be changed for the better in her daughter-in-law. It was well that she thought so, because after the death of Patrick Rogers, Grandma made one of her decisive moves. She divided her husband's legacy among his four children and went to stay with each family as she had a mind. She spent a good bit of her time with Abraham's family. He was the youngest, he had the most forbearing wife and the largest number of children. In his home Grandma had the most scope for her managerial talent, which was considerable.

She undertook to better everybody within reach, not excepting Mr. Abraham Rogers himself. It astonished those who held in awe this white-haired, impressive-looking man to see him accepting her admonitions and directives with some show of meekness.

Grandma's activities were not altogether penitential for those with whom she lived. She had the capacity to admire as well as to criticize, to applaud as well as to deride. She loved to listen to Bill's nearly word-for-word account of any affair that he attended—whether it was a Sunday sermon or "The Prince of Pilsen." He had an excellent memory, a good singing voice and played the violin well. He was both a mime and mimic with a real gift for comedy. When one of his productions—whether a monologue or a drama with a full cast of younger brothers and sisters—went too far and he was banished from the scene, he would comfort himself with the observation, "Well, even if he did send me upstairs, I made the old man laugh first." As the oldest brother, he was apt both to make and to exact sacrifices for the sake of his art. When he was still quite small, and Mollie smaller, one of her dolls lost its pretty head in a realistic dramatization of "Mary Queen of Scots."

Leo was early tall and distinguished-looking and Grandma doted on him. When he took his mandolin on his knee and played for her, he was, as far as she was concerned, irresistible. She took an outspoken pleasure in Elizabeth's good looks. "She is like my sister Teresa," she would say, as one bestowing the ultimate accolade.

Grandma liked to be read to, both to encourage good reading as well as for the pleasure of listening. Her son Abraham read well, his voice, his diction, his interpretation all a gratification to hear. She wanted her grandchildren to be equally accomplished. She would seize upon an available child of reading age and set him to the task. If her standards were not met, she was not one to suffer in silence.

"Josie," she would say to her patient daughter-in-law, "have you ever heard anything as tiresome as that child?" "That child" would know it was time to make a quiet departure.

On Mollie as the oldest daughter, Abraham's joy and idol, Grandma expended considerable effort. When Mollie was younger and racketed up and down the stairs, Grandma made her retrace her steps and re-walk them. Grandma had her parade back and forth in front of her with a book on her head to improve her posture and carriage. As to her appearance, Grandma conceded that Mollie's hair was beautiful. She would not have denied that she had fine eyes. Her nose, however, although straight like her father's, had to the old lady's eyes nothing patrician about it. Grandma's was aquiline. She liked noses with character to them. During one of her visits, she decided that something should be done about Mollie's nose. She would stop by Mollie's room after she was in bed and put a clothespin on that offending feature. How long it stayed on after Grandma left the room was Mollie's secret. Her nose remained like her father's to the end of her life.

All this, one might think, would destroy any ambition that Mollie might have had to be "a real Irish lady," her grandmother's standard of perfection, but it did not. She somehow caught the ideal to which the old lady was so dedicated, no matter how preposterous her approaches to the goal might be. Already Mollie had a talent for seeing what was good in the anomalous mixture of human ends and endeavors.

As Mollie grew older, Grandma kept a vigilant eye on her friends. She noticed that they were not all of the right sort, the sort that Grandma approved.

"Who is that child?" she would ask. "What is her name? Where does she live? In a house or a flat?" To Grandma's thinking, anyone who lived in a flat was a questionable character. Mollie, who realized that flats were in houses, had no difficulty with that line of inquiry.

"Mollie, that boy you are going out with, what does his father do?"

"He's an iceman, Grandma."

"Of course. I know he is a nice man. But what does he *do?*"

But Mollie had already made good her escape with the son of the nice iceman.

Another boy courageous enough to come to see Mollie while Grandma was on sentry duty was also diplomatic enough to propitiate Grandma with a box of candy. She was mollified, took one piece, and broke her bridge on it. That boy was forever an exile from her favor.

In a small house with one or two children, the presence of an outright autocrat like Grandma could have been overpowering. In the big old neoclassical house on Robinwood Avenue which teemed with energy and activity, friends and fun, it acted only as a mild depressant. The older boys felt its effect the least, the younger children—Louise, John, and Abe—the most. But even they could hear the big rosary which their grandmother wore or carried rattling along the upper hall or down the circular stairway and could make their escape or, if cornered, exercise their charm upon her. To this she was not immune. Most of the time, they simply took her for granted as they did their father's notable combination of stern and tender qualities.

When Mr. Rogers said "Go!" his sons went; when he said "Don't!" they didn't; when he said "That's enough!", they had no doubt that it was. Just the same, they loved to be around him, to be chosen to drive with him, to do something, anything, for and with him. What a man he was to go camping with! He was good at anything—putting up tents, fishing, rowing. On top of that, he could recite poems right out of his head and even, sometimes, make them up as he went along. And what stories he could tell! And who could sing like he did? When the family orchestra got going and the few who weren't playing some instrument were at least singing their heads off—his voice was the best thing of all. And when Mollie went to the piano and he started out with something on his own like "Polly Perkins" or "Florence and Paul," he was better than anybody that they had ever heard. It gave you pins and needles when he got going on "The Larboard Watch Ahoy!" His voice was like a bass violin, like a drum. He was really great. They were proud of him.

On Sunday afternoons Mr. Rogers liked a small span of leisure, a minimum of quiet, in which he could devote himself to reading and could learn what his beloved John Boyle O'Reilly had to say that week. Surrounded with babbling small fry, he would finally break into an exasperated roar, "Quiet, you young ignoramuses, while I read *The Boston Pilot!*" The small fry would scatter, little visitors shaken, the Rogers temporarily subdued. Later the same day, the same afternoon, the same man would be the charmer around whom they all gathered, drifting back to have him read or sing to them. The smallest Rogers would climb into his lap, several others would lean against his chair, and the rest came as close as they could without suffocating him.

In the big dining room he presided at meals like a patriarch. Rarely did less than twelve sit down at the long table and often there were twenty. Not only mother and father had their friends to dinner but the children too knew that they could invite members of their own special little coteries. An extra leaf or two might have to be added to the table and that was all there was to it.

With such numbers and such spirits there were, of course, occasional scenes at meals. On these Mr. Rogers drew the curtain. Children whose manners went into eclipse or whose control folded up were banished with a look or a word.

There was one famous occasion when Mr. Rogers was so overcome that he forgot to exile the culprits. It happened as a result of a rainy day. On rainy days, the Rogers children and their friends sometimes took to the attic to amuse themselves. There they discovered or rediscovered all sorts of old treasures. The girls would dress up in discarded finery. Louise loved to take out her mother's pale blue wedding dress and admire it—the interesting bustle, the little buttons that went all the way down the front. It was still beautiful and she loved everything beautiful.

The boys would be into everything. One day they made a great find—a diary which Mr. Rogers had kept before his marriage. There were some tender passages in it about Josie.

"Listen to this!" The boys gathered around.

That night at dinner—at which there were guests, including one of the pretty O'Connell girls, before whom the boys liked to show off—they watched for a break in the conversation. It came.

" 'Today,' " quoted the ringleader dramatically, " 'I bought a bunch of bananas and walked over to see Josie.' "

" 'When I got there, she was playing the piano,' " continued an accomplice.

" 'So I stood outside the window,' " went on another, " 'looking in and watching her.' "

Mr. Rogers, a large man, began to get much larger. This passage of bananas and sentiment evidently sounded familiar to him, although it was basely corrupted by being mouthed by these young villains whom he had fathered.

" 'Later I went in and gave her the bananas,' " concluded the ringleader, knowing from the storm signals that it was time, and past time, to stop.

For a fearful moment Mr. Rogers could say nothing. His florid face flushed to the roots of his white hair, which bristled as if electrified. He looked as if he were about to disintegrate. Then the dam broke, the floods were released.

"How anybody I helped bring into the world could do anything as contemptible as to pry into the private papers of someone else is beyond my comprehension. It is inconceivable to me how a person with a modicum of honor . . ."

Once he had begun, he had no difficulty continuing. He had an excellent vocabulary and a fine delivery. It was an awesome but satisfying performance. The boys ate silently but with good appetites. It was well worth the trouble that they had taken and the considerable risk which they had been willing to run. And one wonderful thing about Pa was that, when he got over being mad, he was really over it, especially if you could get Mollie to talk to him before he talked to you.

Mollie was often the mediator for the boys with their father. Sometimes, especially as they grew older, she was also her father's unappointed ambassador with the boys, helping them to recognize his love for them even when it was expressed in ways that they found hard to understand or accept—ordering their lives, choosing their careers, attempting to direct their interests and form their tastes. Mollie had a way of upholding everybody without condemning anybody.

Her two younger brothers she openly mothered as far as their manliness allowed. They never objected to being helped with their lessons; at any time they were glad to find a sympathetic listener to whom to relay some tale of victory or defeat; they sometimes sought comfort and healing when life dealt them blows, physical or otherwise.

Louise, sensitive to every nuance in human relationships and to every manifestation both of beauty and of ugliness, had the temperament that went with her outstanding musical gifts. This little sister Mollie shielded as much as she could from the normal day-to-day psychological buffeting in a household of five vigorous brothers and a positive father. Elizabeth, Mollie rarely needed to champion. Elizabeth knew how to look out for herself and to make other people, not excepting Grandma Rogers, admire her doing it.

Ned needed Mollie in his own individual way. She did much to provide the atmosphere of affection and admiration which his reticent and sharply perceptive nature required for the development of his considerable gifts. Between these two, so near in age and yet so different in temperament, there was complete understanding and compatibility. Mollie could hardly stand to have Ned criticized, much less punished, and she would threaten Elizabeth not to dare to tattle on him when his performance fell below his father's ideal.

For Mollie to threaten was far from habitual. For her to argue was rare. For her to fight was unheard of. Yet when she was seventy she could still vividly recall the one occasion when she undertook to right wrongs with physical force.

It was a familiar story pattern but in reverse. Two boys in the neighborhood, one big, one little, used to fight. Mollie had watched more than once while the small boy picked on and beat up the big one, who was slow, probably stupid, perhaps cowardly. His small challenger was fast, knowing, and ruthless. The impotent misery of his big victim touched Mollie to the quick. She was witness to just one too many beatings. She suddenly jumped into the fray, copper-colored pigtails flying, Grandma's specifications for Irish ladies completely forgotten. The big boy disengaged himself and let her take over. She turned the tables on his small opponent, taking whatever punishment this demanded.

The sensational news of her intervention traveled fast, flew up the front steps and burst into the Rogers unlocked front door. "Mollie! Mollie is having a fight!"

An older brother was sent to save her if necessary and to bring her home in any case. When he arrived, she had already finished what she had begun. Big boy and little boy had both withdrawn from the field. Aghast at herself, rather than afraid of any consequences, Mollie had taken deep refuge in a tangle of thorn bushes. In cold blood, her brother lacked the courage to go in after her. He patrolled the edge of her retreat unhappily.

"Come on out, Mollie," he urged. "Come on home."

"No," said Mollie.

"Nobody's going to do anything to you."

Mollie shook her head. There were tears as well as scratches on her cheeks. Whether anybody was going to do anything to her or not, she needed time to get over what had happened—not just so much being beaten up outside but being all wild and raging inside as well.

In stair-step formation the Rogers children moved through the local public schools. At the grade-school level the boys attended Agasy; the girls, Bowditch. When they had graduated from the ninth grade, boys and girls were reunited at West Roxbury High School. Mollie was glad to get there, not just to be in high school but because she and Ned would be together. By this time, the majority of the boys were recovering from their disdain of girls and the girls were abandoning their defensive secret societies, in which the members were identified not by special handclasps but by the color of the ribbons which they wore.

West Roxbury High School offered a three-year course leading to a diploma and then, for those interested and able, a fourth year of college preparation. This the Rogers elected. School discipline was strict and upheld by parents. The program of studies was ambitious and the teachers were dedicated and demanding. Their pupils held them somewhat in awe and, for the most part, tried to live up to the high standards which they set, sure that, if they were interested and studious, they would be given additional time and help and, if they were slack, they would meet with little mercy. They were administered strong doses of history, English language and literature, mathematics and science, Latin, Greek, and a modern language. They finished their twelve years of schooling with a marked ability to use the English language both in speaking and in writing.

At school, Christian beliefs and ethics were taken for granted. At home, father and mother alike taught the Rogers children what their Catholic faith meant both through instruction and, even more tellingly, through the values and customs of their home. They insisted upon the children attending Sunday school, although this sometimes meant the reluctant sacrifice of an enticing Sunday afternoon outing or frolic at home. They helped them to memorize their catechism and to prepare well for the reception of the Sacraments.

Once the children had received their First Holy Communion —done rather late as was customary before Pius X made it clear that little children were invited to the Lord's table—they all went together to an early Mass and Holy Communion on the first Friday of the month. On other weekdays nothing so ambitious as a full family exodus was attempted and on Sundays more Masses meant greater latitude of choice.

The night before first Friday, everybody, of course, wanted to go to Mass the next day, but at six o'clock in the morning Mr. Rogers' generalship was needed to get everybody up, fittingly clothed, and on their way in time. Sometimes Grandma Rogers was on hand to give an assist with late risers by applying cold wet washcloths. As a team, she and her son were eminently effective.

Mr. Rogers was largely responsible, too, for the successful launching of the after-dinner rosary. Before it was completed, little Abe might fall asleep and have to be carried to bed. John might get the giggles and have to be banished, but, running his fine eyes around the group, Mr. Rogers would see with satisfaction that all were there to begin.

When the young Rogers gathered around the big table in the upper hall to settle down to their lessons, Ned noticed how Mollie always had time to help anybody wrestling with a difficulty—whether it was an arithmetic problem or a tough passage of French. Nobody could call her a grind, she always seemed to have time for other things besides studying, but she certainly did well at school, not just at lessons, but at everything. Ned was one of the business officers on the monthly *Clarion,* but she was one of the editors. She held class offices, was chosen for the debating team and for the committee on dramatics, and was even elected, plainly on grounds other than any outstanding ability in games and sports, as vice-president of the athletic association. Everybody knew that they could count on her.

Ned was convinced that none of the other girls equaled her. And he was beginning to know quite a few. One of them made him fudge. The mother of another had found out that he liked spongecake and grape juice and whenever Ned showed up at Victoire's house, these goodies made a simultaneous appearance. Other girls let him know how well he looked in his blue and white cadet corps uniform as captain of Company G.

Teen-age social life at the turn of the century was in pack pattern. Wherever the young folk of Jamaica Plain went, whether on summer hay rides or winter skating and sleighing parties, whether to Jamaica Pond or to the Charles River, they traveled in gregarious groups. Whatever they did—boating, ice skating, dancing, driving—they did together. They would return from a winter punging party and invade some home in force, consuming quantities of steaming oyster stew or hot chocolate. They often congregated in droves at the large and hospitable Rogers home, filling the twin parlors, the hallway, the dining

room, and swarming into the kitchen, where all sorts of concoc-
tions would be tried out on the big black coal stove.

The high school Cadet Corps had informal dances occasionally and a big affair annually, beginning with an exhibition
drill and ending with a dance. Whether parties were more or
less formal, Mollie always had more than enough partners. Some
of the girls in her class noticed that if she had a chance to choose
her own escort, she seemed to pick not those who were handsome
or popular but those who did not find it easy to ask or to get
another girl to go with them. She danced well, was admittedly
friendly to everybody and had three good-looking older brothers
—a combination well designed to make her appreciated by boys
and girls alike.

She had become a fine-looking girl, tall and already a little
heavy. Her features were like her father's. There was something
of her mother's clement way in her friendly and livelier manner.
Her smile was a joy to see and her laughter an invitation to share
in it. In repose her face was strikingly thoughtful and, to some,
sad, with a downward turn to the corners of the mouth which
may well have been a physical trait rather than a psychological
statement. Whether due to Grandma's training or to her own
natural buoyancy, she had a light step and a queenly bearing.

At the age when girls not only feel that they must be beautiful but have hope of discovering a magic method to make them
so, Mollie tried several experiments with that end in view.

When visiting at Rochdale, she and her cousin Anne, a slender girl with beautiful dark eyes, heard that eating raw onions
vastly improved the complexion. Onions seemed a simple and
available means to effect such marvels. Anne hated them but
was eager to be even lovelier than she was. Mollie was willing to
try.

Nightly, just before they went to bed, they peeled and ate
their raw onions. By day they searched the mirror and each
other's eyes for results. As the days passed, all they could notice

was a deepening tan, the obvious result of an outdoor summer. The onion treatment for fair and flawless complexions was abandoned.

During the same period, anticipating the combined joy of a dance and a new dress, Mollie tried again. Someone who had obviously never made the experiment, gave it as gospel that turpentine wonderfully whitened the skin. It was an era when to be fair was to be fashionable, to be sunburned was unseemly. Mollie had a vision of her head and shoulders, freshly transformed by turpentine, rising pearly white and phoenix-like from her new gown. She applied the turpentine generously, could not get it off fast enough and went to the dance looking more like a broiled lobster than a pearl. She was already mature enough to laugh at her predicament. It was her final attempt to make any drastic alterations in her appearance.

During her high-school days Mollie's relationships with both teachers and pupils, as well as with her wider circle of friends and relatives, were simple and uncomplicated until a single exception began to develop.

On the school staff was an especially gifted and personable teacher. She had a fine grasp of her subject and taught it expertly. She was exceptionally well read, had a taste for classical music and good drama and was well traveled. In general, the teaching staff showed their pupils austere benevolence rather than warmth or cordiality, but she was unaffectedly friendly, and especially so with Mollie.

She began to ask Mollie to accompany her to plays and concerts, made her small gifts and, as time went on, invited her to her home and, in readiness for her coming, prepared the dishes which she knew that Mollie liked. For the first time in her life, without knowing just why, Mollie became uneasy about her relationship with another human being. She was troubled by the evident affection shown her and by her own response to it. She had never before felt that anybody came between her and God.

Now she did. Once she had faced that, she sat down at her desk one evening at home and wrote briefly to her teacher, thanking her for her kindness and saying that she would not see her again.

The teacher took her at her word. She never replied to Mollie's note or addressed her again except in class or in groups where some exchange was necessary.

As she matured, Mollie had increasing insight into the wound which she must have dealt the older woman. She had little with which to reproach herself in regard to her treatment of others but, even late in life, she still regretted the manner in which she had solved this adolescent problem.

"I was right, but I would do it so differently now. However, we can't be old in wisdom and young in years all at once. And maybe what I think a better way now would not have done then."

In the active, happy home on Robinwood Avenue, the children of the household felt the long lovely days drift by, carrying them gently on toward manhood and womanhood. They had, they assumed, illimitable time in which to do and to be whatever they dreamed or hoped to accomplish and to become. To their parents the years had already begun to hurry along, bearing their children toward a future which would all too soon exceed their own reach.

There were days, occasions, when the flight of time seemed particularly noticeable, such as the warm afternoon in late June, 1901, when Mr. and Mrs. Rogers sat in the audience at the graduation exercises of West Roxbury High School. If they did not say anything to each other about time flying, it was not for lack of reminders.

They had only to look at the alumni violinists who had returned to play for the ceremony. There sat Bill, his violin tucked under his chin, looking mature and manly, already a Harvard graduate and established in the profession which his father had chosen for him. Leo, a Harvard junior, loomed near at hand, taller and more distinguished-looking than ever. There were Ned and Mollie both among the graduates. Even the younger Rogers who flanked their parents on either side seemed no longer so young. The girls were growing up. Elizabeth could certainly not be called a little girl any longer. There was no current Rogers baby. John and Abe, doing their best not to squirm and swivel during the long exercises, were already more boys than children. If they had their way, the whole program would have been cut down to just two of its twelve parts—Mollie's talk and the distribution of diplomas.

All the Rogers, big and little alike, were interested in the essay that Mollie was to present, first because it was Mollie's and secondly because they all felt that they had had something to do with it. She had talked it over with her mother and father and had then taken the topic to the Redemptorist Fathers on Tremont Street to get their advice about it and, once she had written and rewritten it to her own satisfaction, had tried it out on anybody in the family capable of giving it critical appraisal or just willing to listen.

The subject had a certain delicacy in the social and religious climate of the time, especially when presented by a Catholic girl to a predominantly Protestant assembly at a public-school graduation ceremony held in the local Congregational Church. Mr. Rogers was not worried about how it would be delivered or how it would be received. He could think of no one better suited than Mollie to give people a few good ideas on "Toleration," the theme of her essay.

He raised his fine head to hear her begin with an apt and impressive Latin quotation, *"In necessariis unitas, in dubiis libertas, in omnibus caritas."*

Even if it was a quotation from St. Austin suggested as an opener by Father Bloem, the Redemptorist, it was enough like Mollie for her to have made it up herself: "In what is essential, unity; in what is indifferent, liberty; and in all things, charity."

CHAPTER 2

FATHER WALSH

Mollie completed her studies and received her Bachelor of Arts degree from Smith College in June of 1905. Elizabeth, graduating from West Roxbury High School the same month, celebrated that event by going to Northampton to attend Mollie's commencement and to share in the festivities of the week. She was the family's only representative. Mrs. Rogers was ill. Mr. Rogers would not think of going so far without her, even to see Mollie graduate.

For her part, once she had her diploma, Mollie could hardly get home fast enough. To be back in the lovely old Robinwood house, to have the chance to wait on her sweet and patient mother, to feel again the bracing impact of her father's robust personality, to be surrounded with brothers and sisters full of ideas, projects, and demands—it was pure pleasure and she reveled in it.

With the fall, she enrolled at Boston Normal School, taking the course offered for college graduates, and at the end of the year received her diploma. She was invited to return to Smith College the following autumn as a demonstrator in the Department of Zoology. This offered her, in addition to the experience of working with excellent teachers, the academic prestige of the position and an opportunity to follow graduate studies and write a thesis for a master's degree.

If she were going to teach, she now knew that science was her field. For French she had a long-time affection. Literature gave her delight but, once she had studied the life sciences, she knew that she had found her forte and her predilection.

During her junior and senior years, Professor Wilder, the department head, and his assistant, Miss Whipple, had become conscious of Mollie's interest and ability. They found her a thoughtful, thorough student and a skillful, well-organized laboratory worker, unusually patient with those less gifted than herself. She seemed to have the scientific temper. There was a great deal of discussion in the department at that time about evolution. To some of the students with strictly fundamentalist views, it was a soul-shaking concept. Mollie, who saw the universe at rest in the hollow of God's hand, was not overconcerned with how He had chosen to fashion it. It was a marvel in any case. She loved it and was grateful for it.

Back on the campus for the academic year of 1906-1907, she felt at home. There were three other new demonstrators in the science departments. Two of these, Hannah Billings in physics, and Sophia Eckerson in botany, had graduated with Mollie. Among the seven graduate students, three were Smith girls whom Mollie had known. Many of the faculty were glad to see her back again and told her so. Girls whom she recalled in the First and Second Class, as President Seelye preferred to call freshmen and sophomores, were now juniors and seniors. Quite a few of them remembered her, although they were prone to feel that she had somehow gone over to the other side, the faculty, and had now to be treated with a certain amount of distance as well as of deference.

Professor Wilder and Miss Whipple had married. They were

more than professionally correct in observing the formalities of that era, yet worked together like two hands of one body and created an amiable atmosphere in which it was pleasant to be. The year stretched out invitingly for the Zoology Demonstrator. Without being convinced that her path was fixed, Mollie felt that she was on her way. A combination of circumstances and choices had brought her this far. She was evidently going to be a teacher of science. As she settled easily and successfully into the routine of the department, Professor and Mrs. Wilder congratulated themselves that they had recognized her potential and chosen her for the post.

Others at Smith were thinking of Mollie's potential, Miss Hanscom for one. Elizabeth Deering Hanscom, professor of literature, scholar and individualist, darling of the brave and the bright, terror of the timid and inept, was the faculty advisor of the Smith College Association for Christian Work. This was the central religious organization at Smith and embraced all other religious clubs and societies as its departments. A devout Episcopalian, Miss Hanscom was troubled with a Catholic problem brought to her for solution by the president and secretary of the SCACW. Religiously, they said, Catholic girls at Smith were out of things. All of them attended their own church on Sundays, a few even went to services on weekdays, but they had no social entity as a religious group, they had no study clubs and were either unwilling or unable to join those of others.

To these three devout Protestant women, this minority group seemed on the spiritual fringe, so to speak, in evident need of leadership to round them up and solidify them into a working unit with a sense of solidarity and purpose. They had been let go their own individualistic ways so long that it would take real leadership to do this.

What about Mary Rogers? somebody asked. Sitting very straight, with her hair pulled back austerely from its middle part, little Miss Hanscom thought about Miss Rogers. She did not recall her as a particularly brilliant student. She did not even remember that she had awarded her a "D" in American Literature just two years ago, although "D" was the highest grade in the reverse order of marking then in vogue at Smith, and Miss Hanscom was not in the habit of according it lavishly. She had only a general impression of Miss Rogers as neither timid nor inept but a solid and reliable young woman, capable of giving her full attention to what she was doing. Miss Rogers it would be.

Soon after this little conference, Miss Hanscom invited Mollie to tea. Over the dainty ritual of paper-thin bread and butter, dainty cookies, and fragrant tea served in translucent cups brought from the Orient years before in a Yankee clipper, they picked up the threads of mutual acquaintance and interests.

Mollie enjoyed watching Miss Hanscom make and pour tea. Every movement was like a revelation of her mind—deft and definite.

Then, without preliminary, Miss Hanscom suddenly fixed her sharp blue eyes on Mollie and said, "Why don't you do something for the Catholic girls here?"

Mollie looked at her.

"They ought to have some kind of religious organization, activity. Every other group has."

"What did you have in mind, Miss Hanscom?"

"Well, what would you think of a Bible study class?"

"Who would conduct it?"

"You."

Mollie did not have to think that over. "Oh, I couldn't do that. I have no preparation, no qualifications. The girls would think me presumptuous to attempt it, and they would be right." She fell silent. The only formal instruction that she had had in Scripture was the required introductory course which she had followed under the Reverend Dr. Wood during her sophomore year.

Miss Hanscom sipped her tea and waited.

The old dream, the interest that lay still and mute in Mollie's heart, stirred and spoke.

"What would you think of a mission study class?" Mollie asked. "I might be able to do that."

Miss Hanscom thought well of it. It was settled.

Mollie found herself walking away from 32 Bedford Terrace somewhat appalled at what she had done. She thought that if she had more sense and more courage, she would go right back and tell Miss Hanscom that it would be impossible for her to do what she had proposed. What knowledge had she? What resources for information? What hope of finding any?

As Catholics at Smith so often did, she went directly to Father Michael Welch with her problem. He had no books, no materials himself, but he did know of someone who could help her.

"Write to Father James Anthony Walsh," he said. "He's the Director of the Society for the Propagation of the Faith in Boston. We were in Brighton Seminary together. He'll be able to help you. And he will."

Before writing to Father Walsh, Mollie marshaled her thoughts. She had to keep in mind in drawing up any tentative program that her group would be comparatively small. Unlike the Protestant groups, they would have no mission books or periodicals: nothing on Catholic mission theory—theology, methods, techniques; nothing on mission facts—surveys, statistics, studies on fields, organizations, personnel, services; almost no biographies; and no contemporary accounts of Catholic Americans in the mission fields, if there were any. She knew of no mission maps or materials except the *Annals* of the Society for the Propagation of the Faith—a thin and unappealing diet for any college girl. In the Students Building there was a mission library of about one hundred volumes, all Protestant. Doubtless, the only resource that she would find on the whole Smith campus for her Catholic girls would be Robert Louis Stevenson's classic defense of Father Damien, *An Open Letter to the Rev. Dr. Hyde of Honolulu.*

As Mollie saw it, she and her study class would need to concentrate on a few key topics. She summarized these for Father Walsh: 1) the preparation of priests and nuns for the work; 2) mission orders and the field of work; 3) nature of the work done; 4) collection and distribution of funds.

She asked, "Will you tell me where I can get any information (in English, French or Latin) bearing on these lines of thought? And will you kindly send me some pamphlets concerning the Society for the Propagation of the Faith?"

She was clear about her objective and stated it simply: "The particular motive of these classes is to inspire the girls to do actual work when they leave college. . . . By giving the girls what information we can get, we hope to show them how great the work of the Church is, to make them want to keep in touch with that work and to give it their hearty support whenever an opportunity affords now or later."

She had begun to weave the net in which she would be the first to be caught.

"Who knows," she asked Father Walsh in a rhetorical question, "but that the little work we do here may be the beginning of greater efforts in later life?"

A prompt answer came back under the date of October 20.

"Far from bothering me, your appeal gives me great pleasure," began Father Walsh, "in the thought that you will interest the Catholic girls of Smith College in the great work of Catholic Foreign Missions—a work which up to the present time has not been appreciated by the Catholics of America, and which we have reason to believe is fast growing in popular favor."

He commended the points for discussion which she had proposed and added another of his own, "the martyr spirit of our age." He sent her a supply of materials which he thought should be of help for the group, and, for herself, a copy of the *Life of*

Theophane Venard as a gift. He called her attention to the weekly column on the missions in *The Pilot* and to the occasional mission items that appeared in the *Sacred Heart Review*. He regretted that the sources of information in English were so meager. He offered to come to talk to the group being formed, should she be able to muster as many as fifty to listen to him.

He closed his letter with a statement which was certainly an open end for further correspondence. "Don't be afraid to write to me as often as you wish on the subject of this work. I shall look upon it as a privilege and a pleasure to assist you in the effort which you are making and for which Almighty God will give you some reward through the prayers and sacrifices of those whom you are thereby helping."

The Christmas holidays came and Mollie was back in Jamaica Plain on December 20. On top of her usual happiness at being with her family again, was the anticipation of meeting Father Walsh. He had invited her to call at the office of the Society for the Propagation of the Faith while she was home for the holidays, and she meant to accept his invitation. Womanlike, she expressed her estimation of the importance of the occasion by wearing a new winter outfit.

Of Father Walsh's office she knew only that it was number sixty-two on Union Park Street and that Union Park Street was near the Cathedral. Quite unconsciously she had pictured to herself a setting which would express the vigor and efficiency which she had found in the Director's letters.

She found instead a row of clapboard houses which bore their hundred years without grace. If one sagged and gloomed more than the rest, it was number sixty-two. A big sign on the small building announced that here was the office of the Society for the Propagation of the Faith. Another smaller sign nailed next to the paint-peeled door said, "Push the button and walk in." Mollie found the invitation anything but irresistible. Surely the

Father Walsh whom she had come to know through his letters would not be found in a dilapidated place like this? However, she pushed the button, walked in and found herself in a small dark hallway with a door to the right and a narrow staircase straight ahead.

Two pleasant secretaries and an office boy in the first-floor office all looked up to direct her upstairs. She went up the rickety stairway, mindful of the squeaking steps, the quivering banister. The whole building seemed on the verge of collapse, just waiting for her to bring it down.

At the top of the stairs, the gloom broke. Light streamed from a sunny office, a priest sitting at a big desk rose and came to meet her with outstretched hand. She had no doubt either of who he was or what he was.

When they were seated, he on one side of the desk and she on the other, she realized that her dismay at their surroundings had not gone unnoticed and that Father Walsh was amused by it. His small dark eyes shone with laughter. She, on her part, saw how he had done whatever he could to give significance and even beauty to his cramped quarters. His stacks of work were neatly aligned and ready to hand. He had a globe to remind him and his visitors of the world-wide character of his work. Oriental hangings and objects of art spoke of other places and peoples and lent at least visual warmth to the small cold room.

Mollie and Father Walsh talked about their families, their homes, their mutual friends and acquaintances; they discussed the character and progress of the mission study classes which Mollie now had under way at Smith; they agreed on tentative plans for Father Walsh to come to Northampton to address the group that winter. This would be an open meeting to which the whole faculty and student body would be invited.

On his desk, Father Walsh had something which he could hardly wait to show Mollie—the galley proofs of the first issue of *The Field Afar,* a bimonthly beginning publication under the date of January 1, 1907. He spread them out for her to see, giving her a lesson in paging and correction-making and telling her something of the genesis of this project.

In October, just about the same time when Miss Hanscom was making up her mind to invite Mollie to tea, four priests had met in Boston and formed an unpretentious organization which they called "The Catholic Foreign Mission Bureau." The priests were Father John I. Lane and Father Stanton, both apostolic Bostonians burdened with illnesses, Father Bruneau, a French Sulpician teaching at Brighton Seminary, and Father Walsh himself. All were convinced that the time had come for the United States to nurture priestly vocations for the missions and to have a foreign mission seminary of its own. By way of preparation for this, they planned to bring the mission fields, the mission vocation, the mission Church to the attention of the Catholics of their country. This they resolved to do through books, pamphlets, and a periodical, *The Field Afar*. And here it was now, a reality, on Father Walsh's desk.

Looking over the galleys, Mollie had a chance to taste its flavor, to note a few of its capital ideas, to see further into the vision and purpose of the priest who had set out to capture the interest and imagination of the Catholics of a whole nation.

The aim of *The Field Afar* was forthrightly stated on its editorial page—"to deepen and widen in its readers the missionary spirit . . . to strengthen, especially in the Archdiocese of Boston, all work for foreign missions."

Who would do this? "The Catholic Foreign Mission Bureau" —two sick priests, a seminary professor and the busy Director of the Society for the Propagation of the Faith?

As Father Walsh saw it, "Every Catholic who has reached the use of reason is in a position to help, at least to the extent of an occasional prayer, in the evangelization of the world, and if many of us have until now given little or no co-operation to this sublime work, it is largely because the need has not been sufficiently realized since it has not been adequately presented."

Now the effort toward adequate presentation was making a

start. Mollie looked at the man who had taken up this colossal task. She saw a priest of thirty-nine, of middle height and weight, with dark hair and small, lively dark eyes. He had a look at once recognizably Irish, especially in the brow and the long upper lip, but with something Roman and nearly regal in the strong prominent nose. By no means handsome, he was notable-looking. As he sat watching her and waiting for her comments, leaning back a little with his head on one side, his hands folded quietly, his quick and energetic movements stilled, she was conscious chiefly of his regard. When he turned his glance upon you, you had the sensation of being the focal point of an unusual gift of concentration and insight. Had it not been so kind, it could have been frightening.

They talked. Time flew. Mollie suddenly realized how long she had been there, taking up the time of this obviously busy man. She stood up with an apology.

"And I really must be going now anyhow. It takes quite a while to get back to Jamaica Plain."

Father Walsh did not get up. He was not ready to let her go. He looked up at her and said, with startling frankness, "No, no, don't go. Sit down again. I'm trying to form an opinion of you."

Mollie sat down again. She was a young woman of unusual composure. However, she felt uneasy, "dead silly," as she admitted to herself. She stayed, nevertheless, and they talked some more, about what she did not afterwards recall.

When she made a second attempt to leave, Father Walsh made no objection. He did not tell her what opinion he had formed of her, but said only, with a smile, as they shook hands, "I think we are going to be very good friends."

Apparently, manlike, he did not advert to the fact that she too might have taken his measure. From the time when she had walked into his office and he rose smiling and holding out his hand, Mollie knew what she thought of him and thereafter never changed her mind. He was the priest that she had expected and hoped to find.

That winter and the following spring when Mollie was not at her duties in the Zoology Department, she gave a good share of her time to what she already had accepted as a great cause. She translated French letters and articles for Father Walsh to use in *The Field Afar* and, before long, she and members of the study class were portioning out among themselves sections of a French missionary's biography to be put into English—all part of Father Walsh's drive to make his American fellow-Catholics aware of the missionary character and task of the Church.

Because she realized that the girls who came to the study classes were carrying a full scholastic program and could afford little time for any extracurricular activity, Mollie took on the lion's share of the preparation for these sessions. Her group met on Friday evenings, had a list of forty-eight names and an average attendance of twenty-five, which she considered good.

Her methods were informal. She gave a brief presentation of the subject scheduled and then opened the floor for discussion and questions. The topics which they covered included the Society for the Propagation of the Faith; the Mill Hill Seminary for foreign missions in England; the *Missions Étrangères* of Paris; brief sketches of different mission fields, with the students giving short preparatory talks on geographic, economic, and religious factors. Theophane Venard was singled out for special study and so was Father Damien's work with the lepers on Molokai, together with Stevenson's defense of him.

In addition to Father Walsh, who gave an illustrated lecture to which many non-Catholics came, another speaker addressed the group during the year. Dr. William Thornton Parker, a convert who had lived for some time on an Indian reservation, gave a talk on "The American Indian and Catholic Missions."

All in all, Father Walsh was so pleased with the program that Mollie planned and carried out that he presented it in *The Field Afar* of the following October as a model and incentive for other study groups.

Before the end of June, Mollie was again home in Jamaica

Plain. It was vacation time but she had no inclination for vacationing. Instead, she went every day with a light heart to the
hot little offices on 62 Union Park Street where Father Walsh
squeezed in another desk and called it hers. To it came anything
and everything—translations to be made, editing to be done,
topics to be developed into articles, pictures to be removed
from heavy cardboard backing and systematically filed. The
pictures she took home and put to soak in the bathtub. This did
not advance the mission cause appreciably with her brothers and
sisters. They already felt rather long-suffering, for they had
looked forward to Mollie's companionship that summer and
here she was spending all her time running back and forth to
Father Walsh's office.

The day's work was a delight to Mollie and she enjoyed the
long and lovely evenings with her family and friends. She gave
some days, too, to outings and picnics. Ned's canoe was always
waiting at the boathouse, a silent but eloquent invitation. It
took only a matter of minutes to make up a party, and if it ex-
panded, as it often did, they simply hired as many additional
canoes as their numbers required.

They were all old hands on the Charles River and could recall
only one spill. Leo, Ned, and Mollie were just getting under
way together in one canoe. Leo, drawing luxuriously on his
pipe, had stretched out his elegant length in the rear. Mollie
was settling herself, putting a pillow at her back. Ned slid into
his place in the forward end, throwing some brotherly remarks
at Mollie over his shoulder. She threw her pillow at his head,
he ducked, the canoe flipped, and they were all in the water.
When Leo came to the surface, water cascading down his face
from his flattened hair, he still held his pipe firmly between his
teeth. Ned and Mollie thought the vision worth the ducking.

One summer afternoon Mollie told Father Walsh that she
would not be in the next day. "We're going canoeing."

He gave her his quick look. "Would you take me?"

She was surprised. Father Walsh in a canoe? But she answered warmly and without hesitation, "Of course. We would be happy to have you."

"Maybe there wouldn't be room?" Was he looking a little shy at having asked?

"Certainly there will. We are taking several canoes and we can always add another one in any case."

Father Walsh had few holidays in his busy life. The demanding schedule that he had laid on his own shoulders allowed him little leisure. He enjoyed this outing to the full. He had a fund of interesting stories and told them well. He could mimic skillfully. He was a good listener and fell in easily with the plans and projects of others. On the Charles River that day the humor that helped to lighten the full days in the ecclesiastical shanty on Union Park Street was at its best. Mollie was proud of him before her brothers and proud of her brothers before him.

She especially wanted Father Walsh and Ned to understand and appreciate one another. Ned was not easy to know. He kept a certain distance with Father Walsh. On the way up the river, the priest told how one day when he was out, a fish jumped right into the boat with him. Ned scoffed. It would take more than Holy Orders to get him to accept that fish story. On their way home, with the day not yet over, a fish cleared the water, made a shining arc and thumped into the canoe with them both. Ned was taken aback, as if the fish had betrayed him.

Father Walsh chuckled and commented, "The Lord takes care of his own."

Even mutual laughter could not entirely dissipate Ned's reserve. With his sharp perceptions, he already sensed in Mollie's association with Father Walsh and his work something that raised a little fear, a little sorrow in his heart. If he had not yet phrased it, the question was already being formed in his mind: Where will all this lead Mollie? Where will it end?

Accumulating evidence pointed out some answers to the un-

asked question. It was certainly not going to lead to a professor-
ship, or to a career in college science teaching, or even to a
Master of Arts degree.

Mr. Rogers had had a picture of Mollie returning to Smith
in the fall and quietly picking up her M.A. With all the time
that she had been devoting to Father Walsh's work, he took it
for granted that she must have finished her thesis before she
came home.

The thesis, he was soon to learn, was not even under way.

Louise was not surprised. "Who would want to write a thesis,
a whole thesis, on that awful old subject they gave Mollie?
Something about a water bug! Imagine expecting Mollie to
spend her time writing about water bugs!"

It was not just a question of water bugs, however, and Mollie
made that clear to her father. She was not interested in getting
a master's degree; she would return to Smith for another year
as a demonstrator, since she was expected, but then she would
come home, take a teaching position somewhere near and give
whatever time she could spare to Father Walsh's work. Their
conversation on this subject was a memorable one, marked with
fatherly fireworks. Mr. Rogers had to give his disappointment
that outlet. Both he and Mollie understood that, just as both
of them knew that in the end he would accept her decision.

Not only did he accept it but he eventually came to take pride
in it and to see in Mollie's choice some compensation for the
fact that no priestly vocation had fallen to the lot of any of his
five sons.

That Mollie was able to arrange her life over the next few
years as she had hoped to do was evidenced by a Christmas gift
she received on December 24, 1908. It was a bound copy of the
first year's issues of *The Field Afar*. On the flyleaf Father Walsh
had written in his swinging script, "To my co-worker with deep
appreciation of her faithful service." It remained one of the
few treasures which Mollie kept and took with her when she

left Robinwood Avenue for Hawthorne nearly four years later.

Father Walsh spoke and wrote persuasively of the missionary vocation. This may have had something to do with the fact that he learned during the winter of 1908 that he was going to lose one of his two paid office workers. Miss Donovan wanted to be a sister and a missionary. How in the United States, a country so recently promoted from its missionary status, could she accomplish this? Just as there was no seminary for foreign missioners in the United States, so there was no Sisterhood dedicated to foreign mission work. However, careful inquiry disclosed that on the North American continent near French Quebec, a new missionary community for women was just making a beginning. To enter it, Miss Donovan would have to learn French and nursing. Miss Donovan was willing to meet both conditions.

She began to make preparations for her departure. After office hours, she started to assemble her austere trousseau. While at 62 Union Park Street she could sometimes be heard murmuring *"S'il vous plâit," "Merci beaucoup," "Pas du tout,"* and *"Au revoir."* All of which reminded Father Walsh that he needed to look for another office worker.

On the third Tuesday of the month, he used to attend a promoters' meeting of the Society for the Propagation of the Faith, held in the Cathedral basement. One of the most faithful promoters was a retired Irish domestic, a dear old faithful woman named Walsh, who could not write. Her accounts were beautifully done.

That January evening, when she submitted her report, Father Walsh asked, "By the way, Miss Walsh, who does your writing for you?"

"A darling girl named Nora. She lives where I do, just down the street, at the Grey Sisters' Home. Right now she happens to be out of work. Do you think you could do anything for her, Father?"

It was the kind of question that he had heard and welcomed since the beginning of his priestly ministry.

"I might," he answered. "Ask her to come to see me."

Nora came.

"So your name is Shea?" he said, as if that were a compliment to him and a boon for her. "I have three cousins named Shea."

"I wish that I could claim to be the fourth," said Nora.

She smiled at him. Nora smiled on the whole world as if the world had done nothing but smile upon her. It was one of life's miracles that Nora should smile like that. She was the child of a widowed mother who, to maintain herself and her family, had had to work from dawn to dark in one of the Massachusetts mills. Even as a little girl Nora had carried responsibilities, looking after the other children younger than she, preparing their meals and trudging to the mill daily to bring her mother a noontime dinner. To stay alive and well, to have enough to eat and decent clothes to wear, to go to school and learn something, had been the necessary preoccupations of the Sheas. Yet Nora smiled. No hardship had made bitter her sweet nature, and for her the privations of her childhood were only a dark setting for the radiant figure of her valiant and beloved mother.

By the first week of February, Nora was working for Father Walsh, replacing Miss Donovan who, two days after Nora arrived, went off to begin her nursing course before leaving for Canada. Nora followed her to the head of the narrow stairwell, absorbing last-minute instructions.

Miss Donovan ran down the shuddering steps. Halfway to the bottom, she paused and called back to Nora, "Oh, you'll be all right. Just pray to St. Jude. He's hanging on the wall there. He'll do everything for you."

Nora went back into the tight little office. Its files, its mail, its machines, were all hers. She was on her own. It was sink or swim. Well, she had always kept her head above water. Why not now?

A brighter day dawned a little later that week when Miss Rogers came into the office to help out. Miss Rogers knew where everything was and how everything was done. Nothing bothered her. Nothing dismayed her. Nora felt that altogether Miss Rogers was a rather more satisfactory co-worker than St. Jude, with all due respects to him. Her heart was Mollie's from that time on.

The year 1910 was a big year for Father Walsh and his little establishment. First of all, offices of both the Society for the Propagation of the Faith and of *The Field Afar* moved to another old but larger house on Malden Street. Father Walsh was given an assistant, Father James Redican. And in September, Father Walsh went to the Eucharistic Congress at Montreal.

More than six years earlier, Father Walsh had attended a meeting of the Missionary Union, an organization concerned with home missions, held in Washington in the spring of 1904. Several hundred bishops and priests attended. Father Walsh heard Father Price, an austere, tireless, and prayerful missionary from country North Carolina, give a talk on "The Progress of Localized Missions." Father Price heard Father Walsh speak, out of the depths of his conviction, on "Catholic Foreign Missions."

After the discussion following Father Walsh's paper, the two priests were introduced to each other. Father Price reiterated what he had already expressed during the discussion—that he agreed wholeheartedly with the younger priest's idea that participation in foreign mission work would have a good effect on the Church at home in the United States.

From that time on, each was always aware of the other's activities and interests, realizing what convictions and desires they shared. In his periodical *Truth,* Father Price brought Father Walsh's thoughts on foreign missions to the notice of his readers. When Father Price's apostolic school at Nazareth, North Carolina, burned to the ground in 1905, Father Walsh publicized his loss in the hope of winning both sympathy and help.

The two priests did not, however, see each other again until the Eucharistic Congress at Montreal in September, 1910. When they met that day, the desires that had so long been urging them, their long-considered schemes and plans, their half-formed resolves seemed suddenly to fire and fuse. Absorbed in each other, they sat in the lobby of the Windsor Hotel and talked and talked, entirely oblivious of those around them. Before they parted, they had come to a definite decision. Here and there among the clergy of the country a burgeoning interest in a foreign mission movement was becoming faintly evident, but no individual or group seemed ready or willing to begin the undertaking. Both men were sure that it was time, if not past time, to make a start. Together they meant to try.

As a beginning, they would do all they could to interest the Bishops of the United States in the project. Whenever possible, they would go to see them personally.

Not many days later, Father Walsh began a long correspondence with Cardinal Gibbons, submitting proposals and plans for his consideration.

After the day's work was done at five, Nora would have the office to herself and would type up whatever papers Father Walsh had prepared for her. Many evenings the task kept her past her dinner hour, and the dining room where she took her meals would be closed. She did not mind. She went home cheerfully and made herself tea over the gas jet in her little room.

As she ate her lonely meal, she would still be aglow, thinking over the great issues in which she had become so happily involved.

"All because I offered to help old Miss Walsh with her accounts!" She would smile to herself, since there was no one else to smile upon right then.

She knew that Father Walsh wanted this wonderful matter kept confidential until it was time for it to be publicly and authoritatively announced. She did not mention it to anyone, even her new confidante, Mollie. Mollie, of course, already knew about it. Father Walsh did not take for granted ancient prejudices about women and secrets.

The spring of 1911 was a season packed with interest, activity, and events for Father Walsh, Father Price, and all those associated with them. On March 25, they saw their beloved venture launched with a letter from Cardinal Gibbons to all the Bishops of the United States, advocating the foundation of a foreign mission society and seminary and recommending the two priests promoting it. The Bishops were to meet on April 27, at The Catholic University in Washington. The agenda of the meeting included a foreign mission society for America.

That day was a kind of target date toward which were directed the concern and prayers of Father Walsh and Father Price and their co-workers. When it came, Father Price waited in the hall outside the Bishops' meeting room, saying his rosary and, as the day wore on, doubtless fighting off more distractions than he ordinarily had to do. Father Walsh worked quietly at his desk in the Malden Street office, trying to keep his mind on what he was doing, trying not to watch the clock or wonder, as the hours ticked off, why no word had come. Nora at her typewriter, Mollie in her classroom, had but one thought filling the whole background of their consciousness.

About four-thirty, Father Walsh called Nora. She went into his office, her eyes two question marks, her smile quite gone. Whatever had the Bishops been doing all this time? There must have been lots of arguments. She looked at Father Walsh.

He was leaning back in his swivel chair as if he were both tired and relaxed. He had his hands on a piece of paper on his desk. He looked at Nora with his lively dark eyes.

"Miss Shea, the word has come. 'Unanimously approved.' "

If he had expected to see her sunshine smile, he was mistaken. She stood stock-still for a moment without saying a word. Then tears came into her eyes and bounced down her cheeks. She plunged out of the office to have a good cry in the sanctuary of the Exhibit Room. Mollie, returning from school, heard the wonderful news. That same evening, it was in the late papers, nobody's secret and everybody's concern thereafter.

Things moved quickly after that. Father Walsh was released from his duties as SPF director to give all his time to his new responsibilities. A new director was appointed. *The Field Afar* and its force needed new quarters for this interim period. The Washington Press, which printed *The Field Afar,* offered Father Walsh space in their plant on 242 Dover Street until things could be settled. The space, not to be despised at this juncture, consisted of a long storeroom, small and stuffy, unbelievably dirty at the moment and permanently subject to the noise of the printing presses thumping and crashing just the other side of the thin wall.

Nora and Mollie went to work with brooms, wall brushes and scrub brushes. They were stiff and groaning but still good-natured by the time they were finished. They arranged the two desks, the empty file cases, into the semblance of an office and learned to shout at each other at the top of their voices over the noise of the presses.

Everything had happened so fast that the process of sorting out *The Field Afar* business from Propagation of the Faith business had not been completed. *The Field Afar* subscription list and the Propagation of the Faith entries had all been entered on the same cards in the same files. These were needed in the offices of the Propagation of the Faith during the day.

Mollie settled that difficulty by taking the files home, drawer by drawer, at five o'clock each day and bringing them back before nine the next morning. At night she and her family and friends sat around the big dining room table and copied the names of *The Field Afar* subscribers on new cards for a new file.

Years later, at Maryknoll, when *The Field Afar* subscription list had increased far beyond the seven thousand names of that year, Mollie would come across some card written in her mother's or father's hand. It would bring back a rush of memories. She would see again the big table, her father's white head, her mother's sweet face, bent over the cards, her brothers bantering, her sisters and their friends laughing. She would feel again the sense of support and solidarity as they worked together and of accomplishment and relaxation when Mrs. Rogers would bring the night's task to a close with some treat as their reward.

Their fortunes might have altered in the last year or so, but they still had one another, they still had the dear old Robinwood home. The Rogers brothers had lost heavily through some unwise investments. Largely as a result of this, Mollie's father had had a stroke. He was making a good recovery, but he was no longer the sure and vigorous man that he had been. And on his mind were the unfinished plans that he had for his family. There were still two boys to finish college. John was in his last year at Harvard, but Abe was only starting. And what of the generous inheritances that he had meant to provide for each of the three girls?

Mrs. Rogers comforted him: "Nobody can expect to plan for everything all the time. Nobody is expected to."

The way of life in the gracious old house had to be altered somewhat to meet the new circumstances. Mollie made her own adaptations. In addition to teaching and giving her free time to volunteer work for Father Walsh, she managed to make dresses for herself and Louise and to trim their hats at a time when fashionable hats were a medley of birds, fruits, and flowers. Mollie had never done anything like it before; she had only the half-remembered sewing lessons taken at Bowditch School to rely on, but she bought patterns and materials and went to work with that ease which made everything she did seem so simple and inevitable. Louise looked with astonishment at the dresses that she turned out, called them lovely, and wore them with pride.

On the thirtieth of May, Father Walsh and Father Price sailed for Rome to seek papal approval for their plan.

From the SS *Franconia* Father Walsh wrote Mollie, "I will think of you and yours often. I hardly dare to thank you for all that *you* have done, but through you I must thank those who have been copying the cards. Let me know later how many were engaged. . . ."

In his flowing script and telegraphic style, he kept her informed of his movements and of the progress of events.

From Paris he wrote: ". . . arrived last night—same old place —hardly stranger to me now than N.Y. . . . Fr. Price is getting a new shock about every quarter of an hour, although much escapes him since he is not of this world . . . at present I feel absolutely unworthy not to say unfit to go on with this great work—and that I can be no more than a passing agent through whom God will work."

From Rome under date of June 21 he could say: "Things are moving along well so far."

His schedule, even in bare outline, gave some indication of how full were his days:

"Sunday 8:30 A.M. called at the American College and talked with Bishop Kennedy. We went there again next morning but just for a moment, as we were due at Propaganda for the first attack, a conference with the sub-secretary, Msgr. Laurenti.

"Tuesday found us interviewing Cardinal Gotti.

"Wednesday Cardinal Merry del Val, at the Vatican.

"Thursday the Procurator General of the Paris Seminary et al.

"Today we have been drawing up a formal petition which must get into Cardinal Gotti's hands by Sunday, as there will be a meeting Tuesday, and tonight at 8:30 we are to call on Cardinal Martinelli. . . .

". . . God love you and keep you long to serve Him and to

bring joy to all who know you. . . . I don't know how long we
will be here. After this you had better write to Paris, 128 Rue
du Bac, Missions Étrangères. . . ."

On June 29, the feast of St. Peter and St. Paul, Father Walsh
and Father Price were told by Cardinal Gotti that their plan
for an American foreign mission society had been approved.
The next day, a golden summer day, they knelt together at the
feet of Pius X to receive his blessing. Already glowing with the
good news of the Church's approval, they felt their happiness
fill to the brim with the benediction of this sturdy, white-haired
old saint, vested with the tremendous power of the papacy and
endowed with a warm and shrewd fatherliness all his own.

The two priests, each in his individual way, carried that grace
and memory away with them to be their bread of Elias in the
long months and years ahead; for, outside of their heads and
hearts, the Seminary had no existence except as a paper plan.
It had no building, no site, no faculty, no students, no appli-
cants, and almost no funds. It did have friends, from Cardinals
to coal miners. And it had Father Walsh and Father Price.

Back in Boston, Nora and Mollie were overjoyed and bewil-
dered. Things were moving so fast. What would happen next?
Where would the new Seminary be? Where would *The Field
Afar* be transplanted?

During the long hot summer, they worked away at the little
periodical, now more significant than ever. Nora took care of
the business end, Mollie of the editorial. Father Lane came in
occasionally to see how they were getting on.

How much Father Walsh relied on Mollie could be judged
from a cable which he sent to the Washington Press that July.
"Print FA. Rogers fill space."

This he followed up with a letter to Mollie, saying, "I know
that you have used good judgment."

On September 19, both priests were back in Boston. Father
Walsh headed for his office, bringing Father Price with him.
Mollie had brightened the unrelieved grimness of the place

with red roses. They made a cheerful glow on Father Walsh's desk and before the statue of Theophane Venard.

Father Price greeted Nora and Mollie briefly, drew up his chair in front of the statue and went on with his interrupted prayers. Later he plunged out to visit a nearby church.

Father Walsh gave his co-workers some of the highlights of events which he had not already written to them, answering their questions, and taking fresh delight in the outcome of this mission. Finally, he took up the folder on his desk which Nora had marked "important."

At the top of the papers were two letters, one dated June, the other written only a few days before. Both were from a Mary Louise Wholean. Eight years ago, she said, she had heard Father Walsh speak in the parish church at Natick, when she was a student at Wellesley College. He had talked about foreign missions. Now she wanted to know, "Is there any way in which I could serve the work of the foreign missions?"

Father Walsh wrote that day to the Pennsylvania town where she was teaching, inviting her to come to see him when she could arrange to do so.

One Saturday in October, she made a flying trip to Boston and they talked together briefly. To Mary Louise, who had been thinking both of serving the missions and of becoming a religious, Father Walsh made it clear that he could offer her only the opportunity to serve. He could give her no assurance that she would ever be a Sister.

Summing up the understanding which they reached in this brief interview, Mary Wholean later said, "It seemed that I should be satisfied under any conditions, if only I were allowed to do ever so little to help spread the knowledge and love of the Faith . . . given this privilege, I should rejoice under any circumstances. . . ."

That September, shortly after Father Walsh's return, a Miss Sara Sullivan called to offer her services.

If she were thinking of religious life, he asked, had she considered joining the Canadian community at Outremont or the Franciscan Missionaries of Mary?

Her chief thought, she convinced him, was to help the Church in her own country make a beginning in foreign mission work.

In October she gave up her position in the Dean's office at Harvard Medical School and came to 242 Dover Street several times a week to help Nora. She was rather appalled at the dingy noisy storeroom which Nora insisted upon calling an office. She found typing 7000 names for the next issue of *The Field Afar* anything but absorbing. She was somewhat aghast at what she had done but would say to herself, with a little thrill, "This is the life I choose." And she had no intention of turning back.

Miss Mary Dwyer, a clever, generous, and complex woman, owned and managed a business office in Boston and often did work gratis for Father. She made up a third in this trio of volunteers.

By this time, the decision had been reached to locate the Seminary-to-be and *The Field Afar* offices in New York State not too far from the metropolitan city. In October, Father Walsh went to look for a suitable property in that area. Once he had made that move, he came back to Boston more as a visitor than as one returning home. And, as soon as he had found a site, *The Field Afar,* its files, its two typewriters and several desks, and its three new volunteers, would all be going to New York. Nora too might be needed there more than in Boston.

What were Mollie's thoughts as she watched these developments? As she saw the work to which she had given so much, preparing to move elsewhere? As she knew that later but more fortunate recruits would be following it where she could not go?

She did not let anyone at home guess what she felt. She did not abandon the hope of someday being a fourth volunteer in Father Walsh's little group. Yet she could not see when that would be.

She had no doubts as to what she should do. For the present, her place was at home. Only a few years ago, her teacher's salary would have meant little one way or the other to her family. Now she knew that it was needed. To meet his obligations, her father had even mortgaged the Robinwood house, an unprecedented action which weighed heavily upon him and gave Mollie the measure of his critical need.

She had seen and felt this severance from the work she loved coming. She had tried to ready herself for it while Father Walsh and Father Price were still in Europe. To Father Walsh she had written some of her thoughts before he started on his return home. He answered her in a note written soon after his arrival in Boston. With all its restraint, it revealed that the sense of loss was not hers alone.

Dear Mollie—

I may have the pleasure of greeting you before this arrives but I wish to write a few lines to thank you for the letter which you sent to England and to tell you how much I appreciate all you have done this summer.

I have read this morning from Bishop Spalding's *God and the Soul* and some beautiful words on *Silence*—whose argument wonderfully expressed is that the deepest appreciation and greatest powers are voiceless.

In union of prayer and effort I know that you will long continue your devoted service and I will try to help you make it unselfish as I would make my own—a task not without difficulty especially for some dispositions. And yet there is so much more to our credit if in striving for what is more perfect we must struggle to overcome what is weak.

This is no farewell, however. I expect to hover around Boston for at least a few weeks and to fly back frequently.

The F.A. will become monthly in Jan. and I hope to continue its printing at the Was. Press.

Give my best regards to all at home.

As soon as the F.A. is well into the printer's hands I intend to spend an evening at J.P.

Affectionately in Christ,
JAW

PART II

The Finger of God

—◦◦◦—

". . . the longer you live and the more you
see, the more you will become aware of
the finger of God in the guidance of this
work and your own spiritual development."
                              —Mother Mary Joseph

CHAPTER 3

HAWTHORNE

THROUGH THE shortening fall days and into the winter, Father Walsh and Father Price lived with the French Dominican Fathers at Hawthorne, about twenty-seven miles northeast of New York City. Father Cothonay, the Superior, was happy to have them and they could not help but feel welcome; yet as the leaves fell and the snows came, Father Walsh was conscious that Father John Lane, their other associate, was anxious to join them. To provide room for him and, more important still, to establish their small nucleus as an independent and going concern, he knew that they had to have a place of their own where the Seminary could take form and the work of *The Field Afar* could continue and, in time, expand.

Busy seizing every opportunity to make America acquainted with its present missionary opportunity and future foreign mission seminary, Father Walsh was writing letters, giving talks, preaching, seeking out laymen and ecclesiastics to enlist their help, sampling opinions and discussing ideas with his fellow priests. Yet he found time to go house hunting too, giving his full attention to it as he did to whatever was his concern.

By the first week in December nothing had yet been decided in regard to a house for the priests, and he and Father Price went tramping through the snow together investigating leads and offers without success. By that time, however, he had notified Mary Louise Wholean, Mary Dwyer, and Sara Sullivan that they could go ahead with plans to leave their homes in Massachusetts and come to Hawthorne. He had already made provision for these volunteer helpers, renting one small cottage for their living quarters and two rooms in another for their offices. When he found that all three could be ready to come after Christmas, he asked them to begin the new year by making a retreat together at the New York Cenacle and to reach Hawthorne on the sixth of January. Under his direction they would carry on the publication of *The Field Afar,* the lifeline, in his opinion, of the new Catholic Foreign Mission Society of America.

Late in the afternoon of the sixth, newly acquainted with one another, recently guided through the silences, meditations, and other spiritual exercises of a retreat by a wise and gentle religious of the Cenacle, Mother Filippi, and fresh from a closing conference by Father Walsh himself, they chugged into Hawthorne aboard a New York Central local. Their retreat concluded, they had gone shopping in Manhattan while Father Walsh caught the earliest train back to Hawthorne. Looking out eagerly, and a little fearfully too, they saw their spiritual Father standing on the platform, smiling and lifting his hand in greeting.

As they got off the train, he came toward them with his quick energetic step. "Welcome to the three wise women on the feast of the three wise men!"

The hills of Hawthorne were rosy in the sunset as he led them up through the snow. He told them news and developments and chuckled over setbacks and frustrations as they went along.

"Oh, and Nora Shea is getting in later this evening."

"To stay?"

"For a while, to help get the work started. You won't mind having a little extra assistance, I suppose?" he asked, laughing a little.

At the narrow door of the narrow little house poised on a miniature terrace Father John Lane stood smiling broadly. "Welcome!" he called out, his fine pain-lined face beaming on the three of them. "Happy feast! You are welcome indeed on the feast of the first missioners, the wise men."

Father Price came forward from within the house, looking at them over his glasses, nodding, smiling, happy in the arrival of recruits to a work so dear to his heart, but woman-shy as always.

A neighbor and her son were unpacking and washing dishes in the kitchen; Father Walsh led his three wise women out to introduce them.

"The place isn't quite ready, but the essentials are here, I believe," he commented.

Soon the priests were gone, and not long after, the neighbor and her boy. In the fading light the small house showed itself more uncompromising within than without. The windows, the walls, the floors, leaked cold air although a good fire burned in the furnace. Furniture had been marshaled painstakingly from different sources. Some of it had been arranged; most of it still stood stacked here and there in the bare, uncarpeted rooms. Food in paper bags and parcels lay on the kitchen table.

Mary Louise stood numbly, taking it all in, her gray eyes wide. All unconsciously and quite illogically, she had expected to enter a house completely prepared to receive them—carpeted, furnished, and dusted, with bright lamps burning, a cook in the kitchen, and a hot meal ready on the stove.

Sara Sullivan and Mary Dwyer moved toward the kitchen table, peeped into the packages.

"How about supper?" asked Sara. "If you are not overfastidious, I can get something together."

She began to go through the parcels, to look over the kitchen utensils, to investigate the stove. Mary Dwyer shot off to explore and to organize, full of ideas and plans.

Mary Louise, who could wrest scholastic honors from an exacting Wellesley faculty, found housekeeping a cabalistic ritual. She picked something simple and, in her fatigue, fundamental.

"I'll make the beds," she offered.

As she went up the dark narrow stairs, carrying the pain that she took for granted these days, her heart lifted. Father had promised them poor accommodations, plenty of work, and an uncertain future. Well, here it was. But he had shared with them, too, his own motivation, giving it to them in a short formula that welled up in her heart now. As she went looking for the sheets, pulling the beds out from the walls, plumping the pillows, she found herself repeating his words over and over in her mind, "For God and souls."

In the days and weeks that followed, the cottage lived up to their first impression of it. Its arctic cold brought the new residents to the breakfast table in their winter coats, and drove them, shivering, to sit on the radiators between courses at dinner. Its plumbing had nasty and unpredictable habits. They who were dedicated to baths with the enthusiasm of most Americans and had learned to accept the twentieth-century flush toilet as a natural phenomenon, learned in time to cat-wash in a basin half filled with dark water, to care for their inconvenient commodes, and to rejoice with foolish ardor in a clean drink when good water was sent to them from Rosary Hill as a gift from Mother Alphonsa Lathrop, Superior of the Dominican Sisters there and one-time much-admired Rose Hawthorne.

Sometimes their hearts sang and sometimes their hearts sank. Father Walsh's good humor in the face of difficulties and failures and his sympathetic concern with everything that affected them helped to buoy them up. He planned their schedule, drew up their few and simple house rules, proposed principles and ideals to live by, helped them in their office emergencies and stood by in small household crises and disasters. He gave them a series of instructions on the spiritual life based on the beatitudes. He called these volunteer helpers of his "secretaries," for want of a handier title. He got help to bolster up the house's declining conveniences, a teen-age boy to unfreeze pipelines and pump water, laundresses willing to attempt washing almost without water, cooks and then more cooks to replace those who came and left.

The first of these arrived two days after the secretaries themselves reached Hawthorne.

"Come, Sara, look!"

"Mary Louise, quick, the new cook!"

From an upstairs window they watched her come. Large and circular herself, she was rounded off on top with a tiny circle of a hat from which a feather plume drooped and nodded as she rocked along.

"She can't be real!"

She did indeed look like a cartoonist's creation. Her eyes seemed to confer with each other about this possibility, looking inquiringly toward each other across the bridge of her round, upturned nose. But she was real; her dialogue bloomed with life and local color; she cooked like a dream, but she did not last. She had heard somehow that a suicide had taken place in the cottage.

"I don't like ghosts," she said darkly, "and I don't care for sliding panels neither."

"Sliding panels?" Sara asked, lifting her eyebrows.

"Sliding panels is what I said. Just lay awake at night and listen to them."

In the end, however, she admitted that it was her arctic upper room and not the bothersome spirits that got the better of her.

When she learned that lighthearted, friendly Nora was to return to Boston for a time, it was the last straw.

"Good-by to you ladies. Sorry to leave you in the lurch. And good-by to the Klondike—and no regrets."

The little round hat with its drooping, bobbing feather went bobbing down the hill and "the Klondike" saw its owner no more. She had a long line of successors, few who cooked as well, and none so colorful. To prepare meals even for three in that inconvenient cottage was a full-time job, and the secretaries had plenty of work to do in connection with *The Field Afar*.

Mary Louise Wholean, an exact and careful worker with a fine-honed mind and a good grasp of languages, helped with the editorial work, giving attention particularly to missionary articles and letters contributed from the field, many of them in French, some in Italian and German. These she translated and edited. She was responsible, too, for the file of potential copy— articles, photographs, postcards. She was to prepare occasional articles for the daily press and mission notes for the Providence *Visitor* and the Hartford *Transcript*. And like the two other secretaries, she was to help wrap and mail *The Field Afar*, which at that time had a circulation of about ten thousand.

Mary Dwyer was the bookkeeper, took dictation, did the multigraphing, had charge of stock, both office supplies and material for sale—such as the small books and pamphlets which Father Walsh had begun to issue—was responsible for all the ordering and shipping, together with whatever invoicing, listing, and billing these entailed.

From out of Sara Sullivan's balky and antiquated addressograph poured the monthly wrappers for the magazine. She had charge of the subscribers' index and stencils, sent acknowledgments to new subscribers and urged the lapsed to renew their subscriptions. She was housekeeper too and, when they had no cook, did most of the preparation of the meals as well.

Nora Shea acted as Father's secretary and filled in wherever she was most needed. She knew bookkeeping as well as stenography and had a grasp of Father's requirements and habits that none of the others possessed, partly the result of experience, and partly due to a particularly intuitive and sympathetic nature. She was the only one of the four working on a professional basis and salary. She and her family had recently agreed to buy a little home together, and they were all still paying off the debt. If her heart prompted her to throw her lot in with the group, the claims of justice were still stronger, and she postponed volunteering until later.

As Father Walsh planned the work of the secretaries, they had enough to keep them stimulated and on their toes but not enough to overwhelm them. The eccentricities of the cottage caused some loss of efficiency and occasional tension but gave them some good laughs, too. The necessity of filling in for disappearing cooks cut into their time, especially Sara's, but Father Walsh understood all this and did not press them, even if he felt the burden of added work weighing him down.

The sickness that came was of another order. Together with some dispositional difficulties, it was paralyzing for the work and deeply disruptive of their small hive of community life. Indeed it seemed to mark the group for annihilation as a unit.

As the long winter weeks stretched out into a late spring, Mary Dwyer was up and down, at one time full of driving energy, talk and accomplishment and, almost within the hour, drained of physical resources, silent, unable to eat or to work. Sometimes she just disappeared into her room, sometimes she kept at her desk, ate little, or lay on the couch in the dining room, eating nothing while the others had their dinner.

On her way home from the office Sara sometimes stopped in at the little Dominican church and, kneeling alone there, covered her face with her hands and wept. Being one of Father Walsh's secretaries was proving so different from being on the staff in the Dean's office at Harvard Medical School. She thought the priest cold, did not understand the cheer and hope with which he met their shared difficulties or the demands in vision and dedication which he made on the secretaries as well as on himself. She would not go back on her decision, she would stick it out somehow, but it was hard, hard.

Over the past months, Mary Louise Wholean had come to accept pain as her normal companion and bore it without complaint or self-consciousness. She did not, or would not, connect it with death. And yet death was already growing wildly within this woman of twenty-nine, pushing its way into the domain of life in an enormous tumor that was taking over the whole abdominal cavity. By St. Joseph's feast, March 19, she lay helplessly in bed, fearful of awakening the spasms of torment that even for her were a new experience in pain.

An operation held death at bay temporarily. During the critical time of her illness, Father Walsh anointed her and made the trip daily from Hawthorne to New York City to visit her at St. Vincent's Hospital. As she convalesced, he came often, amusing her with his humor, keeping her informed about the work she loved so well, never allowing her to feel that these trips were a tax upon his time.

When she returned to Hawthorne on May 11, she came back to another and more convenient house which included both the living quarters of the secretaries and *The Field Afar* offices. By June she was slowly gaining strength and able to do a limited amount of work. A studious solitary both by taste and habit, she found herself, because of this illness, less able than before to participate in community living. She had already discovered that it cost her far less to pray for others than to take part with them in what was called recreation. For her, pleasure and refreshment lay in doing the work to which she gave herself unstintingly.

Mary Dwyer was still up and down. Sara was tired out and, at times, sharp-tongued. The genial Nora returned from Boston for a while to help out and did much to reduce the mountain of work and to lift the depressed morale.

All this time, Father Walsh had been studying the secretaries. All were devout and conscientious; all, even Mary Dwyer in her oscillating way, were generous and entirely sincere in their desire to further the cause of foreign missions under Father Walsh's direction. Yet he wondered. Working with them, observing them under all sorts of circumstances, he had come to know their temperaments, their points of view, their reactions to community living, to the long haul of day-in, day-out confining work, and to the quick flare-up of emergencies. He had to conclude that among them there was no leader on whom to build for the future.

As spring became summer, he often turned over in his mind what he should do. Should he have some community come to train the secretaries in religious living? Even as auxiliaries, they ought to have some religious formation other than that which he could give them in his instructions and conferences. What if no other recruits came and came soon? Could these few hold out?

As early as December, 1911, he had introduced to his readers the subject of a new American community of women for foreign mission work. He still had out feelers for new recruits, especially through priests in the Boston Archdiocese. Now and then too he let fall a bit of Irish *comether* in *The Field Afar*—a stimulating bit of news about the secretaries maybe, an allusion to their service and value, or again a baited bit of information.

But what to do with the recruits he already had was his most pressing concern. First of all, a leader was needed. If Mollie could come to join the secretaries, Father Walsh was convinced that this biggest problem would be solved. He had noticed the nearly magical effect her presence had produced when she had visited them over the weekend of Washington's birthday. Sara had met Mollie casually. Nora, of course, knew her well.

The other two were acquainted only through hearsay. Yet all three seemed different while she was there. The tone rose, the air lightened, work went like holidaying, and a sense of well-being filled the shabby little house and crowded offices. Nora bubbled over. Mary Dwyer was interested and stimulated. Mary Louise Wholean shone in a subdued but contented way. And Sara smiled her lovely, special smile, challenged, relaxed, and amused.

As July first, the expiration date for his agreement with the secretaries, approached, Father Walsh knew that, leader or no leader, he must come to some decision in regard to the group. First he talked things over with Mary Louise Wholean, outlining the possibilities. Although the secretaries themselves indulged in occasional speculations about a vague new order, he thought a new order the least likely of all developments. He had earlier broached the subject of bringing in the Franciscan Missionaries of Mary; now he went through other alternatives with her. Like the other secretaries, Mary Louise had come to Hawthorne primarily to further the work, not to become a religious. She admitted that now they all had the thought and hope of forming a new order.

As for herself, however, she summed up her dispositions briefly: "I shall be satisfied whatever is done, or if nothing is done."

On Sunday, June 23, at his regular weekly conference, Father Walsh laid before the secretaries the possible future courses open to them as a group.

"There appear to be three possibilities," he said. "First, as a group you might develop into a new order. Secondly, you might come under the guidance and jurisdiction, at least during a formative period, of some already established religious group and be absorbed into their ranks or aggregated to them. And, finally, you could, of course, remain as you are."

He then went on to discuss these possibilities. The first he

canceled out as apparently impossible under their present circumstances. "You have no one qualified to act as a superior. I
could not myself in fairness to you and to the work that lies
ahead make myself responsible for training you as religious.
Once the students for the seminary arrive, more and more of my
time will be taken up with them. That day lies only a few
months off." The third possibility left the little group with no
security, no means for future development. To him then it
seemed that the most practical plan was to invite some group
such as the Franciscan Missionaries of Mary to train them and
then in some way to aggregate them to their own community
as auxiliaries.

In his direct but kindly way he went into the matter of their
future as individuals. To give each a chance to rest, to gain a
new perspective on their life at Hawthorne, and also, if they
wished to do so, to bow out gracefully, he had made up his mind
that they should all take two weeks' vacation at home during
July, returning for the rest of the summer, if they wished to
come back, and by September making a clear-cut decision
whether or not to remain. This plan he now laid before them.
He let his quiet, searching look rest upon them, and concluded:

"I want you to consider individually whether you are to continue in the work. Put these questions to yourselves in the days
ahead, especially while you are at home, and consider them
well. 'Do I feel a strong desire, or only willingness, to do this
work? Have I the necessary physical strength? Do I know my
own shortcomings? Are my habits so firmly fixed that I could
not put myself under the will of another?' "

In Mary Dwyer's heart lay an uncomfortable residue of indulged eccentricities and demanding emotionalism. Already it
was forming into a small but flinty core of animosity. She herself called it a cloud and felt that Father Walsh was responsible
for raising it between them.

*   *   *

The day Sara and Mary Dwyer went away for their vacation, Mollie and Nora arrived from Boston and came panting up the hill to join Mary Louise. However hot and tired they were, they brought with them laughter, an aura of home, and a blessed sense of normality. It was summer, schools were closed, teachers vacationing. Mollie found no reason and no wish to prevent her helping out at Hawthorne until it was time to go back to the classroom.

It did not take her long to get into the midst of things. The morning after her arrival, Katherine, the cook in office at the moment, given to tears and misfortunes as well as to good works, strained her back and collapsed over the coal scuttle. The secretaries were just about to go down the hill to Mass.

Mollie turned back, put down her missal as if her mind had already been made up for just this contingency.

"You two go on," she said, and to Katherine, patting her shoulder, "and you go up to bed. . . ."

"But breakfast . . ." wailed Katherine. "There isn't even a fire in that nasty stove yet."

"Don't worry about breakfast. We won't starve. Go on upstairs to bed. I'll be up in a few minutes to see you."

By the time the others returned from Mass, Mollie had a fire in the stove and a good breakfast all ready for them. Katherine had had her back rubbed, her breakfast in bed, and her spirits revived, and was finding life far less melancholy.

Mollie went down the hill to the priests' house after breakfast to have a short talk with Father Walsh before he left on one of his innumerable trips. That done, she walked up the hill again, went to the office and began her assault on the mass of work accumulated there by tackling the stencil file. She was glad to be there, and her contentment reached out to embrace and encourage those around her.

"These are happy days," Mary Louise set down in her little chronicle; "even the cat is so glad to be here that he has given

up his wild ways. He used to regard humans as his mortal enemies and, while he stayed around to secure our food scraps,
would at the same time threaten us with teeth and claws. Now
he rests contentedly in Mollie's lap."

Sara Sullivan and Mary Dwyer soon returned and then there
were five, with work enough now for twice that number. Mollie
found the office routine as pleasant as ever, delighted in Father
Walsh's large vision and practical plans for the future, and happily lost herself in serving and supporting others. When the
cook fell sick, she added the duties of housekeeper and nurse to
her share of the office work, lightly catching up and carrying
along those extra duties which Sara had found so wearing and
worrying. Yet she could see no way of giving herself entirely to
the work before the following year, if then.

Early in August, at Mother Alphonsa's invitation, the secretaries and one of the two Brothers who made up Father Walsh's
entire male auxiliary staff went up to the Cancer Hospital at
Rosary Hill to sing for the patients. Mollie and Mary Dwyer
were the vocal mainstays of the secretaries. The others leaned
heavily on their strength and picked their way carefully along
the notes. Brother Thomas McCann, with his amiable fun and
golden tenor, covered himself with glory and shed radiance
over his fellow concert artists as well.

Thanking the performers afterward, Mother Alphonsa managed to get Mollie off to herself. In their short acquaintance
these two women had developed a deep affection and reverence
for each other. From the beginning Mother Alphonsa had
shown her kindness to the secretaries in all sorts of thoughtful
ways. From the first time that she met Mollie, she had been
drawn to her.

"Stately youth," she observed, in her positive way, "and
energy. There is the bright star for the future in Father Walsh's
'holy group,' as the patients call them."

Mollie saw in Mother Alphonsa the charm of a great legend

and felt the magnet of her personal holiness and dedicated charity. It was hard to realize that this white-habited figure, this aging reticent religious committed to plain speaking, direct action, and an almost frightening personal poverty, was the once imperious, spoiled and lovely Rose Hawthorne, daughter of Nathaniel.

Described in her auburn-haired youth by an enthusiastic admirer as "a peach blossom in the sun," she still retained the temperamental vigor and, in a translated form, the enthusiasm of those earlier years. Foundress and Mother General of a new Dominican community dedicated to nurse the cancerous poor, she had, at fifty-eight years, made her vows for life only three years ago. She knew all about beginnings.

Now she bent her acute blue eyes on Mollie and said, "Father Walsh is very happy to have you here this summer—happy and relieved. You know that, of course."

"Father is always so appreciative of anything done for him—beyond anything it deserves."

The blue eyes grew a little more intent. "Has he told you just how much having you here means to him and his work?"

He had, and recently. "He has spoken of it, yes." Mollie's serenity clouded a little.

"He fears that this beginning will come to nothing if you do not join them."

"I don't think that I am that important, Mother." He had put the case to Mollie in almost the same words.

"Father Walsh does."

"But there are reasons why I cannot stay. I really must go home."

An urgency born, not of Rose Hawthorne's old imperious ways but of strong conviction, made Mother Alphonsa lean forward and say, "You can't leave. You must stay. You must."

Mollie was silent, troubled. Mother's voice was like the urging of her own heart. But how can I? she thought.

"What is it? Financial?"

Financial? Yes and no. No, not financial in those indefinable and manifold bonds that fastened her to home by love, gratitude, honor, and duty. The financial was a straightforward problem, at present insoluble but simple. But what of her father's aging powers, her mother's increasing physical weakness, their declining fortunes, the big house which had begun to empty of the children who had once filled it with friends and laughter and who would now be marrying and making homes of their own? Her service and support, her presence, were needed there as never before. Her father's financial reverses simply put a fine point on the goad that drove her affections to supply everything she could for them who had done everything for her. She was the oldest girl, "the old reliable," as even Father Walsh called her. She was needed . . . Yes, needed, but not indispensable. No one is. She came back to the plainer problem.

"Yes," she said, "it is financial. There are obligations."

"How much money would you want? How much do you need?"

Mollie laughed ruefully and answered as one calling attention to an obvious impossibility. "If I had two thousand dollars I could stay."

"Two thousand dollars," repeated Mother Alphonsa, and she said nothing further.

A few days later Father Walsh asked to see Mollie. He held out to her a note from Mother Alphonsa.

She read it, amazed and aghast. "But I can't take it."

"She says it is a thank offering," he remarked gravely.

"Oh, but I couldn't think of accepting it. Look at her own burdens, caring for all those sick people, trying to build, supporting her own Sisters. If I had ever guessed what she had in mind . . ."

In the end, Father Walsh's quiet reasoning and Mother Alphonsa's sweet but unyielding insistence overcame Mollie's resistance. Mother Alphonsa would not let her feel indebted for the gift, but turned the tables so completely as to put her in the position of a benefactress.

"We Sisters," she wrote, "have been marvelously helped in the last year and a half, and I wanted to make a thank offering. Your clear and just mind will recognize the good sense in my desire to make your gifted and precious self the key to blessings for ourselves."

Whatever Mollie might not need for her own purposes could be, and later was, turned over to the infant work poised so lightly on the razor's edge of financial nothingness. Characteristically, Mother Alphonsa attached no conditions to her gift.

Before Mollie went home to tell her people of her intention, wind up her affairs, pack, and spend a few weeks with her family, she saw the hilltop of Our Lady, that Maryknoll which thus far had existed only in a name, blossom into reality. And she had her glad part in bringing this about, making the purchase for Father Walsh.

Father Walsh had talked, thought, planned, purposed "Maryknoll," but until then he had only a few rented houses and his own vision. His first attempt to buy property for his future seminary at nearby Pocantico Hills had been effectively blocked by Mr. John D. Rockefeller, who apparently had no liking for an institution as his next-door neighbor.

On August 14, Father Walsh, together with Monsignor John J. Dunn, director of the Propagation of the Faith of New York, and Mollie, motored to Ossining to look over a property for sale there, a modest farm of ninety-nine acres.

The priests wore dusters and scarves, Mollie wore a motoring veil to keep her large hat anchored. Dust rolled off the road behind them and farmers gentled their shying horses onto the grass as the party raced by at twenty miles an hour.

The farm immediately won their hearts. Its woodland and

fields, its height, its sweeping view of the magnificent Hudson and the blue hills beyond all seemed to express in physical terms the spiritual character which Father Walsh wanted for his society and its work. He felt not so much that he had found a place as that he had simply recognized his Maryknoll on sight. "This is it," he said to himself. "This is Maryknoll."

His exaltation did not prevent him from going carefully through the four buildings on the property—two homesteads at some distances from each other, a carriage house with quarters for hired men, and a barn. All except the barn were in need of repair, but all seemed basically sound. After a second look on another day and reassurance about the source and supply of water, the purchase was made and duly celebrated with a supper of Boston baked beans.

In the years ahead and far ahead, hundreds of young girls, fresh from parting with their families to become Maryknoll Sisters, feeling a little numbed, heart-wrung and homesick, would find in their newly acquired Mother, the head of their community, the person above all others who seemed to understand exactly how things were without being told and to enter completely and consolingly into their feelings. Experience had taught her what that severance meant.

While at home, Mollie wrote gratefully to Mother Alphonsa, revealing in a way unusual to her the grief and strain she felt at parting with her family.

My dear Mother,
        Father Walsh has forwarded your letter and it finds me still overwhelmed.
    Just today you must let me thank you. One must recognize Divine Providence in this, realizing that all comes from Him, but nevertheless it is right to appreciate and love the instrument through which He works. Truly we are all tools in this great workshop—fashioned for different ends—ready for the Master's use. You have been blessed with great gifts, but the priceless pearl is the tender mother heart through which the Mother of us all sent so

great a blessing to me. And you must not scold or even frown, if in my heart I feel that I am in some measure your child.

I can do nothing in a material way to thank you—but so long as I live and long after if possible, at least a *Memorare* will be offered for you each day—a trifling thing in itself but powerful when laid at our Lady's feet.

It is quite different to dream of giving up one's family and friends—when a glorified picture of heroic self-sacrifice lures the mind to dwell on it—and actually to face all that it means. Yet I have not hesitated for a moment. Personal grief is nothing. Sorrow comes from hurting those we love.

My people have been most generous . . . and after the first passionate outbreak, unselfishly gave me up. Each one is striving to do all the little things they know I love, and we're all saying good-by to the places that hold such dear memories of childhood. It is good to feel their love closing about me. My heart is a ragged old thing these days.

I shall go back on the 9th and perhaps you will let me see you someday.

Please pray for me, for the greatest ordeal faces me.

Gratefully and affectionately,
Mollie Rogers.

Just about the time that Mollie wrote to Mother Alphonsa, little Miss Shea, Miss Margaret Shea, came calling on her at Robinwood Avenue. Miss Shea thought that she had never entered a home with a warmer, friendlier atmosphere. And indeed the old house had bloomed again. The brothers rallied around, teasing and joking. Friends and relatives poured in and out. The old songs were sung. Louise played. Elizabeth set herself to recall and reproduce the dishes Mollie most enjoyed. Father beamed and laughed. Mother went about smiling that quiet smile which enveloped everybody.

It was she who opened the door for Miss Shea and said, "Why, come right in, dear. Mollie is expecting you."

Little Miss Margaret was not exactly nervous, not precisely afraid, but just a little keyed up. She had come from nearby Melrose for an interview with Miss Rogers. She wanted to help

Father Walsh with his work for foreign missions. She had called him when he was in Boston recently to discuss the possibility, and he had referred her to Miss Rogers, saying that whatever decision they reached together would be satisfactory to him.

Miss Shea had half expected to find Miss Rogers in a sort of convent. She had formed a dim picture of Miss Rogers as a nun-like figure, quite correct herself and quite concerned about the correct way for young women to speak, act, and dress—especially young ladies interested in offering their services to the cause of foreign missions.

Dressed all in black with long sleeves, stylish, of course, but quite subdued naturally, Miss Shea had permitted herself a modish white hat with a small bunch of purple violets. The complete costume amounted to half-mourning and stood above reproach.

Mollie came quickly into the room, all vitality and welcome. She wore a summery dress with short sleeves and had her lovely chestnut hair swept up in a pompadour. Miss Shea felt a little breathless.

What a lovely little thing, Mollie was thinking. Those clothes —can she possibly be a widow? I thought she said *Miss* Shea. And she looks so young.

They sat down to talk.

"I've *always* wanted to be a religious," said Miss Shea, looking back, it would seem, over decades of longing. "And I've made inquiries. But none of the communities have seemed just right. For me, I mean. I talked to the Good Shepherd Sisters and when they told me about the girls and all, why, I admired them *tremendously,* but I knew that I could never do that. I have dear friends in the Holy Child community and my confessor thought that I might like to be one of them, but they *teach.* And I can't *teach.* I'm not *trained.* Then Father said maybe I could enter as a lay Sister, but I told him 'Oh, no! I could never do *that.* I don't want to have to carry *coal* all my life!' "

"Carry coal?"

"You know, coming up out of the cellar with it—for the kitchen stove."

"Oh, I see."

"And the Sisters of Charity, the cornet Sisters, I *did* think I would like to be one of *them*. And I called on them, but the Sister I talked to told me, 'Go away and come back in a year. *Then* we'll consider it.'"

"Why was that?"

"She thought that I was too *young*."

"She did? How old are you?"

"Why, I'll be *eighteen* in December!"

"What kind of work can you do?"

"Nothing much. I do love children. . . ."

"I do too."

Her confessor, it seemed, thought that Margaret might offer to work for Father Walsh's project without, however, committing herself for any definite period because of her possible religious vocation. She presented his point of view, a little anxious as to how it might strike Miss Rogers.

"That seems much the wisest plan, Margaret," said Miss Rogers, smiling at her. "Let's just go together and see what God has in store for us."

Brother Thomas tickled the big bony horse with his whip. "Gee-up. Come on there! Clk! Clk!" The carriage curled away from Hawthorne station and went rocketing through the village, a fat spiral of golden dust unfolding behind it. The old horse stretched out his neck gallantly, pumped along at a rocking gallop and did his utmost to look well bred.

Mollie and Brother Thomas laughed and talked together. Flushed with excitement and anticipation, Margaret tried to take in everything as they bounced and clattered over the country road and the long shadows of late afternoon slid soundlessly over them. It was September 9, and Mollie and Margaret were coming to Hawthorne to stay.

"Is it far?" Margaret asked anxiously. It would be dreadful not to see it until the last minute.

"What's that?" yelled Brother Thomas, as their carriage shivered and danced and a spray of stones slapped against the floor boards.

"Is it far—the convent—I mean, the house?"

"Far? No, no. Not far at all. We'll be there any minute now, if we get there at all."

"How far is it?"

Brother Thomas gave the horse another little stimulant with his whip, and then made a lordly gesture with it in the general direction of Hawthorne's upper rim.

"See that place up there?"

"Why, yes! Is that it?"

"Like it?"

"Why, I had no idea it was like that, such a big place. Isn't it wonderful!"

"Wonderful is the word," said Brother Thomas.

The old horse had slowed down as the hill lengthened out, but Brother Thomas urged him into a trot and they swept into the driveway at a good pace and made a broad turn. As if from a merry-go-round, Margaret saw steps, porches, windows, a few staring, surprised faces flash by; then they swept right out again.

"Tch. Tch." Brother Thomas shook his head. "I must have made a mistake," he remarked apologetically. "That seems to be Mother Alphonsa's place. But your house can't be far from here."

They drove on and came to a little cottage standing among trees on the rim of Hawthorne's green bowl of hills. Four women came running out to welcome them. Mollie was surrounded, exclaimed over, embraced, pelted with questions and bits of news. Margaret, once Mollie had drawn her forward and introduced her, hung back, a little overcome by all this exuberance and seniority.

Sara Sullivan came over to her, took her suitcase, and led her inside. "Maybe you would like to see your room and get settled," she said.

They went up together to a tiny attic room with sloping walls. Margaret took it all in on a held breath, ran to the window and looked out. She could see only the sunset sky, the blackening trees and the rounded hills. She looked at the scene and Sara looked at her. A moment passed. The peaceful view, the slanting, spare little room spoke to Margaret's heart.

She turned around, her face full of delight. "It's perfect, just perfect. I never dreamed I would have anything like it."

The little pucker between Sara's brows smoothed out. Her brilliant smile responded gratefully to this unlooked-for enthusiasm.

"We didn't know just what kind of person was coming and what she would think of such accommodations. I'm so glad—and relieved," she concluded, "that you like it."

A few days after they arrived, Father Walsh returned from making his yearly retreat. One of the first things he did was to place Mollie in charge of the secretaries. It was not a surprise to anyone, as he had already led the others to expect it and had let Mollie know that he looked to her to bolster up and sustain the group.

Characteristically, however, he wanted first to know the secretaries' wishes and to have everything clear and in writing. Each of the five received a brief note asking her to answer two questions: "Do you wish Mollie to direct you, i.e., under my direction? Will you do your best to practice obedience to her, or rather, to the authority invested in her, even if occasional commands seem unreasonable?"

All of the answers were in the affirmative.

At this time Mollie was twenty-nine. So was Mary Louise.

Margaret was seventeen. The other three were all older than
Mollie, Nora by only a few years, but Sara was thirty-seven, and
Mary Dwyer forty.

Mollie accepted this charge as she accepted every opportunity
for service held out to her by Father Walsh, giving her entire
good will and fine intelligence to carry out his ideas and to
bring success to his plans. To take charge or to cook, to wrap
the magazine or to write a story, to fill in anywhere she was
needed—it was all one to her.

Only a day after Mollie's appointment, the secretaries saw
at Mass and later met in the office the first of the six Seminary
students expected for the fall term. Handsome, with grave
dark eyes and an engaging smile, he was Francis Xavier Ford of
Brooklyn. Following their first encounter with this young boy
who years later, as a Bishop in South China, would die a martyr's death in a Communist prison, Mary Louise offered the
opinion, expressed in her old-fashioned way, that Francis Xavier
Ford's appearance "suggests possibilities of much strength and
zeal."

On September 18 the Fathers and their handful of students
moved to "Maryknoll," as Father Walsh was already calling his
farm on the hill above Ossining. After a period of straightening
up and settling down which Father Walsh crisply defined as
"chaos," just as things were beginning to fall into normal lines,
they woke up one morning to find that their faint-hearted cook
had departed and left them breakfastless. Father Walsh had only
to tell Mollie what had happened. She set out immediately for
Maryknoll, undismayed at the prospect which had sent the cook
hurrying out for a pre-dawn train.

Hannah, who had been cooking for the secretaries, joined
forces with her the following day, and together they turned
out three robust meals a day, with occasional evidence of Mollie's special touches. They mowed down pots and pans, stocked
the ever-gaping provision shelves, met the usual unusual situa-

tions—unexpected guests, late and early dinners, the lack or delay of supplies—as these came up.

They slept in the old farmhouse or lodge down the hill from the Seminary. The farmer and his wife who still occupied it offered each an unprepossessing room and a large sagging bed. At the end of a long day Mollie would sink into hers too tired to stay awake and battle the cockroaches and bedbugs which came out in the dark to take possession of the ancient farmhouse.

One evening after the third meal of the day had been successfully turned out, Mollie went, tired and hot, to sit on the back steps of the Seminary and let the lovely evening air and the beautiful outlook refresh her before she returned to finish up the tag ends of the day.

It was dusk, the time when at home her brothers used to come pounding up the steps, slamming the front door, knowing their mother was home and asking if Pa had come in yet and whether dinner was ready or not. On just such evenings, too, as they grew older, some of them might be out canoeing on the Charles River. Their picnic basket empty, the sunset colors fading from the sky, they would dip their paddles rhythmically in the darkening water and, singing, head for the boathouse and home.

She had not been sitting there long when a file of dark figures came around the corner of the house—the priests and students out for a short walk on this peerless evening. The Fathers saw Mollie, lifted their hats and bowed; the boys tossed pony nods in her direction; and the well-fed line passed on down the hill and out of sight.

They had all had a very good supper, Mollie thought, and a very good dinner, and a fine breakfast, too, if you wanted to go back that far. Why hadn't anyone bothered to mention it? Why doesn't anyone ever remember to say anything about food to the people who prepare it unless there is something the matter with it?

Not given to self-pity, she was as near discouragement as she

could come. "Oh men!" she said to herself, and got up to go
back to the kitchen. But she never forgot that people who create
meals deserve commendation just as much as painters, poets,
and philosophers—and need it more.

CHAPTER 4

ST. TERESA'S

O N OCTOBER 15, 1912,—with the air of an Irish king bringing visiting royalty to his favorite castle—Brother Thomas drove into the shaggy old farm with the brand-new name of Maryknoll. Pulling back on the reins as if he were checking a matched pair of pure-blooded Arabians, he brought the ancient carry-all to a halt. The solitary nag between the shafts breathed deeply and rocked to and fro on his knobby legs.

Brother Thomas made a regal gesture. "Well, here we are! Home, sweet home. Be it ever so humble," he began to sing, "there's no-o place like home."

Like kittens in a basket, three well-cooled secretaries popped out from under their covers in the old vehicle and began to work their way from under their belongings. These transplants from Hawthorne felt that this inconsequential shift of person-nel—three today, three more tomorrow—made up a really mo-mentous occasion, for themselves if for nobody else.

They knew that they were not coming to a well-prepared house. Mr. Jenks, the farmer, and his family had just vacated it the day before. Part of his furniture, awaiting a moving van,

still clogged the lower rooms and hallway. Carpenters and
plumbers were already at work making repairs and dirt. Mollie,
with her position as head cook at the Seminary, had no time to
work any transformation in this hodgepodge.

One after another the three secretaries climbed down stiffly
from the carry-all: Margaret red-cheeked, bundled in a horse
blanket and snuggling the cat; Mary Louise, gray with chill in
spite of the carpets under which she and Anna Towle had
hidden from the wind; Anna Towle herself, a newcomer, with
a beautiful youthful face, snapping brown eyes and striking
white hair, carrying, of all things, an armful of summer hats—
as out of place, season, and use as April's daffodils. She made
straight for the Seminary kitchen, saying "Where's Mollie?"

Mollie came out, put her arms around each one of them and
hurried them in to warm themselves by the kitchen stove. She
had it bumping and bubbling with big jolly pots which, with
the full oven, sent a fine circulation of tantalizing odors soaring
around the room. Margaret's mouth began to water.

"When the priests and boys are served," Mollie said, "we'll
have our supper right here at the kitchen table together, as snug
as you please. There won't be a stove in our own house for a
few days more at least."

After they had attended Benediction in the Seminary chapel
and had made a very good supper, they walked down to the
Lodge together. To commemorate the day of their coming and
to honor the great Carmelite whose feast it was, Father Walsh
had already christened the old house "St. Teresa's."

In the dim light, with a surf of flying leaves breaking around
it and its protecting stand of trees writhing in the wind, the
old Dutch colonial house looked at once less dilapidated and
more ancient than by daylight. Out of one of those dormer
windows tunneled into the steep sloping roof a white-capped
maidservant of the seventeenth century might call out to ask
their business; along the railing of the narrow second-floor gal-

lery several of General Clinton's red-coated British soldiery might lean down to look at them inquiringly; and before the many-paned windows of the first-floor rooms a file of friendly Mohican Indians might conceivably drift by as silently as smoke in the wind.

The latest of many generations to seek shelter under those rafters pinned together with hickory pegs so cannily and so long ago, the secretaries stood outside silently a moment. Then Mollie opened the door, went ahead into the darkness and lit a kerosene lamp, and the others followed her in, knowing that they were home.

The next day the rest of the secretaries arrived, and in the days that followed they had much to do. They settled in, workmen or no workmen. In an upstairs room Anna Towle's cheeks grew pink as she laid out cassock patterns, cut out yards of black material and drove her faithful old sewing machine at such a pace that it thundered away like a miniature thrasher and poured out cassock parts onto the newly scrubbed pine flooring.

Downstairs in a large room to the right of the front door— which might have been the common room of a one-time inn— all the paraphernalia for editing and publishing *The Field Afar* was assembled, arranged, and rearranged. Here and there among the files, tables, and machines, strategically placed secretaries took up the pursuit of their several occupations. Mary Dwyer leaned over her books, making careful entries, or stood hand-turning the multigraph machine. Its clashing rhythm, together with Sara's banging addressograph, did nothing to help Mary Louise concentrate where she sat among her manuscripts, composing and editing. At her typewriter, tapping out Father Walsh's letters, Nora was always tuned for his quick call. Margaret went where she was most needed, abetting Mollie in her many house-improvement projects, getting the meals for the secretaries, working at one task or another in the office. Mollie herself would come to her own desk in the office when she could or when she must, beginning bravely on one of the several piles marked "urgent" and looking forward to making an end of them all so that she could go back to scraping the four coats of paint off the secondhand altar just received or relieving the small parlor and dining room of their melancholy with paint and pictures.

With its rusted pipes, loosening plaster, rough floor boards, and leaking roof, the old lodge challenged Mollie's homemaking ingenuity and taxed Father Walsh's feeble finances to bring it into repair. And it was just too hospitable. Bugs, rats, rain, cold —it welcomed them all.

Mollie's thirtieth birthday passed almost unnoticed in a flurry of fumigation. Even in this first state of upheaval and reclamation and in all its various stages thereafter, the old house had charm and character, and Mollie gave herself cheerfully to making the most of its good points. After all, she loved it—it was as funny, provoking, and interesting as Grandma Rogers— but she loved it most of all because it was the cradle of a great hope.

The secretaries' days were crammed with activity, but they made every jot of their little free time yield its full payload of enjoyment. Without sports, games, musical instruments, their recreations were full of fun and often of song. The ways in which she and her family had enjoyed themselves at home provided a wellspring on which Mollie now drew. If there were no violins or piano, there were combs and tissue paper, and with these and such voices as God had given them the secretaries orchestrated. Once upon a time Mollie had sat fascinated and absorbed while her father read aloud. Now in the evenings she would sometimes read to the others for fifteen minutes or so. Then after they had been lifted out of their fatigue and preoccupations by the enchantment of the story and the pleasure of her voice, she would put the book aside and they would talk together, their hands busy with mending and darning. The present was absorbing, the future engaging. Their conversation ranged back and forth between the two.

Sometimes Father Walsh came to join them, telling them of his hopes and plans and the activities and events of the day, his small dark eyes alight with enthusiasm or amusement, his quiet laughter bubbling up as he recounted some domestic setback. He had a way of converting trouble into fodder for fun, as his *Field Afar* readers well knew. The quiet fading away of farm hands and cooks moved him to make observations such as "Poor John! His imagination, a delicate instrument, was easily affected." "Cook number 'what?' has folded her tent and quietly stolen away." He spoke of "necessity's sharp pinch" without sighing: "*The Field Afar* office needs an attachment for a typewriter and a typewriter for the attachment."

No one looking at him as he sat there could find in his attitude or expression the weight of work that rested upon him: the final editing of *The Field Afar,* the administration of the Seminary and the close following of its exacting schedule; the buying of farm animals and equipment; the banking, investment, and disbursement of funds; the dealing with crews of men working on drainpipes, cisterns, septic tanks, and the repairs and additions going forward on both the Seminary and St. Teresa's; his increasingly heavy correspondence which he always ambitioned to answer the day that it was received; the entertainment of guests, and finally the time gobbled up by emergencies such as the failure of the "guaranteed" water supply and the falling ceilings in the old lodge. One great gob of plaster thundered down all over *The Field Afar* office just as it was beginning to grow into its new quarters, and all the equipment and workers had to be moved elsewhere while the whole room was replastered.

Yet Father Walsh never became so deeply immersed in all these activities and concerns that he could not stand aside and look at Maryknoll's strong but uneven growth with humor and awe. His faith and his restraint lent him the advantage of a spectator, and he watched the miracle of God's providence develop before his eyes with wonder and thanksgiving in which the secretaries shared.

As the winter set in, a whole series of "firsts" stretched out before the newcomers to Mary's Knoll and remained to sparkle in the memory as clearly as the string of icicles that so often hung along the edge of St. Teresa's long sloping roof.

On All Saints' Day the first High Mass was sung in the small Seminary chapel. Father Price celebrated the Mass. The boys sang with plenty of heart and some accuracy. Father Walsh played the organ, his musical sensibilities happily dulled by his joy. And the secretaries sat in their corner and found it all a marvel. On November 21 the first six of many hundreds of seminarians to come went up to the altar to receive the cassock and cincture from Father Walsh's hands. Watching them, the secretaries were deeply moved at this simple ceremony. And Anna Towle, who had made the cassocks, found her eyes checking cuffs and hemlines. For all of them who had worked and sacrificed to bring it about, the occasion was both a sign of promise and a reward.

How quickly the high points of that year flashed by: the first Thanksgiving, as old-fashioned in their country place as a Currier-Ives; the first Christmas, poignant with a sharpened awareness of Bethlehem in their midst—the secretaries making their way through the snow and silence to midnight Mass at the Seminary and in the morning waking up to take part in the first Mass said in their own house, a Christmas gift indeed. Soon an anniversary, January 6, was upon them.

With the anniversary came their first community retreat, preached by Father Henry Borgmann, a Redemptorist deeply interested in Maryknoll and its future, a friend and advisor to Father Walsh, and Sara's former director. The secretaries had to sandwich their work in between his talks, but found them both stimulating and enjoyable. It was the first retreat that Mollie had ever made and she reaped a rich harvest from it. Her simple, uncomplicated approach to God found Father's frequently repeated maxim, "Know thyself; know God," eminently normal. She had no tendency toward those "baby devotions" which he urged them to avoid or to abandon. She found it no hardship to love and to try to imitate St. Teresa, as he advised them to do. His instructions on the Mass and the missal moved her to have the secretaries begin early the use of the missal. Later the practice of the *Missa Recitata* was also initiated.

Before lengthening days and occasional thaws even hinted of spring, Father Walsh began to stock his farm to provide for the future of his growing family. He invested in cows, sheep, pigs, and chickens. Mary Dwyer, who kept the books, let the other secretaries know that after this outlay of funds the Society's capital stood at just eighty-seven dollars. The secretaries, of course, depended on the Society. She was aghast.

Mollie went over to the barn with the other secretaries to make the acquaintance of the new members of the family. As they patted the smooth flanks of the bossies, exclaimed over the dark faces and thick coats of the sheep, leaned over the pig pen and marveled at the porkers' size and appetite, counted the chickens and tried to calculate the number of eggs they might expect, Mollie's enjoyment was unmixed. She never doubted Providence and she never questioned Father Walsh's wisdom. And she could recall one day at Hawthorne when he had just five dollars to his name and had handed over the whole of it to be spent at the parish church fair.

Early in March the word suddenly came that Mollie had prepared herself to receive but still found heartbreaking to learn. At the foot of the stairs in the old Robinwood Avenue house her father had suddenly fallen. When the family ran to him, he could not speak. He was in bed now, paralyzed, very ill. Could she come? Father Walsh said that she could and should.

After she reached home, her father rallied, grew worse again, lingered for weeks, at one time begging her brokenly not to return to Maryknoll, at another retracting his request. She stayed, took over his nursing at night. When he was wakeful in the early evening, he would find it restful to have her nearby. It eased him to see her sitting by the lamp with her sewing in her hands, or even just to know that she was there. And whenever through the long heavy hours of the night he woke, he would find her beside him ready to anticipate his wants and wishes. His helplessness and dependence brought out something new in their old close relationship. If he leaned upon her as never before, she loved him with a compassion which his masterliness had never needed or evoked.

Yet something of his old imperiousness remained. He would not allow Elizabeth's marriage to be postponed because of his incapacity, and so Mollie saw her lovely young sister marry on Easter Monday and go away on her honeymoon.

Back at Maryknoll the apple trees bloomed like brides all over the hilltop and Father Walsh and his short string of seminarians formed a miniature procession and went out to bless the fields and flocks and orchards. Mollie stayed on at home until the day after the Ascension, when, with that consoling feast still fresh in everyone's mind, her father died.

In November of 1913, *The Field Afar* began to refer to the secretaries as Teresians, a name given them quite informally because they lived in St. Teresa's Lodge, and because they had developed a special devotion to the great Carmelite. It was more meaningful than "secretaries" and less clumsy than "women auxiliaries," but it signified no change in the status of the group. By then the secretaries were habitually addressing Mollie as Mary Joseph, a name which Father Walsh found more fitting for her as their directress and which she herself loved as paying tribute to the two patrons to whom she was most devoted. Yet things were not so formal that the Teresians did not occasionally slip back into the old nickname. With all its associations, it fell from their lips like an endearment.

Even if the Teresians were still just laywomen, they had begun to look like something else—"Heaven knows what!" some of them thought.

Before the secretaries moved to Maryknoll, they were well dressed laywomen wearing the clothes they had brought with them and sweeping up their hair in the popular pompadour. After they had settled in at St. Teresa's, Father Walsh decreed that the darling pompadours must go. They went. He thought that the hair should just be pulled back into a knot at the neck. It was. Father thought that a uniform would be good. "Something like that gray dress you brought with you," he said to Mary Joseph. Soon all the Teresians were wearing something like Mary Joseph's chambray, only plainer.

The first day they put these on, they were rewarded for their conformity by Father Walsh's chuckling observation, "I am strongly reminded of my visit to Sherburne prison."

Brother Thomas was less controlled. "Who are these old ladies in gray?" he wanted to know. "Who are they, anyhow?"

The impression made on a visiting prelate from Venezuela was hardly more encouraging. "I see," he observed in carefully enunciated English, "that you are halfway between ladies and Sisters."

During the early days of the evolution no Teresian could find it pure pleasure to go to the village or to the city. Deprived of her pompadour, she disappeared into the crown of her hat like somebody falling upward into a hole. She endured it, stuffed the hat with tissue paper, or tried to borrow a better. Over her uniform she put somebody's coat, always out of style, often out of season, and rarely a good fit.

When he saw a small group of Teresians making ready to invade the startled outer world, Father Walsh laughed softly and shook his head. "You certainly have courage to go out," he tactfully remarked.

The village youngsters were at first dazed, but quickly rallied. "Suffragettes! Look at the suffragettes!" they cried.

Although habit and veil would both eventually work out to be sensible and seemly, not all the proposals and products in its evolution were a success.

At one time Father Walsh returned from a trip during which he had met some members of a new community. He considered that they had outfitted themselves in a practical way and that their headgear might serve as a model for the Teresians. He set out to describe it to Mary Joseph.

"They look very neat," he said. "They wear a sailor hat—outdoors, I suppose. And they keep their hair in a kind of fish net."

"A sailor hat and a fish net!" cried Mary Joseph. "Father, what an idea!"

"It looked very sensible to me."

"Sensible! How would—how would even Margaret there look in an outfit of that kind? In a sailor hat and a fish net we would never get any more recruits. If we are going to attract young girls to join us, we ought to have something a little becoming."

"Mary Joseph, the sooner you take the word 'becoming' out of your vocabulary, the better."

But the subject of the marine headgear was not brought up again.

At another time Mary Joseph wore a newly designed bonnet and veil for Father Walsh to view and bestow his vote or his veto. He approved. In due course the whole group blossomed into similar bonnets. Father Walsh came upon them en masse. The impact proved too much.

"Everybody has a headache today?"

"A headache?"

"Yes. Aren't those headache bands?"

"Father," said Mary Joseph firmly, "those are bonnets—bonnets just like the one which I wore and you approved."

"Did I?" He looked genuinely surprised. "It certainly looks different in dozens."

When Father Walsh tried to put into effect the idea he had almost from the beginning—to have some religious Sisterhood train the secretaries in the principles and practice of community life—he did not find competent and willing educators rushing forward to meet his need. He received offers from several laywomen to do this, one holding out to him not only the boon of her services but a considerable amount of money as well. Wisely he found himself unable to accept either.

He was particularly keen to have the Franciscan Missionaries of Mary take the responsibility. They had the missionary spirit that he would like to see developed in the Teresians. However, his negotiations with this community and four others as well came to nothing.

A sixth brought success. In June of 1914, Mother Germaine of the Sisters Servants of the Immaculate Heart, at Scranton, Pennsylvania, consented to send three of her Sisters to live at St. Teresa's and to form and direct the Teresians. Both Bishop Hoban of Scranton and Cardinal Farley of New York approved the arrangement. It was doubtless no easier for Mother Germaine than for others in similar positions to detach three Sisters from the activities of her community and assign them to this task. She was generous and apostolic enough to do it, nevertheless, although some of her own Sisters thought it imprudent and ill-timed, since Sisters were lacking to staff their own schools adequately. Together with Father Walsh and Mary Joseph, she made plans. Mary Joseph found her large-hearted and kind. She had Mary Joseph visit with her for several days at the Motherhouse at Mt. St. Mary's and talk things over.

It was decided that during July all the Teresians should make a retreat at Mt. St. Mary's, as the Marywood Motherhouse was then called. After that, as soon as it could be arranged, the three Immaculate Heart Sisters should go to St. Teresa's to begin the novitiate. Sister Stanislaus would be the novice mistress, and would be assisted by Sister Gerard, who would have charge of the kitchen, and Sister Domitilla, who would supervise the laundry.

Since the fall of 1913, Mary Dwyer had been acting as book-keeper, secretary, and housekeeper at the Venard Apostolic School, the nucleus of a junior seminary begun at that time in Scranton by Father Walsh. Even the virtual independence of this position and the play it gave her considerable abilities left her dissatisfied.

While in Scranton, Mary Joseph was grieved to find how much Mary Dwyer's discontent had overflowed into criticism of Father Walsh's way of developing the group of women aux-iliaries. She had managed to speak her mind to some key people. She had emotional force and a kind of deadly logic that was completely but not always obviously unreasonable. Here and there she had made an impression.

The difficulties which she created for Father Walsh pained Mary Joseph more than any of the suffering which Mary Dwyer caused her personally. The enthusiasm which the older woman had expressed at Mollie's coming had long waned. Although she still maintained that she had no personal feelings against Mollie and never found anything to criticize in her generous and self-forgetful ways, she yet made her position as directress as difficult as possible. She refused to recognize Mollie's au-thority, insisted upon receiving assignments and instructions di-rectly from Father Walsh himself, and drove hard to impose her own ideas on the group.

Mary Dwyer had two key complaints. First of all, the Tere-sians lacked definiteness. They had no real rule, no status, no stable organization. More than once Father Walsh had changed his statements, and evidently his mind, about the character and purpose of the group. What future did they have? What were the so-called Teresians, anyway?

Mary Dwyer's second indictment concerned the composition of the group itself. Some were trained and some were untrained for secretarial, editorial, or clerical work. Either the group should be two-pronged, with office and domestic workers in separate categories or, better to her mind, restricted only to the trained, the intelligent, the educated. Margaret was used as a case in point: she had no professional preparation of any kind.

"Regular Sisters and lay Sisters? We will never have any such division among us if I have anything to say," Mollie maintained quietly. "Of course, Margaret has no training for any specific work. How could she? She is only eighteen now. But she is young enough to learn anything."

About their standing and stability she could have reminded Mary Dwyer that Father Walsh had never promised them religious life or status and that he, more than they, had to trust in God for the development of every facet and phase of Maryknoll. She knew, however, that reasoning served little purpose and so she said simply, "You know as much of the future as I do. God has provided thus far. Why should He fail us now?"

As the arrangements with the Immaculate Heart Sisters went forward, Mary Dwyer came to a kind of armed truce. A change might result in things going more according to her mind in the future.

Before she had returned to Maryknoll, however, Mary Joseph had quite unexpectedly sailed for Europe.

Julia Ward, a retired couturière to New York's theatrical and fashionable world and a benefactress to many Catholic institutions and enterprises, had added Maryknoll to her list. To this successful woman of little formal education, genuine business ability, grande dame manners, and patrician tastes, the Teresians were indebted for all sorts of practical gifts—from screens for St. Teresa's to winter coats and hats for the Teresians. She had made up her mind to go to France during the summer of 1914 with Lourdes as her main objective. She had made up her mind, too, that Mollie would make an ideal companion. Too wise to issue an invitation directly, she approached Father Walsh.

He, on his part, saw immediately the advantages of such a pilgrimage. He recalled what his own trips to Europe, to Rome, had meant to him—to the catholicity of his Catholicism. He thought, too, that with their magnanimous prop removed for a time, the Teresians might come to value Mary Joseph more and to share more of her burdens. He enlisted their co-operation.

When the invitation was finally extended, Mollie found herself faced with a solid front of approval and a formal resolution insisting that she accept signed by the Teresians and Father Walsh himself over his handwritten title "commander-in-chief." Mother Germaine approved, so did Cardinal Farley. Almost before she could realize what had happened, she was aboard the liner *France* with Julia Ward, beaming with satisfaction, at her side.

The harbor was fog-bound when the *France* steamed confidently seaward, showing as little concern for the weather as the Americans aboard manifested for the man-made storm rising darkly over Europe.

"You will adore France," Julia assured Mollie in her high-pitched intonation. "Paris, of course, will not be at its best in the summertime—but the Château country! And Lourdes! Lourdes will be heavenly!"

It was July 15, 1914. Less than a month ago the heir-apparent to the throne of Austria-Hungry, Archduke Ferdinand, and his wife Sophie had been shot to death by Serbian revolutionaries.

Americans, unaware of the significance of the murder, felt sympathy for the bereaved royal house and took for granted the indignation of the government of Austria-Hungary; then they turned back to their own concerns, sure that this critical European situation, like a half-dozen others in the last decade, would somehow compose itself. From the Vatican, Pius X warned, appealed, and found no comfort, no response, among the great nations.

At Lourdes, meanwhile, people of all nations, even the Far East, were converging to honor their Lord and their Lady and to demonstrate and experience their brotherhood as fellow Christians.

Julia Ward and Mollie were there, joining the thousands who made their way to each of the three churches layered one above the other on rocky Massabielle. With the multitude, they followed the Blessed Sacrament in the daytime procession from grotto to esplanade and back, watching the touching blessing of the sick.

Mollie was struck not only by the sick but by those who tended them as well—observed the faithful and courtly stretcher-bearers, wearing their harness of distinguished service and manipulating their burdens as if they bore Christ Himself; the thoughtful nurses and attendants, deft and cool in the face of sudden hemorrhages, terrible paroxysms of coughing, sinking spells, spasms of agonizing pain. Everywhere the sick were made beautiful by their own courage and resignation and by the love which surrounded them. And the well were ennobled by their own compassion.

Mollie and Julia attended Mass and Benediction at the grotto, spent most of the day there.

In the evenings they were part of the long human stream that wound its way from the grotto through the esplanade and up the sweeping horseshoe ramps until the night was saturated with candlelight and song. With thousands of other pilgrims they sang the haunting theme of Lourdes, *Ave, Ave, Ave Maria*. Around them, to the same rhythm and melody, people sang to the same Lady in French, in German, in English, in Flemish and in Dutch, in Portuguese and in Spanish, and in other languages Mollie could not even identify. War seemed far away.

Then suddenly, like lightning, the news of war flashed into that place of peace. During the early part of July, Austria-Hungary, having satisfied herself of Germany's support, pressed Serbia to make amends for Archduke Ferdinand's death and, unsatisfied with Serbia's partial concessions, declared war on her on July 28.

Russia mobilized to support Slavic Serbia. Germany, standing between Russia and France, allies of one another and enemies to her, resolved to strike before she could be struck. On August 1, she declared war on Russia and on August 3, on France. On August 4, Great Britain announced herself at war with Germany. On August 6, Austria-Hungary declared war on Russia. Other nations followed, choosing the side from which they had most to fear or most to gain.

Almost simultaneously the war machines meshed into gear. Julia and Mollie gathered with the townspeople in the square of Lourdes and heard the Mayor read the mobilization orders.

On August 4, a river of living gray flowed swiftly over the border of Germany into Belgium toward Liége—the well-trained, well-equipped armies of the Kaiser on the way to outflank France.

Although far from the area where the battle was forming, the little town in the gateway of the mountains felt the overwhelming impact of the war in its own way. The pilgrims, the stretcher-bearers, the attendants, the nurses, the sick, came from all over Europe. The trains were immediately requisitioned to carry the men called up for service to their mobilization centers. Sons and fathers in Lourdes, as elsewhere all over France, were already saying hurried good-bys. And the sick waited sometimes for hours on the station platform until trains could be spared for them.

By August 10, Julia Ward managed to acquire two passes from France to Italy by way of Toulouse and Marseilles, a hired car and a chauffeur, and two bearded Coptic ecclesiastics. Stranded pilgrims too, these Churchmen were anxious to reach the Mediterranean and return to their diocese in Egypt.

His Excellency, Most Reverend Maximos Sedfaoui, Bishop of Minia, was a striking personality with distinguished manners, iron-gray beard, and high-crowned headgear veiled in black. His companion and Vicar General, Monsignor Basil Bistauros, with the large plumlike eyes of an ancient Egyptian statue, was hardly less arresting.

As the little car rolled eastward down the mountains, through the hills, over the lovely vineyard country stretching away in long undulations or in green-lined tableland to the pale blue horizon, the Coptic churchmen talked about their country and their Church.

The Bishop held title to ancient Hermapolis, a center of influence and religious worship in Egypt more than two thousand years before Christ. The moon god Toth had been adored there. With the desert to the west and the Nile sliding by its eastern flank, the city held on to existence while dynasties flourished and decayed and left behind only the mastaba-tombs to keep from extinction kings and consorts, royal sons and daughters. All else became a wisp of lingering memory, recorded in fragments of stone.

According to a legend recorded by Palladius, other royalty had come to Hermapolis—the Holy Family during their Egyptian exile. Though they did not remain, the followers of Christ and His doctrine came there early and seemed to secure a firm hold. The great St. Athanasius had once made the city his home. Not far away, eastern monasticism grew up like a desert flower.

Early, too, came the parasitic Monophysite heresy, waxed strong, weakening its host and outlasting even the Moslem penetration. To the Bishop it was no neat set of textbook distinctions, but a contemporary problem.

Before the Bishop and his Vicar General had made their adieus, Mollie no longer found these bearded Copts so strange. They had come to seem as completely and normally Catholic as Boston's Archbishop Williams, who had once leaned down to anoint her forehead with the chrism of salvation. For the first time she really knew what Greek and Coptic Uniates were—not a group separated from so-called Roman Catholics by different liturgical observances, but completely one with other Catholics all over the world in the same sacraments, doctrine, mission, and destiny. She was well launched into the educative experience which Father Walsh had expected of this European journey.

Meanwhile in Rome, Pius X, stricken down more by sorrow than by sickness, was failing fast. Mollie and Miss Ward had hardly reached the Eternal City when the great bells of St. Peter's began to ring and, as the day slid softly away, church bells all over the city caught up the message and passed it along. "Your Father Pius is dying. Come pray for him. The Pope is dying. Pray." As night fell, the whole of Rome seemed to be on its knees.

In the early morning of August 20, having received the Sacraments with great faith and in deep peace, Pope Pius X died. The next morning his body was brought in solemn procession and placed before the altar in the chapel of the Blessed Sacrament in St. Peter's. It was elevated so that the thronging people could see it easily. Like the others, Mollie and Julia worked their way into the basilica and up to the chapel. There they lingered as long as they were permitted. Dressed in full pontificals and with the insignia of his office—the white pallium with its black crosses—around his shoulders, the Pope looked benign and princely even in death. Above the catafalque hung the triple crown which he had accepted with tears and left without regret.

The two women attended one of the three Pontifical High Masses of Requiem celebrated in St. Peter's for the dead Pope. They joined in the spontaneous prayer of the thousands who filled St. Peter's and made its nave and dome re-echo their petition, "St. Pius, pray for us!"

Because of the war in Europe, it was not easy to secure reservations on a ship bound for the United States. While Mollie and Julia waited, they got to know well much more of Rome than Mollie had ever hoped to see: all those magnificent and melancholy ruins of a great pagan capital and those material records —in stone and in marble, in brick and in mosaic, in underground chapels and in lofty basilicas—which silently tell the story of Christianity.

Everything about Rome affected Mollie deeply and drew her more closely into the bosom of that wonderful masterpiece, the Church, which Christ fashioned for our salvation and sanctification. It gave her happiness to see that, like St. Paul, the Church knew how to do without—as the narrow deathlike tunnels of the Catacombs attested—and how to abound—as the basilicas rising into the blue Italian sky like crowned arcs of prayer gave testimony. To find the glorious murals and statuary of Michelangelo and the majestic remnants of Greek and Roman art caught up in one wide, worshipful embrace to be offered to God and preserved for men, made her heart glad. Everything she had felt about the use and value of the beautiful, the reverence for whatever is good in man and in his works, she found confirmed and blessed. But out of many impressions two remained with her vividly all her life.

For her, the great oval shell of the Coliseum and all that she had read and heard of the martyrs and confessors was made strikingly imminent by the realistic pictures painted around the inner walls of the fifth-century circular church, *San Stefano Rotundo*. These heroic-sized representations of the suffering martyrs made some turn away out of pity or distaste. Mollie felt deeply their dreadful and glorious message. She had never been one of those who, separated by time or distance from martyrs and fortified by a dull imagination, could speak facilely of martyrdom. Now she felt more humbled and worshipful than ever before in the face of such suffering, such courage.

"This is what it was like," she said to herself. "These are the things they suffered."

Going with Julia to see a sick friend at the Hospital of the Company of Mary, Mollie went into the chapel to visit the Blessed Sacrament. Before the altar a white-veiled, blue-habited novice knelt praying. Presently another novice came forward, the two genuflected together, the first one left the chapel and the second took her place. The meaning of the little pantomime seemed clear—the changing of the guard. Something formed in Mollie's heart, part hope, part prayer, part decision.

Later, talking with one of the Sisters, she asked, "Do your Sisters take turns all during the day praying before the Blessed Sacrament?"

"Yes, we do," replied the Sister. "While we are working, someone is always praying for us. One or two of our own Sisters. When we go through the city to visit the sick and the poor or when we make our rounds in the hospital taking care of our patients, someone is praying for us—that we will be safe, and good, and do our work well—she prays, too, for the people we are trying to help."

How beautiful, Mollie thought; if only we too could do something like that. She pictured the chip of a chapel and the handful of women in the old farmhouse at home. Not now. Maybe later. As the numbers of Teresians increased, ten-, twenty-, fifty-fold, this fugitive thought, this half-expressed desire would blossom into two great blessings for her Sisters: perpetual adoration at the Motherhouse and a cloistered branch of the community.

A Pope is not yet buried when preparations begin for the

election of his successor. The Cardinals converged on the Vatican, made themselves inaccessible behind locked doors, and Rome waited.

Mollie and Julia went with the rest of Rome to stand in St. Peter's Square and look for the little puff of white smoke from the Sistine Chapel chimney which would announce that a Pope had been elected.

They saw the diminutive new Pope, Benedict XV, valiantly upright under the weight of his magnificent robes, carried shoulder-high into the Basilica for his coronation to the shouts of thousands. They knelt in one of the great audience chambers and received the potent blessing of his fragile hands. Each of these experiences Mollie put away carefully in her memory to share with all those whom she could bring to Rome only in her heart. Years later she could still tell the novices of the impressions of those days.

"All this helped us to appreciate the Church, to realize what Rome means to us. The Church is our Mother and that comes home to you in Rome as in no other place."

On her return from Europe, Mollie found the three Immaculate Heart Sisters from Scranton already at Maryknoll and the other Teresians making month-old efforts, generous if awkward, to acquire the sedate ways and pretty virtues which they themselves considered proper to novices. During that first month they had all gone through a period of discouragement.

With Mollie home again, her bags full of remembrances, her head brimming with impressions and experiences, her heart overflowing with gladness to be with them once again, they took new heart. When she joined them in all the novitiate exercises, listening to the instructions that began each day, adopting all the practices suggested, carrying out the penances, observing the unaccustomed old-world formalities between subject and superior, the new yoke seemed to lie more lightly on them all. No one who had not already learned something of Mary Joseph's tastes and opinions could have told that these ideas were not in every case her own.

Her position was one which required a delicate balance of submission and authority. Sister Mary Stanislaus was novice mistress and, since there was no house superior, filled that office as well. Yet Father Walsh required Mary Joseph to retain her responsibilities as directress of the Teresians. To her Father Walsh looked for the Teresians' work assignments, for supervision of *The Field Afar* office, the care of guests, and to a large extent, the administration of the temporalities of the community. He took it for granted that she would continue to share with him the task of interviewing and admitting candidates and look out for a number of other matters which routinely fell to her lot.

The Teresians had all come to Maryknoll to further foreign mission work through co-operating with Father Walsh. The immediate means of accomplishing this was the publication of *The Field Afar* and all the tasks which that entailed. Father Walsh naturally expected the work to be done. He looked upon it as Maryknoll's lifeline. The groups within the Maryknoll family were already growing in a way that drove him to arrange and rearrange, repair and alter his housing plans to make some kind of provision for them all. Somehow all this growth and activity had to be financed.

The magazine's subscription list was increasing, as all hoped it would, but that entailed more work—on typewriters, stencils and stencil files, multigraphs, and addressographs. Every magazine that went out was folded and wrapped by hand—the hand of one of the ten Teresians. And every letter, appeal, reminder, that went out was inserted by hand—the hand of one of the ten Teresians. Normally, a novitiate would not be burdened with such a work program. For the Teresians, it could not be helped; without that work their little society could not even continue and indeed would have no immediate reason to exist.

Father Walsh favored a program which gave plenty of time

for prayer but allowed for solid blocks of uninterrupted hours for work. Sister Stanislaus, on the other hand, with the thought of sanctifying the day throughout with prayer, interspersed work time with religious exercises and utilized work hours for conferences with individual Teresians. Through Mary Joseph, Father Walsh made suggestions and adjustments. Her position made for a complex relationship between the Novice and the Novice Mistress and could not have been easy for either. Mary Joseph wanted to be, like the others, simply a novice, a real novice, and, except for the unusual role which her retained authority imposed upon her, she was. She did not desire privileges or seek for exceptions, she asked for her personal permissions, and received Sister Stanislaus' corrections and instructions with candor and good will. She was anxious to use to the full the opportunities of this period, so long awaited.

Of her conferences with Sister Stanislaus she said years afterward, "Mother thought I was proud, and no doubt she was right."

When Sister Stanislaus remarked one day that she would not require as much of the Teresians, because of the age level of the group, as she would have expected of younger novices in her own community, Mary Joseph was troubled.

"We ought to be no less generous. Please do not spare us, Mother. We want to do everything that we should."

Too delicate and earnest to be a fun-maker herself, Sister Stanislaus was tolerant of the Teresians' exuberance and unconventionality. They had original ways of celebrating feasts and observing birthdays. The newest and liveliest Teresian, Mary Letitia, under the title of "the Crawford clown," had a whole repertoire of song and dance and operatic burlesque which she was glad to supply on short notice. Irrepressible, she once presented Father Walsh with a nosegay of vegetables after he had given an illustrated talk on the martyrs of the Paris

Foreign Mission Society. Whatever he thought of the gift, he accepted it with grace.

In the spring the farm animals bore their attractive children and Teresians trooped down to the barn to admire the calves, the lambs, the piglets, and the baby chicks. Sister Domitilla's feast came in May. When she came to the table that morning, she found an astonished pink and white piglet, freshly laundered and wearing an Easter bonnet, occupying the place next to her at the table. He proved such an agreeable guest that he was allowed to remain for the meal before being demoted to pigdom once more.

Sometimes an extra load of work, instead of depressing the Teresians, seemed to make them effervesce. After a full day with laundry tasks still facing them at night, they would round up a wheelbarrow and interrupt their chores to take each other, and even Sister Stanislaus, for rides.

When St. Teresa's feast came around with a whole free day— the only one that they really counted on during the year—they seemed to want to pack it full of as many activities as possible. Should they hike? Put benches in the open Ford truck and go for an outing? Play games and run races? Give a show? Concoct sodas? They tried them all, never singly, but always in combinations. Even Mary Louise Wholean, who could not take part in anything very active, enjoyed it all in her quiet way and tried not to bemoan the backwash of work which resulted.

The days of the novitiate, in spite of Mary Dwyer's aggressive discontent, passed happily and swiftly. The Teresians learned even more from watching the Sisters live the religious life than they did in being instructed about it. They were encouraged by Sister Domitilla's lighthearted Christian way of accepting life's ups and downs. To Sister Gerard, the Sister placed in charge of the kitchen, they were particularly drawn. Thin, beautiful, and composed, she was wholly dedicated to her religious life.

Her example had especial weight when the Teresians came to learn that she was also quietly carrying the considerable burden of ill health.

The Teresians were beginning to look forward to making their vows. Openings in the missions had already been held out to them enticingly as possible fields of labor. Then suddenly the blow fell.

On the feast of St. Thomas, March 7, 1916, after about a year and a half of their two-year novitiate had been completed, Father John T. McNicholas, a friend to Father Walsh and all Maryknollers, came to enroll the Teresians as Dominican Tertiaries. At that time, it had already been decided that they would adopt the rule of the third order of St. Dominic. Before the white-habited Dominican began the little ceremony, he looked at them kindly and without preliminary told them what he himself had discovered:

"I hope it will not be a disappointment to you to learn that your status is not canonical. According to a recent decree, permission to start any religious congregation must come from Rome—a fact to which Cardinal Farley did not advert and which even the Apostolic Delegate did not appreciate until I called his attention to it.

"Although this means that technically your eighteen months' novitiate does not count, I am sure that what you have learned from the good Sisters of the Immaculate Heart will be invaluable and will help you in whatever supplementary training may be necessary."

They all sat silently, absorbing it, realizing that somehow they would have to start all over again.

"All bodies starting out to work for God have sufferings and difficulties," Father McNicholas concluded, "and so I am not surprised that this trial has come to you."

Father Walsh, who had come with Father McNicholas, spoke briefly of his gratitude to the Teresians for their services, predicted that in years to come they would look upon their present disappointment as providential and invited them to pray daily to the Holy Spirit for all that still remained to be done to realize their hopes.

Margaret, who had always wanted to be a Sister and who had loved the experience of being a novice and the thought of making her vows, realized with surprise that the older and better-schooled Immaculate Heart Sisters were much more disappointed than she, who was usually so sensitive. They knew far better than she the usual orderly process of preparation and training for religious life. She, on the other hand, had come, as Mollie had proposed to her in the parlor on Robinwood Avenue, "to see what God has in store for us." This was part of it. She looked at Mary Joseph's untroubled face and thought that she did not really mind.

In June a carefully prepared petition was sent to Rome through the Archdiocesan Chancery. It asked permission to inaugurate a Sisterhood and to open a novitiate. It was returned in August; it had been addressed to the wrong Roman congregation; it was re-sent.

In July, with the ultimate prospect of the Teresians becoming Dominicans and nothing immediate settled in regard to their status, Father Walsh released the Immaculate Heart Sisters and they returned to their own community and again took up their share of its works. Mother Germaine's understanding and concern and the Teresians' gratitude for all that she had done for them herself and through her Sisters helped to soften their mutual disappointment. Mother Germaine wrote encouragingly to Mary Joseph:

"I realize that as yet things are uncertain for your little band, but take courage, God will be with a work that exists entirely for His honor and glory, and in His own good time, His loving hand will lead you from darkness into light."

With the Immaculate Heart Sisters gone, the responsibility for the immediate direction of the Teresians again rested fully on Mary Joseph. She was "a shepherdess under an overseer," as

Father Walsh described their relationship. He, as well as the Teresians, had expected the time between the leaving of the Immaculate Heart Sisters and the coming of the Dominicans to be short, a matter of weeks perhaps. He spoke to the Teresians of the value of such a period:

"A time like this *interregnum* will give you an especially good opportunity to show your spirit, and at its close you may find yourselves, individually and collectively, on a higher plane than ever before."

The Teresians were not soon to become Sisters. The "brief *interregnum*" lengthened out into months and years.

During this period Mary Joseph never afflicted others with her fears or self-doubts, and in time they came to consider that she never experienced either. Her faith in God certainly overrode her distrust of self, but she was not always as much at ease in her place of authority as her tranquillity and buoyancy led others to suppose. She felt that she, who was just learning about the religious life herself, was not the one to attempt to educate others.

Writing several years later of this time to the Dominican Father Thomas à Kempis Reilly she said, "Indeed we owe her [our Lady] more than can be estimated. . . . At St. Teresa's one of her greatest gifts has been her maternal watchfulness. No one more unfitted spiritually than I could have been selected to guide the little flock here, and it was she who kept us in safety during the years when we had no experienced religious with us to give us what aspirants to the religious life need and had a right to expect."

Meanwhile, she kept up the generous pace that she had set for herself, never asking others to do what she had not done. Indeed she did not expect them to keep up with her. She took it for granted, and everyone else did too, that whenever a need arose she would take care of it, whatever it might be. Somehow it seemed to be just the thing that she wanted to do at the time.

She would fill in for the cook at the Seminary or at St. Teresa's, take over the management of the laundry, help with Father Walsh's correspondence, do the preserving, houseclean the Seminary, make herself available to guests whenever they came. In the spring and summer they came often. Whether they were visiting missioners, potential Teresians, benefactors, or the relatives and friends of Teresians, she received all with the same warmth and courtesy. Her own family, her brothers particularly, surprised her in the midst of house painting, cooking, or cleaning. They could harbor no illusions about the nature of her executive position.

One night about eight-thirty Margaret was just finishing her chores. She was tired. The sight of the spotted kitchen floor fretted her.

"Mary Joseph, I just have to do that floor. It's a sight."

Mary Joseph put her arm around her and gave her a little pat. "You go to bed. Never mind the old floor."

In the morning Margaret found the floor immaculate. She thought of the stories she had read about angels helping out religious, especially obedient religious—who went to bed, for instance, when they were told. She left the kitchen and went to find Mary Joseph still in the chapel making her thanksgiving after Mass.

"Did you see the floor?" she whispered.

"Sh-h."

So she knew!

They went out and looked at it together. Even with the morning sun slanting across it, it was satin-clean. Margaret was thrilled with the angels' efficiency. She waited for some pronouncement from Mary Joseph.

It came. "It does look good, doesn't it?" she said. "And it shouldn't. Do you know what I did to it? I just threw soapy water over the whole thing and swept it all out the kitchen door."

The Teresians' Directress acted as infirmarian, especially when the duties were heavy. All throughout the fall and winter of 1916, Mary Louise fought a stubborn but losing contest with death. As the new year began she was bedridden and growing emaciated almost beyond recognition, but she had not yielded up her dream to continue the work to which she was so devoted. All Maryknoll knew that she was dying except Mary Louise herself. Francis Ford came to St. Teresa's back door to ask if he might give Mary Louise a message to take to his mother. His mother, he knew, was in heaven and Mary Louise, he was sure, would be going there. Seminarians shoveling snow around the Lodge tried to be as quiet as they knew how in order not to disturb the sick woman. Fellow Teresians were permitted few and brief visits to her room. Yet Mary Louise continued to hope—or long—for her recovery.

Mary Joseph took on the duties of night nurse and watched and prayed over the unequal battle, bringing such serenity and insight into the sickroom that the dying woman hung on to her presence as if she might drown without it. By day the tired night nurse carried on as much of her usual work as she was able, and snatched what rest she could.

When, on February 19, death finally came to Mary Louise, it found her ready, her resistance laid aside, her own dream of serving God abandoned fully and finally in favor of His plan for her. It was a great victory and a great grace. From it Mary Joseph drew much consolation even while she felt keenly this first death among her companions.

The month before, the Teresians' first petition to Rome had received its answer: they were granted permission to organize as a society of pious women without vows. They could not, of course, begin a novitiate. Father Walsh told Mary Joseph at once, but the news was not given out while Mary Louise lived. And Mary Dwyer was no longer at St. Teresa's to be further antagonized by this fresh failure. In April of the previous year she had returned to Boston and had re-established her former business.

In March, Father Walsh summarized for the Teresians the result of the petition and the general state of their affairs. Margaret, who looked at Mary Joseph to see whether the stars still shone and the sun was yet on his course, saw that she looked very tired. The great eyes were deeply circled, but still steady and benign, the lovely mouth a little firmer perhaps, but still gracious and ready to smile. Although the answer was not just what they had expected, evidently everything was all right. Mary Joseph did not seem to mind.

The day after Father Walsh had told Mary Joseph of this grant of privilege which was really a refusal of their petition, she wrote him a brief note to let him know that all was well.

The shock of the announcement—which was almost pain—is over and I can see things more clearly.

Did I thank you for all you did yesterday? I should have, and you felt my gratitude, I am sure. There never was a Father so thoughtful, so self-sacrificing as you!

I believe that the Teresians as a body will willingly accept the decision. To do otherwise would be to wound the Head of which we are the members. It will be a good test of our Catholicity, our vocation, and our self-love. May God bless you and your work in proportion as He humbles and tries the beginning here.

What people say ought not to affect us. Probably priests and Sisters will hear us less readily. Yet we know that if it is His will, God will make our efforts effective.

May we still keep the Blessed Sacrament with us? How lost we would be without It!

. . .

Please don't think I am going to burden you with notes. This will take less of your time perhaps than if I tried to talk to you. I hope so.

Faithfully in Christ,
Mary Joseph.

1-18-17

Worn out by Mary Louise's long illness, Mary Joseph remained tired all that late winter and spring. Soon pain and illness came to be her boon companions, as though they had transferred their allegiance from one Teresian to another. She had always been healthy. At home it had been almost unknown for her to be sick. Her brothers used to admire and praise her stamina in that inverted way which brothers have. "Mollie, you are not built like a hippopotamus for nothing," said one of them fraternally.

Now she embarked upon the first of a long series of illnesses that would space themselves over the rest of her life like the way of the cross. They would not prevent her working nor take away her joy in doing, but they would make it all much harder to accomplish. And as she grew older and took on more flesh this burden was increased. When she had to submit to care and hospitalization and surgery, she would do so with such humor and relaxation that many, even the Sisters who nursed her, had no realization of her pain and weakness. The effortless way in which she detached her mind from herself and fastened it on the concerns and needs of others, particularly evident toward the end of her life, was the product of long habit as well as of charity.

During the spring and summer of 1917 she made a slow and difficult recovery from an abdominal operation, at one time burning with fever and weighed down with pain, at another improving only to relapse again. After several months, the body finally responded, sealed off the infection, and she was able to take up her full round of activity.

While she was in the hospital, the dark shadow of the European War lengthened until it touched America. In January, Woodrow Wilson had severed diplomatic relations with Germany. On April 2 he called a special session of Congress, requested that it recognize a state of war between Germany and the United States. On April 6 Congress gave that recognition.

What that would entail began to spell itself out even before the Selective Service Act was passed in May. News of enlistments began to come in from all sides. To Mary Joseph, the war had always been more imminent than to the other Teresians. As she remembered the call to arms and the leave-takings at Lourdes, she thought of her own five brothers.

Just at the time the sky darkened over America, however, a ray of light shone on the Teresians. From April to August of 1917, Sister Mary Ruth of the Dominican Sisters of Sinsinawa, Wisconsin, came to stay with the Teresians. Released for a period by her Mother General, Mother Mary Samuel, at Father McNicholas' request, she used the short time well. She taught the Teresians, who were certainly Dominican Tertiaries and one day hoped to be Dominican Sisters as well, Dominican prayers and customs, as well as the fundamentals of Dominican spirituality. After Mary Joseph returned from the hospital, they had time to discuss and work over the proposed constitutions together. Then in the late summer Sister Mary Ruth was gone again, to take up her new duties as Vicaress in her own community. She and Mary Joseph had much in common, and during their brief association formed a lasting friendship.

At this time Father Walsh was planning to set out for the Orient to find a mission field for his priests. The teen-age students whom the Teresians had watched arriving at Hawthorne and Maryknoll with their hair slicked back and their quietest manners laid on were beginning to look like men—and like priests. Noticing the shining neophytes who moved about him at Mass, Father Walsh could hardly identify them with the rag-tag lot who turned out for the daily manual labor period in a flame of colorful cast-offs. Whether he saw them out on the grounds in white ducks and frock coats, in striped trousers and cutaway coats, and in whatever else they picked out of the "mission barrels"; whether he watched them in well-brushed cassocks bending over their books or standing up in lonely diffidence to practice their oratory on their fellow students—he was apt, these days, to think of China whenever he looked at them. He wanted Maryknoll to send its first missioners—some of these young men—to China.

Before Father Walsh's departure for the Far East, he helped to formulate a second petition for the inauguration of the Teresians as a religious community. Soon after he left, this was forwarded to Rome. And the waiting went on. The Teresians, however, never felt that they were marking time. Their full and busy lives left them no time or inclination to mourn over their delayed hopes. The months between the launching of the second petition in the fall of 1917 and its refusal in the spring of 1918 sped by, lightened by the electrifying news at Christmastide that Father Walsh had found a mission field for his Fathers in South China.

The year 1918 was an especially active one for the Teresians. Their program of utilizing to the utmost Maryknoll's own farm produce to feed the two communities and to save funds fitted right in with the war program to "Hooverize." They pickled, preserved, and canned as never before. They turned from cabbages to tomatoes, from tomatoes to corn, from corn to grapes, from grapes to crab apples. And they managed on the side to make clothing for Belgian refugee children. And *The Field Afar,* of course, was turned out as usual.

They prayed as well as worked and often, because the work filled the whole day, they prayed while they worked. During that summer the thirteen who had been at Maryknoll the longest made private vows—for them a renewed dedication and for the others reassurance and encouragement.

Over the years potential candidates had kept finding their way up Sunset Hill to discover what the Teresians were all about and to learn whether they would like to join them and, if so, whether the Teresians would take them in.

Not everyone who came to apply was accepted and not everyone who was accepted stayed. There was the question of health. There was the question of temperament. Some could not put up with others or could not themselves be borne. A candidate whom the seminarians unerringly tagged as "Mournful Minnie" had a short run. There was the question of character traits. A single visit by one scintillating young woman in the early years sufficed to make Mary Louise remark dryly, "A candidate called—one of those remarkable people who can do anything and everything—and lose no time in telling you so."

Some lacked the patience or the vision or the faith to take up or to continue a life which assured them nothing except an opportunity to work for God. They wanted definite and even immediate prospects—vows after two years' novitiate, mission assignments on the next year's agenda. Some found that they had loved only the image or idea of religious life, but cared little for its reality. Some never came at all. Understandably, prudent directors counseled them to go elsewhere and join a real religious community.

Before November had brought the longed-for Armistice, October let go the first terrible whiplash of influenza-pneumonia. It snaked across crowded military encampments, reached into cities and towns, and spread across the countryside. It proved virulent enough to strike down people of every age, the strong as well as the weak, and totaled up an appalling number of victims.

The first siege of the disease touched Maryknoll lightly. Later when it returned in January of 1919 it bore down hard. The majority of both communities became ill. By the end of February the worst was over at the Home Knoll, although convalescence for most proved slow and trying. As those at Maryknoll got better, others at the Venard Preparatory Seminary near Scranton began to fall sick. One student and one fine young priest, Father Massoth, died. During the last week of February, the Teresians had recovered enough to send two of their mem-

bers to help out the Franciscan Sisters at Graymoor, where all
the professed Sisters except one were ill at the same time.

The war's end had lifted a weight from hearts all over America. Brothers and husbands and sons, cousins and friends and
fathers came home to their families. A hundred and twenty-
five thousand, of course, would never return. Of Mollie's five
brothers, three had been in the service, and the end of the
conflict found them still well and safe.

Among those who had lived through the combat, many had
been forced for the first time to think seriously of the meaning
of life and to weigh its values. Youngsters just finishing high
school would no longer be faced with the patriotic appeal to
sign up immediately with the armed forces. Would not all this
mean an increase of vocations? Father Walsh thought that it
would. In gratitude to God for victory and peace, the American
people would surely be looking for ways to thank Him. Would
not this mean added support for what lay closest to His heart,
the salvation of souls? Father Walsh thought that it would.

One morning less than a week after the Armistice, he came
into *The Field Afar* office and announced, "Well, I've bought
the field."

No one had to ask what that meant. "The field" was a piece of
ground next to the Seminary property. It would extend the
Seminary grounds to the brow of Sunset Hill, give an unparal-
leled view of the Hudson and the western hills, provide room
for expansion—an area on which to build the permanent Seminary without having first to demolish the various assorted
houses in which the Maryknoll family lived and worked.

Father Walsh showed the Teresians around the new holding
and, a few evenings later, came over to St. Teresa's to spend an
hour with them. While they sat around him, he outlined his
hopes and plans for the future Maryknoll. That evening they
caught a glimpse of the white heat burning behind that quiet

enthusiasm of his which never failed or flagged. They were happy all over again to be part of Maryknoll. The postponements and delays in the development of their own group threw no shadow over their joy.

The moves to gain for the Teresians the status of a religious Sisterhood revealed more and more fully the conditions that would have to be fulfilled to make this possible. Mary Joseph received a progressive schooling in what all this would eventually mean in regard to the Teresians' relationship to the Catholic Foreign Mission Society. The one-time secretaries would be required to have financial independence and autonomy of government. As a congregation devoted to missionary work, they were to state their purpose broadly enough to include, not only work at home and in the foreign missions under the direction of the Maryknoll Fathers, but with other societies and ecclesiastical authorities as well. It was not easy, especially at first, for Mary Joseph to accept all this and the increasing responsibility it would entail for her.

Following a discussion with Father Walsh about the proposed ends of the future community, as these were to be stated in their petition to Rome, she wrote him that evening:

> I fear I disappointed you this afternoon and delayed you by my stupidity and stubbornness. If Father McNicholas keeps the idea of the last suggestion, working for the C.F.M.S. and other foreign mission works we may choose to adopt, I am sure all will be satisfied.
>
> Measure our love for the Society by your own. Such cannot easily be turned into new channels. . . .
>
> I hope you know that I fully appreciate that whatever we have done well was due to your guidance and splendid intellect. Of ourselves we could accomplish little. Perhaps that is why I am so fearful of working away from the Society. But God will send the right one to us since it is evident that we must be independent and leave you free.

I feel as though my heart was heavily burdened. I need your prayers so much. . . .

God bless and keep you!

Affectionately,

MJ

In June of 1919 a third petition was sent to Rome, expertly formulated by Bishop McNicholas of Duluth, the same Dominican cleric who had encouraged the secretaries from the beginning to become Dominican Sisters. Over the years, whether at Rome or in the United States, he had done everything possible to advise and encourage and help them.

Due to the Bishop's influence and her own magnanimity, Mother Mary Samuel of the Dominican Sisters of Sinsinawa accepted the responsibility for training the Teresians. In July, in anticipation of a favorable answer to the third petition, she sent Sister Fidelia to them. No formal novitiate could be started, of course, but Sister Fidelia could help the Teresians to learn and live the life outlined in their tentative constitutions drawn up two years earlier during Sister Ruth's stay at St. Teresa's.

A thin little parchment of a woman nearly sixty years old, Sister Fidelia at first sight dismayed some of the less valiant Teresians. Her future novices looked at her large nose, big glasses, small eyes and long pale face, and made mental ejaculations. "Glory! We are in for it now!"

They found, however, that they had acquired a treasure, a woman singularly well equipped for the task given to her. Balanced, just, she distinguished easily and precisely between what belonged to the essence of religious life and what pertained to individual community custom. She knew how to suggest, when to take a stand, what to let be. Her concern focused on essentials. Undemonstrative as she was, no one could question her devotion to her task or her affection for her charges. She had an abiding springtime in her old heart. Sometimes her digestion or her joints protested, but she kept up the pace of daily religious life and met its extra demands more than halfway. She even joined the Teresians on their rare but rugged picnics, wanting to do—and no doubt to suffer—no less than the others.

With Sister Fidelia's guidance, the Teresians could be sure that, given their own good will, their religious formation would go quietly and steadily forward. Although their numbers had grown, their work had not lessened due to the increase in *The Field Afar* circulation and in the Seminary personnel. It was not always easy for Sister Fidelia to plan and maintain a regular religious order of the day when *The Field Afar* had to be wrapped and mailed within a few days, or farm produce had to be canned and preserved before it would spoil, but together she and Mary Joseph and all the Teresians did what they could so that the group might live and serve God like real Sisters until they could actually become such. Unfailingly at night prayers they asked God to bless them with "Roman approval."

Again Mary Joseph was a novice. Thirty-six years old now and used to governing the Teresians under Father Walsh's direction, she accepted the old role gratefully and completely. She still held the same responsibilities she had retained under the Immaculate Heart Sisters and beautifully reconciled the two positions of novice and directress. The Teresians long remembered the lovely relationship between the two women, their affection, and exquisite mutual courtesy.

"Sister Fidelia, may I give the Sisters some instructions about the work?" Mary Joseph would ask.

In September of 1919, only a year since he came smiling down the front steps of the Seminary to begin his long journey to South China, Father Price was stricken with appendicitis and died in a Hong Kong hospital on September 12. From all over the United States people offered Maryknoll their sympathy for his loss. Some felt that it would have been wiser to keep a man of his age at home in the first place. He had asked earnestly to be one of the first group of missioners, and Father Walsh hesitated to deny him the privilege, particularly because of his years of mission experience in North Carolina, which should prove invaluable in guiding the young and untried missioners under him. Now they would have to make their way without him.

Although he had been for a time the Teresians' confessor and had given them occasional conferences, Father Price was little known to some of them. A number of them had never heard him speak of anything except our Lady and Bernadette. He was kind but distant toward women. Some of the group could not escape concluding that, as Eden had spoiled his taste for apples —he would not eat them—it had also impaired his filial feeling for Eve and deprived him, except in the case of our Blessed Lady and Bernadette, of any excessive enthusiasm for her daughters. In heaven they knew he would forgive and forget the part that woman had played in the sad events of the lesser Paradise and that they could count on him to remember them, together with all Maryknollers, before the throne of his Queen and theirs.

CHAPTER 5

SISTERS AND MISSIONERS

O N FEBRUARY 14, 1920, Mary Joseph returned from a short stay at Trinity College, Washington, where she had gone to give a mission talk. She found St. Teresa's Lodge bubbling over with high spirits and the good news that the Teresians were to be real Sisters at last. They ran from every direction trying to tell her about it all at once. Mary Frances, who had answered the telephone and received the message on February 12, prevailed by right of her stellar role and strong voice.

"Imagine," she exclaimed, "he said—Monsignor Dunn, of course, I mean—'I've been trying to get the Seminary for I don't know how long and they don't answer. I want to speak to Father Walsh. I have a very important message for him. From the Archbishop. From Rome. Can you take it to him?' 'Certainly,' I said. 'Right to him?' 'Of course, Monsignor,' I said. 'Don't tell anyone else first. Don't stop for anything, understand?' 'No, Monsignor,' I said. Then he *told* me! Now I ask you, how could I go rushing right over to the Seminary without saying a word to anybody? What would they think? So I told Sister Fidelia. And then Mary Teresa had to know. And then we *did* get word to the Seminary. And then we got everybody together here and told them all about it and they put me on top of the table and made me announce the whole thing—as well as I could remember. I was so excited!"

"Did you tell Mary Joseph," Mary Teresa interposed, "that you yelled 'Hooray!' and did a dance right on top of the table?"

"At a time like that, who would mind?" Mary Frances wanted to know. "I was carried away, carried right away! Isn't it wonderful, wonderful?"

It was. And when the official document came, Mary Joseph loved every syllable of its staid legal language: "We in virtue of the aforesaid faculty . . . erect by this decree into a diocesan religious institute and declare it to be so erected the pious society of women who carry on the work at the Seminary at Maryknoll. . . ." At the close, something of Archbishop Hayes's paternal interest prevailed over the formalities: "With the certain hope that the aforesaid institute will continue to give generous aid to the foreign missions, We lovingly impart to each of the Sisters our Pastoral Blessing."

The year of canonical novitiate began immediately. After the near decade that had gone by before, it flashed past like a month. Of those who had persevered, some from the very beginning, what can be said? However carefully and precisely defined by theologians in the abstract, a religious vocation in the concrete remains a mystery, especially to those granted such a boon. Looking at the retreating backs of the Marys and Minnies who gave up, any Teresian could rightly say, "There, but for the grace of God, go I."

Mary Joseph recognized and meditated on the mystery, and more than once spoke of it, but never more tellingly than when at last she made her first vows:

"No one of us dares to consider deeply why such graces have come to us. We are only more than ever conscious of the fact that the work here is wholly God's, and that in His omnipotence

He has chosen His weakest children to accomplish it for Him."

The key to the steadfastness of the candidates who persevered could certainly not be found in their similarity. They were not cut according to the same pattern or hewn out of the same backgrounds. They were not of equal gifts and had not all had the same advantages, but to Mary Joseph they were all "my own dearest ones." She understood, respected, and enjoyed the individuality of each, and was masterly in finding the work and place into which each would fit. Meanwhile she encouraged them all to learn new skills and activities and to become as versatile as possible. She let them know that she did not expect this to be done without some mistakes and failures. If God is pleased with honest effort, why not she?

As the Teresian family grew, its heterogeneity continued to flourish.

There was Mary Letitia Crawford, on her way to becoming Sister Ambrose, as full of energy as a hand grenade, impetuous, blunt, lively, and warmhearted. When her family came from Massachusetts to visit her, her very uniform crackled with zest and joy. When they went away, her grief fountained over and splashed down on her round little bosom with such heartiness that the world was inclined to weep with her. Even the self-possessed Mary Louise used to be half-amused and half-touched to find her own eyes filled with reflected sorrow.

There was Mary Magdalen, who was to add Sister to her name. Patrician and gracious, she seemed as remote from the Manhattan which was her home as if she had never heard of it. She had left behind with complete finality wealth and prospects which few young women ever have the opportunity to renounce. Not many were so unassuming as she, and no one more voracious for poverty and self-denial. She loved Mary Joseph's noble and generous ways but thought she would be vastly improved by being more mortified.

There was Kate, Sister Philomena to be, who was born in

County Leitrim, had the complexion and innocence of a baby and the strength and walk of one of Eire's legendary giants. When she turned off a faucet with a firm hand, the washer shrieked and died. She was equally strong in regard to her principles, and before she came to Maryknoll lived and worked in Manhattan as untouched in her simplicity as if she were still a child at home in Ballinamore.

As a teen-ager she had crossed the Atlantic on the *Columbia*. Her magnificent five feet ten, black hair, and lovely fair complexion attracted an admirer. He came to sit beside her, attempting to lead her vast shyness out into the open field of conversation and compliments. Kate looked at her large feet and shuffled them carefully back and forth; she rocked a little from side to side as though replies were stuck somewhere inside of her and had to be carefully dislodged. When she spoke, she blushed and stammered and mumbled. Communications broke down. The man finally gave up and got up. "You certainly are handsome, but good God—!" he exploded.

Kate was decisive enough later when she heard an unknown priest give a talk on the missions and Maryknoll in her New York parish church. Straightway she applied to the Teresians and was accepted.

When the day came for her to receive her uniform, she was ecstatic and voluble. Her erstwhile admirer would never have credited her with such eloquence. As she got ready in her little dormitory cubicle, other Teresians could hear her soliloquizing, "Well, *Deo gratias!* I always wanted to be a Sister, and now I am one! *Deo gratias!* I'm not going to talk after night prayers anymore. I'm going to renounce all the pleasures of earth. From now on I'm for heaven alone!"

The invisible audience in their own cubicles meanwhile were thinking, "More power to you, Kate, so say we all—only not out loud, please."

She was with the initial twenty-one who entered St. Teresa's small chapel on February 15, 1921, and went forward to the altar to make their first vows as Maryknoll Sisters.

Among them, both Massachusetts and Irish lineage were well represented. Besides the two Rogers, Sister Mary Joseph and her blood sister Louise, now Sister James, there were three who had arrived in the Hawthorne days—Sister Teresa (Sara) Sullivan, Sister Theophane (Nora) Shea, and Sister Anna Maria Towle. To these had been added during the intervening years at Maryknoll—Sister Catherine Fallon, bringing her dignity, her mature years, and her business experience; Sister Ambrose (Mary Letitia) Crawford, endowed with both a quick intelligence and instantaneous reactions; Sister Patrick Maher, with a memorably fine face and intellectual and social tastes and habits reminiscent of Mary Louise Wholean's; Sister Dolores Cruise, quietly dedicated to becoming as faithful as humanly possible to the way of life which she had elected; and Sister Thomas Bresnahan, a good household organizer with broad shoulders and capable hands. Sister Anthony Conway from Danbury, Connecticut, carried the flag for the other New England States. Like five others in the group of twenty-one, she had been born in Ireland.

New York State, in a pattern long to be reproduced in the ranks of Maryknoll Sisters, claimed the next largest number: plump and good-humored Sister Francis Davis from Brooklyn, well cushioned for years of manifold experiences in country China, which included being captured by bandits and being in the center of wars, both small and world-wide; young, fresh-faced Sister Agatha Davin, with sparkling blue eyes and a heart of warm compassion for every living thing on God's earth; cheerful Sister Rose Leifels from Schenectady, schooled for office work but ready for anything; Sister Elizabeth Thompson, Maryknoll's first nurse; Sister Margaret Mary Slattery, Athens postmistress and soon to be Maryknoll's own first postmistress and first local catechist; tireless Sister Michael Conlin from

Manhattan, who would long be the chief saleswoman for mission-made handwork; and Sister Rita Bodkin and Sister Philomena (Kate) Flanagan, both of Ireland by way of the big city of New York.

The first two to enter from Pennsylvania were Sister John Troy from Norristown, who, in large part because of her distilled kindness and gentle diffidence, was to become one of Maryknoll's most redoubtable promoters; and last but not least, the gifted Sister Paul McKenna from Reading.

For each Sister, as she said the short formula of vows so long anticipated, the years of waiting and preparation, the delays and disappointments, the hardships and heartaches, served only as a setting in which this day of days shone like a pearl.

Not making their profession of vows with their group that day at Maryknoll were four Sisters already working among the Japanese—Sister Magdalen Doelger and Sister Aloysius McDonald in Los Angeles; Sister Gemma (Margaret) Shea and Sister Gerard Gallagher in Seattle. Three of these four were also from the State where Father Walsh had done his first and most comprehensive gleaning.

Once the Church had given her approving nod and some Sisters had made their vows, the young community would grow quickly and its projects would proliferate. Opportunities, decisions, and obligations soon began to multiply. Even in the first year of 1921 the new Mother Superior found herself in an expanding circle of interest and activities that would grow wider, more diverse, and more complex with the years.

In March of 1921, less than a month after her profession, she was on board a train bound for the Pacific coast. The two Sisters in Los Angeles and the two in Seattle had foregone the canonical novitiate, the year of required special training, to initiate the work there, accepting the possibility of an indefinite delay of their own profession as a result. Their generosity had its reward, however, and a dispensation made it possible for them to make their vows. Mother Mary Joseph went to attend their profession and to acquaint herself with their work and circumstances at first hand. She remained in both places long enough to come to know the people whom the Sisters served and the program which they were following.

She was interested too in the possibilities for expanding the work and in the increased personnel which this would necessitate. At Los Angeles the Sisters would soon have to staff completely a grade school as well as a home, both for Japanese children.

The situation there looked particularly promising, although it had grown up out of the heart of a complex situation. A group of pious Japanese women, who wore a habit and lived in community but had no canonical status, had already been engaged in the work. According to the Bishop's decision, they were given the option of disbanding or joining the Maryknoll Sisters, whom he had chosen to replace them. The proposal was only part of a wide program to prune out a mushroom growth of small communities founded without ecclesiastical approbation. Yet, because the Japanese women of this group were foreign-born and the decision came at a time when a certain coolness was already seeping into relations between Japan and the United States over their China policies, the situation was particularly sensitive and for the Japanese women especially trying. Out of the whole group only one decided to become a Maryknoll Sister. The rest sailed back to Japan and in time became a well-established and useful community.

When, in June, Mother Mary Joseph returned to Maryknoll and her Sisters came laughing and hurrying out of several scattered houses to surround and welcome her, they found standing in her broad shadow a smiling, bowing, formal little Japanese, who managed to look at once timid and self-possessed, childlike and shrewd. Mother's insight into the situation of this woman so unlike herself had already established a bond between them. Now she drew her forward kindly, proudly.

"Your new sister, Sister Marianna Akashi," Mother said, presenting to them the first Oriental to enter their community.

She was the first of a number of others from the Far East— Chinese, Filipino, Japanese, and Korean—who would in the coming years make their way to Maryknoll to become religious missioners. All of them Mother loved and appreciated, recognizing in each the rich gift of her particular nationality and culture as well as of her unique individuality.

In August, a second group of novices would make their vows and bring the total of full-fledged Sisters to thirty-eight. With this increment in mind it was possible in June to designate Sisters to increase the staff both at Los Angeles and Seattle and, besides that, to begin work in the Orient.

On June 28, the day before the Fathers would celebrate their tenth anniversary, when everybody was already agog with preparations to make that occasion a big event, all the Sisters knew that Mother and her Council were in session. In the crowded quarters where the Sisters worked shoulder to shoulder, ate elbow to elbow and slept in cots an arm's length away from one another, secrets had short lives. Besides, Mother had little inclination for closeness and caution. She liked to share her hopes, her plans, her dreams with those who shared her life and work.

So everybody was aware that the door to Mother's small office was closed and that behind it she and her four Councilors were at work on assignments. As the Sisters met each other in doorways, on the paths from one house to the other, or arrived at their desks, typewriters, tubs, stoves, and sewing machines, they all had but one thing on their minds. "Aren't you excited?" "The Council is really sitting?" "Right this minute maybe they are discussing you!" "Who do you think will go to China?" "Who—me? You're probably the only one *that* will occur to. Rush right over and tell Mother before it's too late."

That afternoon after the little ceremony during which Sister Marianna Akashi received the habit of a Maryknoll Sister and before Benediction of the Blessed Sacrament was given, Father Walsh gave one of his brief but telling talks for the occasion. He did not receive the attention usually accorded him.

The soul of conciseness on all occasions, he was mercifully briefer than usual. Suddenly he had a small sheet of paper in his hand, looked at it and then at them and began to read off places and names. "To the Venard . . . to Los Angeles . . . to Seattle . . ." Long before he reached the seventeenth and last name, the question had sprung up in many minds, "What about China? What about China!"

"To China . . ." began Father Walsh.

Nobody seemed to move or breathe.

"Sister Mary Paul, Superior."

"Ah-h." It was not really an exclamation, hardly a sound, just an intake of breath. Most of the Sisters had guessed that one. Sister Paul McKenna's dark eyes held no surprise. She had always hoped and expected to go to China. And very recently Father Superior had broached the subject of this particular assignment while they were working together on the "Maryknoll Junior," a children's supplement to *The Field Afar.* To be in charge of the first group of Sisters to go to the missions . . . She could teach, she could write, she could organize . . . but to find herself set down in vast China—like lonely Jonas in Nineveh— to start a mission without language, background, experience and, it would obviously have to be, without much money! She was dismayed, looked it, and said so.

Father Superior gave her a strong dose of comfort. "The weak things of this world hath God chosen," he said quietly, thinking of himself as well as of her. To that she had no rejoinder.

Now she sat in chapel alert and composed, a little paler than usual.

"Also, Sister Rose . . ."

Sister Rose Leifels of Schenectady had had a busy afternoon. She had taken Father Superior's dictation, typed his letters, and brought them to him for signature. At ten to five he began to sign them.

"Don't go," he said. "Sit down and wait for them here. You can seal them as I finish." She shifted a little nervously from one foot to the other as he gave her a kind and level look. "You want to get to the ceremony, don't you?"

"Oh, yes, Father."

"Well then, let's do this the quickest way."

That was quite a look he gave me, she was thinking. And he never had me sit down in here like this before to finish up the mail. My hands are all thumbs. Maybe he has something to say to me. I wonder what.

But he said nothing, only looked at her once or twice again in the same thoughtful way and then, before she had finished, took himself off to be on time for the ceremony. She hurried over late and, all the seats in the small chapel being taken, stood in the doorway to hear him give his short talk and announce the names of those assigned.

When he read the second name, she started. Glory, for a minute I thought he said me, she thought. Somebody looked her way significantly. Did he? Did he! He couldn't have. It's impossible!

"Sister Lawrence . . ."

Sister Lawrence Foley of Fall River, Massachusetts, too was disbelieving. It can't be, she kept saying to herself, it's too good to be true. *"Sister Barbara, Sister Imelda, Sister Monica."*

Sister Barbara Froelich of Merrill, Wisconsin, and Sister Monica Moffatt of Fall River, Massachusetts, both looked pleased and a little dazed. Sister Barbara even laughed a little, soundlessly, her blue eyes sparkling. "Nobody guessed me," Sister Monica thought; "I never even guessed myself."

Sister Imelda Sheridan, while inflamed by the general ardor, was not wholly changed from the auburn-haired child who always kept a safe distance between herself and Scranton's Chinese laundryman and who joined the Maryknoll Sisters at seventeen without feeling any attraction to faraway places. She had wanted to be a Sister at any cost, had feared to dally and delay over her vocation. "Lord, make me a Sister before I am nineteen," she used to pray. Aided by prayer, determination, and pastoral advice—"Don't send your picture, child; they'll think you're an infant!"—she reached St. Teresa's well before attaining that advanced age.

Now that she had reached nineteen, God was going to make a missioner of her, too. Her future ability to love and live with her adopted people, to identify herself with them, to speak their language as though she had been born to it, were not obvious to anyone that day, and least of all to herself. A little frightened, she reached for her hymnal and found the pages for the Benediction hymns.

The first departure ceremony, brief but meaningful, took place on the twelfth of September. Archbishop Hayes presided. Bishop-elect Dunn attended. Bishop Cassidy of Fall River was the speaker. Father Walsh, of course, took part. The ceremony was planned as a small private affair. However, old friends like Julia Ward and some of the Sisters' relatives and friends crowded into the small fieldstone building—wonderfully transformed from laundry and cannery into a bright and airy chapel for this great occasion—and overflowed into the chairs arranged for the community on the grass outside.

As the six Sisters went up to the altar to repeat the vows which they had first taken so short a time ago and to receive from Father Superior their mission crucifixes, symbolic of their dedication and sacrifice, the hearts and eyes of their Sisters followed them.

To all, this first reaching out to the mission fields in the Orient was both marvelous and overwhelming: to some of those who had waited for this day through long years of setbacks and uncertainties, it had a dreamlike, almost unsubstantial quality; to others who had come to the community but recently it seemed more like actuality than the daily cleaning, cooking, early rising, rule learning, magazine wrapping, class attending and frequent chapel going—all still so unfamiliar to them. These recent recruits caught their breath now to see their daydreams rear up before them like Chinese pagodas, solid and sky-high. A few more tomorrows and they too would be reaching out to receive their own mission crucifixes. They did not mind at all that Bishop Cassidy talked about martyrdom and being ground to powder to become the wheat of Christ. They were in that uplifted mood from which the untried are apt to view the sacrifices of others.

Mother, with her mind on the Sisters' families, who had enough to face in the present without being projected into the possible future, wished heartily that the Bishop would be a little more cheerful.

Regardless of whether the preacher's theme gloomed or sparkled, Mother was well satisfied with the assignments and the ceremony and confident of her fledgling missioners. In the weeks before they took their leave, it seemed that she could not do enough to show them what they meant to her. She planned little programs to give them pleasure, helped to prepare special meals, gave them little gifts, went with them to New York to shop and to secure their tickets and passports.

She was manifestly happy in this new undertaking for God, content with the Sisters chosen to go. Just the same, at the last when she stood on the station platform and watched them glide out of sight framed in the train window, she felt sharply the deep pang which she was to experience over and over again when, at her asking, her Sisters would set out for work and suffering and separation which she herself could not share with them. They had all been so brave, so restrained. Only when they came to say good-by to her did the tears slip past their defenses.

They were gone only a few days when Father Walsh too set out for the Orient to make a round of the Fathers' missions in South China and to investigate the possibilities for new fields. Although Mother was glad that his mission visitation at this time would take him to China just when his guidance would mean most to the Sisters, she felt keenly, as she always did, the withdrawal of his sustaining presence.

His absences, his increasing workload, his growing society of seminarians and priests, even the mighty pile of fieldstone shaping into an unfinished but majestic seminary, were all teaching her slowly but surely the responsibilities which she carried must become increasingly her own. She knew the enduring quality of his fatherliness, that it would never fail her or her Sisters; yet she realized too that both she and they must absorb less and less of his time as the weight of his work and his age grew heavier.

His day of departure, crammed with work to the last minute, was so well planned that characteristically he had time, in seeming leisure, to meet the Sisters in a body and outline for them his itinerary and then to shake hands with each one, saying something appropriate as they came up to wish him Godspeed.

The one-time Teresians were now a rapidly growing Sisterhood. One summer evening Mother noticed almost with a start how big her religious family had become. She was sitting outside with them all, resting and talking and sewing after the day's work. Gathered in gray lines and clusters and little knots of postulant blue under the darkening trees, the group looked wieldy enough until they stood up together to play one of the old-time ring games and found that they could not manage it because they were too many.

"How can you play 'Farmer in the Dell' with about sixty people?" somebody wanted to know.

In December, Mother enlisted a helper or two and set herself to make the community's Christmas pudding. The session with the Boston Cookbook and the multiplication table having been completed, they marshaled their ingredients. When finally Mother sat surrounded with pounds of milk-soaked bread crumbs and suet, big brown paper bags of figs and citron, packages of raisins, bowls of beaten egg yolks and snowy egg white, all incensed with the pleasant aroma of nutmeg and cinnamon, clove and mace, and presided over by an impressive bottle of wine, St. Teresa's old kitchen could offer no container big enough to hold it all. Laughing, the pudding makers pre-empted a brand-new galvanized washtub. Into it the final climactic mixture was poured.

That year of 1921, seventy-six Sisters, most of them novices and postulants, kept Christmas at Maryknoll. When Ellen McMahon, later Sister Lumena, arrived late on Christmas Eve, she brought the roster of the entire community up to one hundred fourteen. Of those not at Maryknoll, six were in China, forming a small nucleus for the work that would grow so well there, and the others were divided among the three houses in the United States—at Los Angeles, Seattle, and Scranton.

Before Father Walsh left on his tour of duty, he had told Mother Mary Joseph that the Sisters might take over St. Joseph's, the changeling barn, as soon as the seminarians could be moved out of it to their stark but impressive quarters in the unfloored and unplastered Seminary. When he returned in March of 1922, he found the Seminary full of men and activity and St. Joseph's, newly painted by the Brothers and seminarians and gleaming after a recent scrub and polish by the Sisters, already re-filled with white-veiled, gray-habited novices.

To accomplish this in time for his homecoming, seminarians and Brothers, Sisters and novices and postulants, farm mules and wagons and wheelbarrows had all played their part. It was a mass movement, a super-production. It looked as if they were putting on a dramatization of the Jews leaving Egypt for the Promised Land—taking the Pyramids with them.

St. Joseph's was the nearest thing to a real novitiate house that the Sisters had ever had. Everybody was thrilled with it. It was spacious, had good lines. Even before the carpentry and painting were done, Mother and Sister Fidelia went through it together, entranced. A refectory into which all of them would fit at one time. A kitchen big enough to work in. Cells and beds for about forty. And for now, until more arrivals would necessitate converting it into a dormitory, a real community room.

"I want it to be a real nursery of saints," Mother told the sweet old Novice Mistress, a good candidate for sainthood herself.

Within a few years the Sisters filled every one of the old houses on the compound as the Fathers relinquished them and withdrew to their hilltop stronghold, the new Seminary, safe from evacuation at last. This continual filling and overflowing of additional houses made the growth of the Sisters' community seem even faster than it was. Increase in numbers brought increase in work capacity, too. Some Teresians could remember when a dozen of them took days to wrap and mail *The Field Afar*. They were amazed to discover that one September day in 1922 they could and did hand-wrap twenty-two thousand magazines between one-thirty and three-thirty in the afternoon.

People are attracted to something new—a new baby, a new scientific theory, a new dress, a new political movement, a new religious society. From the beginning Maryknoll had attracted many visitors. They continued to come, and in increasing numbers: missioners of many orders and societies and from many lands, ecclesiastics from the new world and from the old; benefactors and relatives of the students, the priests, the Brothers, and the Sisters; young men and young women interested in becoming Maryknollers; priests and religious eager to learn more about the work which they were already helping in generous and practical ways; representatives of all kinds and fields of Catholic action drawn by Father Walsh's sustained enthusiasm for everything Catholic. Every growing shoot, every leaf, it would seem, of the great old tree of the Church drew him to admire, protect, and, if he could, nourish it. The Sisters shared and enjoyed all: friends, fellow workers, celebrities. Father Walsh made the rounds with them, showing them off to his religious family and showing off his Maryknollers to them.

Among those who came during 1923 were two distinguished converts: Dr. Kinsman, a former Episcopalian Bishop, who gave a series of talks to both seminarians and Sisters; David Goldstein, a Jew, who brought along his mobile unit, the "Catholic Truth Van." Father Bede Jarrett, the already famous English Dominican, came to tell Maryknollers about the conditions of the Catholic Church in England. Archbishop Fumasoni-Biondi, then Apostolic Delegate to the United States and later to become Secretary of the Church's Congregation of Propaganda, the division of the Church's administration directly concerned with its missions, was one of the most notable churchmen who visited that year. Mother Samuel of Sinsinawa returned once more to renew acquaintance with the Sisters, in whom she never lost interest.

Visitors came from close at hand, too. One of the first of Ossining neighbors to call at Maryknoll was the keen and courtly chaplain at Sing Sing prison, Father William E. Cashin. In every sense a man's man and adequate for his difficult work at the prison, he had an almost womanly intuition into the concerns and needs of others. He became a lifelong friend to all Maryknollers and, after the death of Maryknoll's founder, the ecclesiastical superior of the Sisters.

One particularly beloved guest would come no more. In February of 1923, Mrs. Rogers died. Every visit which she made to St. Teresa's had drawn the Sisters closer to her. They loved to sit with her during their brief stretches of leisure time, to draw her out about home and family and Mollie, and to learn her own sane and solid views. They knew that they owed much to her quiet strength and gentleness, her beautiful manners; they daily enjoyed the counterpart of them in their Mother Superior. She delighted them too because all unnecessarily she would champion them against her daughter and could not withhold commenting upon her Mollie's surprising development.

"When I learned that Mollie was to be in charge of all of you, I was happy. I thought she would be so good to you. I never dreamed that she would keep you in that hot laundry all day, that she would make you work so hard."

Then they would rally to defend their Mother: "She really works harder than any of us." "She would do it all herself if she could."

Word of her mother's serious illness reached Mother Mary Joseph on the evening of February 11, the feast of our Lady of Lourdes, just as she was about to give a little illustrated talk to the Sisters about Lourdes. She found that no train was available until after the talk could be finished, and decided to go ahead with it as planned before leaving. Her sister Louise, Sister James, went off to get their things together.

As Mother came to the front of the room to begin her talk, some of the Sisters had already learned what news she had received. The others heard it from her own steady lips before she began, "Here at Maryknoll all of us have a special love for Lourdes . . ."

Her face had the same repose that they saw in it daily; the large eyes under their heavy fringe of lashes were untroubled; her long-fingered, expressive hands, quiet and relaxed. And when the lights went out and she stepped aside to comment on the shifting pictures of the places which she remembered and loved so well, her voice came through the darkened room with all its usual strength and richness, communicating a sense of peace and stability.

Little Miss Shea—Sister Gemma since 1920—had often wondered about Mother's poise. Her self-control did not seem an outward denial or repression of feelings which ravaged her inwardly, but a kind of harmony of the whole personality to which principles, emotions, and habits all contributed but to which a loving faith probably gave most of all. Thirty-five years later, she was still trying to fathom it, to express it.

"I really don't know how to describe her," she said. "She was complete. She was never anything but noble in any situation, never less than herself. I cannot say the same of anyone else I ever knew."

--⋙{ CHAPTER 6 }⋘--

IN THE EA   med little disposed   spicious, they
watched t   heir neighbors
—either h   ld not forget it
or had been allies and

The United States was drifting, rather than climbing, toward
an eminent place among the reduced number of great powers.
She liked to excel but not to lead. Unhappy about Wilson's postwar experience with European diplomacy, exasperated with
their own unacknowledged inexperience in international affairs,
and fretted by Japan's adroit and successful moves in the Pacific
Islands and in the Orient, diplomats and politicians leaned
strongly toward isolationism.

Americans seemed to turn blindly from the sharpened patri-
otism, the genuine if irrational idealism, and the lingering
anxieties of the war years to concern themselves with more man-
ageable material things—business, large and small, technical
progress, the urbanization of the country, the distractions and

pleasures of city life, the still-new radio, the improved roads and cars.

In the Orient great China was in ferment. Long heckled and bullied by nations stronger than herself, she was becoming more and more fearful of the growing shadow of Japan's postwar power and prestige. With a northern party and a southern party contending for power and no central government strong enough to give her even the semblance of unity, she was a helpless giant upon whom her own war lords preyed, scrambling and intriguing for her cities, wrenching apart her provinces, converting her great rivers into highways for pirates, reducing her people to poverty and terror. In the south and in the north alike hidden Marxist growths were already forming in her great body, one attached to Sun Yat-sen's southern political party, the Kuomintang, the other spewing political agitators from a small study group in the University of Peking. In the south, Chou-en-lai, a young Marxist revolutionary, stood ready to head the political department of the Kuomintang's Whampoa Military Academy and to indoctrinate its cadets as soon as the school should open in 1924. In the north, the son of a Hunan farmer, a former student and librarian at Peking University called Mao Tse-tung, was already dedicating himself to political agitation and the organization of China's laborers. No one then saw the future of these young men or of China, but all could see the confusion, the violence, the cross-purposes and double-dealing, the cynicism, selfishness, and callousness which drained the country of life and left her open to the subtle advances of Bolshevism.

All in all, the times did not seem auspicious for missionarying, and China appeared one of the least hopeful fields for missionary endeavor. But the world has her troubles in every generation and the work of the Church must push ahead as it can, sometimes in great leaps and bounds, sometimes by inches. In this tradition, Maryknollers trickled steadily into South China. By 1923 the priests were sending their sixth group, the

Sisters their third. And throughout the United States, high school boys and girls dropped by school libraries to have a look at the pictures in *The Field Afar* or crouched over copies at their desks at home to read with burning hearts what Father Walsh had to say about the pity of China, the modern marvel of Japan, the wonder story of Korea's faith, the tragic waste of American money on get-rich-quick schemes, the importance of Oriental students in the United States, the doings of Mary-knollers in training at the Home Knoll or at work in China, and the need, the great need of young, dedicated American hearts to take up such a life here—now—today. Their response was out of key with the times: They wrote to Maryknoll in brief, to-the-point letters. "How does a fellow get to be a missioner?" "What do I have to do to become a Maryknoll Sister?" "I think I have a mission vocation. Now what?"

The year of 1923 was no time for traveling in China either, if you were looking for comfort, safety, and pleasure. Since Mother had other things in mind, she decided to visit her Sisters in South China that year. The twelve already there were divided between the British metropolitan port of Hong Kong and the old-world Chinese city of Yeungkong, a focus for contention between opposing war lords. Six more Sisters were to join them that fall. This third departure group consisted of Sisters Dominic Guidera, Marie de Lourdes Bourguignon, Matthew Conlon, Miriam Schmitt, Patricia Couglin, and Ruth Riconda. Mother decided to make the trip with them.

Making a start in South China had not been easy for the Sisters. They were full of generosity and enthusiasm and Sister Mary Paul, their superior, was able and resourceful. In the racial and social composite of Hong Kong and Kowloon, however, they found themselves, if not welcome, certainly not sought after. Was it because they were occidental, or because they were American, or because they were Roman Catholic, or because they were new and untried, or because they were all these things together? Their one work, which looked then like an inconsequential school of few pupils, was just wobbling along on weak infant legs toward an uncertain future. An invitation, then open, for them to staff a government hospital in the colony was a little later to be withdrawn because of local opposition.

At Yeungkong, in Kwangtung Province, the other group were just finding their place in the work of the mission and the life of the people, still handling the language awkwardly and only just learning the customs and thoughts of their Yeungkong neighbors, but they had Father Francis Ford as their pastor and a mission already humming with charitable activities as their field. They were almost completely isolated from the Sisters at Kowloon, not by distance but by slow and uncertain travel. Junks might sail before or after the hour or day scheduled; they might be commandeered by soldiery before you could get aboard or even after you were partway on your journey. After two days of waiting or a week of interrupted travel, you might yet have to return to your point of departure, whether Hong Kong or Yeungkong.

Once reached, Yeungkong presented a social mosaic far simpler than Kowloon's, but its physical exactions were greater. It had few comforts and conveniences, no Western-style shops where English was spoken and British and American goods were handled. It was medieval in its pace, narrow streets, unconcern for cleanliness, democratic way with animals. It was very nearly medieval in its methods of defending itself with gates and walls against marauders. A city well placed for commerce and custom collecting, it made a juicy plum for contending war lords, who used bribery or violence, as the occasion dictated, to secure or maintain their hold.

Bandits in the hills just outside the walls and along the riverbanks made forays according to need and opportunity. The Sisters never quite came to distinguish between armies and outlaws, and in this incapacity many of the Chinese themselves shared.

All this cost the Sisters no lives. But as Mother made plans to sail from Seattle with the Sisters assigned, a cable announced that Sister Gertrude, the nurse at the Yeungkong dispensary and less than a year in China, had died of typhoid on August 21.

Mother felt that one more reason had been added to those which already determined her going. As the head of a religious community, she was required to visit its houses. And she had long realized the value of first-hand mission knowledge for the direction and expansion of the community's mission work and the formation of its Sisters. And now that one of the little company in South China had died so soon, she ached to companion and hearten the others, sharing their grief in this first unexpected loss.

In September, she left Maryknoll together with seven young Sisters bound for their new mission in South China. To the original group of six, Sister Richard Wenzel had been added to take Sister Gertrude's place. With them went twenty-one-year-old Agnes Cogan, sister of Maryknoll's Sister Mary de Paul, on a tour of faraway places.

Lively, pretty, and fearless, Agnes was sure that she was going to have the time of her life. The trip itself would take her to places which few other Americans would ever reach; being with Mother, whom she loved, was a boon she appreciated. A solicitous and somewhat possessive father had generously underwritten her trip and that of her irreproachable chaperon.

As she sank into the seat on the train, Mother took a deep breath of fatigue, contentment, and sympathetic understanding. "Well, that's over." Characteristically, she did not bring her home burdens with her but resigned them completely to those who must stay behind and deal with them. She turned to the present and the Sisters about her, putting her head back and smiling around at them all.

They were thrilled to be with her and glad to be on their way to China, but some were deeply shaken by the final wrench of parting. Subdued, they stayed about her like people who have been chilled and seek the warmth and restoration of a fireside. No one could languish long with Mother around. The matter-of-fact way in which she accepted the sorrows and reverses that came to her gave no indication of the delicacy of feeling that she had for others. She knew that these new missioners had been abruptly uprooted, but she did not call their attention to it. The theme, "You have left home and country," so familiar to apostolic ears, received no emphasis in that little company. Instead, to give joy and alleviate any heartaches that might exist, she planned little treats, surprises, and expeditions.

At Seattle, they spent about a week, crowding into the small Maryknoll convent there. Then, almost before they knew how it had all happened, they were standing at the rails of the SS *Jefferson*, roped with broken paper streamers and waving, waving, waving, until they could no longer see any answering gestures from the human dots that lined the shrinking pier.

The *Jefferson* was crowded, and among her passengers carried a complement of twenty-two missioners. There would be no lack of Masses aboard with five priests, including two Irish Columbans, Fathers McAuley and Murray, and three Maryknollers, Fathers Fletcher, Cleary, and O'Melia. Father Cleary was on his way to Korea. All the other priests, together with Brother Michael of Maryknoll, two Sisters of Providence, six Sisters of Loretto and seven Maryknoll Sisters, were bound for China. Fathers Fletcher and O'Melia and Brother Michael, as well as the Maryknoll Sisters, were missioned to the south and would debark at Hong Kong; all the rest were to remain in the north and would leave the ship at Shanghai.

After a stopover in Victoria, the *Jefferson* put out to sea in the night.

In the morning, for those up to face it, the sea showed itself in a march of great, shifting, blue-green hills against which the ship drove, straining and rearing, to plunge down their far side and fetch up at the base with a lurch that sent the stomach cringing into some part of the body where it had no business to go. Lashed with rain and clad in runnels of racing, pouring foam, the ship pushed her course westward, game but complaining, a mite of solid challenge in a thunderous liquid universe.

No interval of gentle breezes and sparkling friendly water had allowed passengers to acquire sea legs. That first morning proved divisive, separating sailors from landlubbers, without respect for age, creed, sex or state of life.

Could it be only yesterday that Mother had, with motherly prescience, prepared them for the weather to come? "It's quite likely, my darlings, especially since it's the first ocean voyage for most of us, that some may be seasick. For a while at least. If we are, there's nothing anybody can do about it. We'll just have to put up with it. And we mustn't expect our two Sister nurses to be running around waiting on us. They are both tired and need a good rest, and it's just possible that they might not feel so well themselves." *Just possible!*

The first morning only one priest offered Mass. Standing uncertainly before the altar improvised on a large victrola in the social hall, he was assisted and steadied by a fellow priest. Over the golden rim of the paten, he could look straight ahead through the wide window with its draperies and green plantings to the prow of the ship and the backdrop of alternating sky and sea beyond.

After that first day, except when the weather took on real ferocity, all five priests were usually able to offer the Holy Sacrifice, the first Mass beginning at seven and the last at nine. Not all who wanted to could attend, and some who arrived gallantly left suddenly. Mother was a good sailor herself, not perfect, like several of the others, but very nearly so. And the high winds and heavy seas moved her to admiration rather than to fear.

For most of the passage the weather continued stormy, but the days were full of good humor, new and stimulating experiences, satisfying companionship, song, prayer, and contentment of heart. Time on shipboard spun away like the ship's wake.

As the days passed, within the tiny universe of the ship a little solar system established itself and revolved about Mother. No time ever seemed to be the wrong time to approach her. She was as accessible as the out of doors. She and Sister Jane, the superior of the Loretto Sisters, talked over mission work and mission life together. She provided the focus for the little knot of religious who gathered to say their prayers or to chat and laugh together. When passengers wanted to exchange pleasantries, they stopped at her chair. If the young Fathers had something to suggest or share, they made directly for her.

And as thoughts turned back to the Home Knoll, a daughter would urge her to speculate, "What will they be doing at Maryknoll now, do you think, Mother?" Or if anticipation sprang forward into the future, "What do you suppose China is really like, Mother? The people, I mean."

Agnes would come darting back like a bright bird, cheeks flushed and blue eyes pinched together with laughter as she deposited choice tidbits of her shipboard experiences, "Am I your little pet, Mother? Because if I'm not, I should worry. I'm Signor Toldano's. He calls me 'pet,' 'little pet,' right in front of everybody. And do I hate him for it!"

In the evenings, during second dinner, when the ship seemed peculiarly their own and the clouds lowered and darkened with the coming night or when occasional sunsets blazed and faded and the stars showed, singly at first, and then in groups, and finally in frosty battalions, all the Sisters and priests formed a habit of congregating on the deck if they could manage it, or indoors if the storm made that impossible, and then they would sing together many favorite hymns and songs that they had known and sung at home.

As they neared the islands of Japan, the mountainous seas dropped and the rain gave place to a mild drizzle.

During the long days on shipboard Mother had thought back on what Father Superior had written and said about the Orient, about what she had studied and what she had heard from missioners and travelers, about the pictures which she had handled and sorted and gone over until she knew them almost by heart. She was aware that now she could learn a little of what all of these secondhand sources could not teach. And so could these young Sisters with her. She wanted to learn it with them and to share it with them as far as the short weeks ahead would allow her.

Her first glimpse of the Far East was the sight of one of its greatest natural disasters. On September 1, a large area running south from Tokyo had been struck by a devastating earthquake. Throughout the five nightmare days and nights following, it was shaken with aftershocks and pounded with seismic waves. Beyond the reach of the water, fires raged unchecked. In Tokyo and Yokohama alone, ninety thousand died.

On October 5, when the *Jefferson* nosed cautiously through a drizzle of rain up to an improvised pontoon pier, her passengers stood aghast at the ship's rail, dumbfounded at Yokohama's awesome ruin. Over its dreadful face, pocked with mounds of rubble and overturned streetcars and trains, scarred with the jagged shells of burnt-out buildings, with twisted, erupted car tracks and gaping fissures, moved a few figures, mute and solitary and purposeful—the stricken Japanese, already engaged in the awesome business of bringing back to life their dead city. Once ashore—at their own risk—the ship's passengers found their first impression confirmed in terrible detail.

The earthquake had not reached Kobe, the next Japanese

port at which the *Jefferson* called. There Father Patrick Byrne, Maryknoll's first missioner in Korea, came down to the pier to meet them. Nothing about him that day suggested that he would spend long and useful years both in the mission field and at Maryknoll and eventually die a martyr's death as a prisoner of the Korean Reds during the winter of 1950. Mother tried to hide the shock and concern which his appearance gave her. She found it hard to reconcile her memories of the gay and energetic young priest who had left Maryknoll only months ago with this wasted and pithless man, leaning on a cane in an effort to hold himself erect. "Why, he looks like an old man," she thought. "What has happened to him? Why didn't we know?"

Questioned, he admitted that he had not been so well. He had dysentery. His stomach was mutinous. He was confining himself now to eating lightly of a few things that gave him the least trouble.

"Eating lightly," thought Mother. "He looks half-starved."

Together with the Fathers, she persuaded Father Byrne to go on with them to Shanghai for medical care, pointing out how he could also do some necessary buying for his mission there. He was not hard to convince.

She wrote to Father Walsh: "I know you would have done as I did had you been here. I could have wept when we met him. He was so physically weak and, most surprising of all 'pepless.' At the mere suggestion of going to Shanghai with us, he brightened up. . . . He has come up wonderfully, eating well and amusing us as of old."

At Shanghai, Mother had her first look at China. To her, as to many others, the Orient and China had somehow become almost synonymous, as if China itself were the very essence of the Orient. As such it had a special place in her heart. Like many another traveler from the West, she had her first encounter with the stark poverty of the Far East on her arrival in Shanghai's busy port. Before the *Jefferson* could dock, a covey of

sampans maneuvered around the ship to catch the prized garbage which had been saved up for them. Dipping, jockeying,
each boat looked like a floating nest of hungry birds, bodies taut,
necks outstretched, empty baskets held as high as poles and thin
arms could reach. When the garbage began to pour from the
ship's side, the fury of activity, the shrieks and depredations, the
sharp brief quarrels, and the pitiable harvest reaped by these
human gulls filled the heart with pity and dismay. Mother
watched long and silently. What she felt then found expression
in all her later dealing with China's poor, China's beggars,
China's burden-bearers. She would pay coolies twice what was
customary because her party had so much baggage or because
she was so heavy to pull in a ricksha or because the man was so
pleasant or looked so thin and tired, or because what was customary was not necessarily what was just. And she would give,
and give sometimes when others thought it unwise.

"Mother, look how they make straight for you. They can tell
that you are an easy mark."

"Well, even if they don't need it," she would say, half firmly,
half apologetically, as she put something into the hand of a
clamorous woman with a child in her arms, "I will give it in
honor of the Christ Child."

For some it costs to give; for Mother it cost to withhold.

Later on, when she was in Kaifeng during January, she and
her little party were dogged and importuned through the narrow streets by a stream of ragged and filthy beggars. It was impossible to give to all. It would have been futile, and perhaps
dangerous, to attempt to give to some.

"They are professionals, Mother. Don't attempt to give them
anything," she was warned. "Once you start . . ."

She did as she was asked, but when naked and shivering children thew themselves in the way, using their little bodies like so
many pale and eloquent tongues to plead their cause, she could
hardly bear it. What did it matter if they had been stripped of

their rags and sent out naked in the chill of winter just to wring her heart? In any case, they were cold and, worse still, loveless. For how could anyone who loved a child submit it to such agonized necessity of body and spirit? She could not forget them.

The day that the *Jefferson* docked at Shanghai, Mother and her Sisters had another opportunity to see at close quarters the effects of extreme poverty at Mr. Lo Pa Hong's Hospice of St. Joseph. They found in the famous Catholic layman himself, however, at least a partial answer to the puzzle and pity of the great city's fairy-tale wealth and debasing poverty.

First they had some good-bys to say. At Shanghai the little company of missioners broke up. The Columban Fathers were debarking there. The Sisters of Loretto, with Sister Jane at their head, were to start off on the last lap of their journey to Hang-yang to begin their missionary work. The two Sisters of Providence, Sister John Henry and Sister Margretta, were setting out to join their Sisters already established at Kaifeng. Father Byrne and Father Cleary, after some purchasing for the mission and a physical check-up for Father Byrne, would go north to Korea together. Mother hoped to see them all again before returning to the United States and said so, but for the others it was a decisive parting. And they all felt it.

Mr. Lo Pa Hong, tall, broad, dignified and, beneath his quiet Confucian courtliness, dominant and positive, soon detached his party from the welcomers at the pier and had them on their way to see St. Joseph's Hospice, the darling of his heart. He had initiated the huge project and kept it going with his money and influence. The Sisters of Charity managed it for him. It housed about thirteen hundred—the great city's offscouring, whatever it could not use or did not want. He himself led his visitors through. Sister Wagensperg, an Austrian gentlewoman of exquisite refinement and kindness, went with them.

They were shown the hospital, schools, workshops, playgrounds, and a handsome chapel that would seat a thousand.

Mollie at Six

The Rogers Family

Holiday Hikers at Smith
(Mollie third from left)

Graduate of 1905

Father Walsh in His Boston SPF Office

St. Teresa's Lodge

Teresians Working on *The Field Afar*

Dialogue with the Calf Hibernia

Teresians Trying Out a New Design

(Left) Mother Mary Joseph with Sister Rose in China—1923

(Below) Leaving the Motherhouse for the Orient—1940

Receiving an Honorary Degree in 1945
at Regis College from Archbishop Cushing

Looking at the Decree of Praise from Rome
Mother Mary Joseph with Mother Mary Columba—1954

Mother Mary Joseph—Autumn 1955

They saw orphans, some well, some ill; the old and crippled and blind; the insane, for whom no special hospital existed; drug addicts; sick prisoners, brought by guards from jails where no provision for illness was made, still wearing their leg irons and entrusted to the keeping of the Hospice.

Mr. Lo Pa Hong explained it all in French, what the ills and needs of the people were, how the establishment was financed—one third by the municipality, one third by the police, and the other third, his responsibility, secured by St. Joseph. Sister Wagensperg kept pace with his energy and his French, supplementing with flawless English for the sake of the visitors.

Mother had heard much of Mr. Lo and his Hospice through Father Superior. Yet this face-to-face meeting made a new and deep impression on her.

Writing home of this encounter, she said, "We felt like novices in the art of prayer and love of God after listening to him and seeing what he had accomplished."

As they went through the wards, someone asked the Superior, "How can you manage so many?"

"Mr. Lo would say that St. Joseph does the managing," she answered, laughing a little, "and he does. We will be receiving more, now that the cold weather is beginning. Mr. Lo has men go out with lanterns each night to pick up those who would die from exposure if they were not brought in out of the cold."

After this tour through the Hospice, Mr. Lo Pa Hong took the missioners to his home for dinner.

Here the priests and Sisters met the bowing, pleasant-faced family. However, since it was a proper Chinese household, men and women did not dine together. Mother and the Sisters were given into the charge of Mrs. Lo, who presided at their table, while in another wing across the court, Mr. Lo entertained the priests and other gentlemen. Conversation did not flourish because of language difficulties, but faltering French, good feeling, gestures, and guesswork helped to bridge the gap.

It was a day of abstinence, but Chinese ingenuity could, without exhausting the possibilities, devise a dinner of many courses. With pigeons' eggs, sharks' fins, gelatinous bird's-nest soup, the famous buried eggs some of which resembled green jade and others, yellow marble, the dinner marched on for about twelve courses and presently came a something, surely a dessert, which suggested rice pudding. The Sisters looked at each other knowingly, took heart and ate with the fervor of relief. They were at the end.

Agnes, who had been unobtrusively spiriting portions of what she could not manage out of sight somewhere below the table top, had earlier murmured, "My kingdom for a potted plant!" Now she relaxed. All was nearly over. But it was not the end. The dinner swept on majestically for a dozen more courses, ending with a flourish of French pastry.

On the way back to the ship, Agnes made two observations: "They are adorable people." And a little later on, "With me, eating has become a lost art."

The *Jefferson* was due to dock at Kowloon, Hong Kong, on October 15. Maryknollers aboard celebrated the day, St. Teresa's feast, with a sung Mass, their hearts full of anticipation.

As soon as she was free, Mother went on deck. The ship seemed to poke along, although the scenery was full of change and beauty. They passed treeless but green islands ringed with white surf, moved in slow majesty through the narrow defile of Lyemun Pass where, all along the streaming rocks on either side, the turbulent waters threw themselves upward in an endless array of fountains. Then the waterway opened out into a sheltered blue-green highway. On the left the high-backed island of Hong Kong kept the China Sea at bay. On the right a mighty paw of the vast China mainland stretched out into the water, all webbed around with bays and inlets and coves.

The ship moved on, pacing out her time carefully. There was plenty to hold the attention now. Among the outlying islands

Mother had seen a few high-pooped junks moving like Spanish galleons under sail, gallant and graceful in a dromedarian way. She had caught glimpses of homeward-moving fishing fleets sailing through distant curtains of morning mist or had seen them briefly close at hand, frisking along beside the ship like ponies passed by an express train. Once the liner had gained the quieter waters within the Pass, boats began to multiply. Sometimes you could look right into the sampans. You could see how slight was the trousered woman frantically sculling to head her little craft safely into the ship's wake. You could see an unattended two-year-old staggering about a deck full of family gear like a small drunken quartermaster, and, if you had a quick eye, you could observe, too, how a busy but provident father had made him safe from drowning, if not from harm, by tethering him to a broad strip of bamboo, his life preserver; and you could not miss noticing that his young mother already wore a smaller baby fastened securely upon her slender back. You could take in, set out for you, coming to meet you, as it were, on small water-borne stages, a whole galaxy of little dramas presenting the story of great China's ingenuity, humor, and endurance.

In the vanguard of the crowd on the pier, white sun helmets were waving. Soon Mother could make out Maryknoll's Father Francis Ford, Father Bernard Meyer, and Father William O'Shea, brown and cheerful. Some distance away and checked by the barrier, she caught glimpses of Father Frederick Dietz and Father Robert Cairns and near them, the Sisters, their upturned faces brimming with welcome.

"Mother, the Yeungkong Sisters are here too! Look. There's Sister Francis. There, waving her handkerchief. You can see every crease in it. She's kept it in shape for the occasion."

Mother laughed too, her voice warm with the gladness of this reunion; but she was thinking, as the faces took on sharper definition, they haven't much color left, and how thin some of them look.

But there was nothing regretful or subdued in the way she welcomed them and they welcomed her. Each felt that she had come home.

In the days that followed, the Sisters drew contentment from just having Mother with them, enjoying things, talking things over, doing things together. They would tag after her when she was in the house and could not help but begrudge the generous portion of time that must be allowed to guests and the visits and trips which she herself had to take.

She would declare at the breakfast table, "Today is going to be a quiet day and I'll get at my mail." And before they had left the refectory, the first of a string of callers that would continue all day had arrived.

She went for four days to Canton, calling on Bishop Four-quet, who had asked to see her. There, as well as in Hong Kong, she visited the establishments of other missionary societies, and learned whatever she could of their organization, work, and methods. Sister Paul and Sister Imelda went with her, as well as Teresa Yeung and her younger sister Mary, both stanch Catholics and faithful friends of the Sisters.

Mother had some shopping to do. She wanted to find something lovely and suitable for Maryknoll's booth at the coming Vatican Mission Exhibition; she needed silks for vestments and for shrine and altar backdrops; and she had hopes of starting a little salesroom at Maryknoll, where products of the Sisters' handwork could be sold. She and Teresa went bargain hunting through old Canton.

Small and fragile-looking in her lovely Chinese *saam*, with her shining blank bangs, darting movements, and vivacious face, Teresa looked elfin but had the endurance of a water buffalo. A Westerner would take her for a twelve-year-old, but she was a mature young woman who could bargain like an Arab.

Canton in those days was full of Sun Yat-sen's soldiers—
young, truculent, and pistol-conscious.

"The city has been taken by the Army of the Republic," they
told Teresa. "Shops are closed to foreigners."

"I live in Hong Kong. Does that make me a foreigner?"
Teresa wanted to know. "The lady with me here can see the city
while I bargain."

Mother and she enjoyed each other's company and certainly
gave the Chinese plenty of fun. They offered a striking contrast
as they stood side by side, signaling for rickshas, or walked together through the narrow streets of silks and ivories, of linens
and silver. Mother could not understand the comments that
bystanders, shoppers, storekeepers, coolies, and beggars tossed
back and forth. Sometimes Teresa laughed out loud and sometimes she flushed. She did not translate. In a time when foreigners were none too popular, the observations were, as a whole,
peculiarly without malice.

"What is this now that occupies the whole street?"

"See for yourself. One of those big foreign devils."

"All have plenty of money. All very wealthy, the foreign
devils. Much rice is needed to feed such fine strong bodies."

"This one full of benevolence also. Like the Lord Buddha.
Observe the face."

"True. Very much heart."

"Somebody makes a great profit on the street of silks today."

"Perhaps yes, perhaps no. Notice the small one."

"Ai-yah! The little one looks as simple as a goldfish. But she
is a carp, very smart, very smart."

Once they had entered or been enticed into one of the dingy
little shops, it erupted into activity. The proprietor, his son,
his father, or maybe his sister's boy or his wife's brother, sprang
agilely back and forth from counter to shelves, making magic
until the dusty little place broke into a rainbow as they unrolled
cascades of color—soft peach and springtime green, just blues

and regal reds, warm gold and true black, the glow of orange and persimmon, plum and pomegranate, all wrought with exquisite designs of flowers and fans, dragons, gardens, pagodas, steeds, knights, ladies and peacocks, bridges and summerhouses and willow trees, and good-wish symbols for luck, prosperity, long life, and happiness.

Surrounded with silks like clouds of cherry blossoms, waterfalls of wisteria and trellises of firecracker flowers, Mother would stand a little bemused.

"Of course I want them all. But we must be practical. What do they want for this? And this? And that exquisite blue one?"

Teresa would then engage in a fascinating haggle with the shopkeeper, the number one man, and announce a few minutes later, "He start to talk price now."

The shopkeeper would catch up an armful of beauty to make it change tones as he handled it, letting it droop over his hand like a caress so that he and the silk together could plead their common cause. He would propose a sum. Teresa would show herself unmoved except for an air of slightly shocked disbelief. Her lips would go down, her eyebrows up. The comedy would play itself out, scene by scene. At one time the shopkeeper would make a wide motion, threatening to sweep his rainbow back on the shelves again. At another Teresa would start for the door, using both hands to make little circular erasing motions which the shopkeeper understood perfectly: he had not said anything yet.

"Don't you think, Tessie dear," Mother would interpose, "that we ought to give him what he asks? Surely this beautiful stuff must be worth all of that and more."

"Mother, he start too high to begin with. He think because you are a foreigner he can ask for anything—anything. We show him."

Finally the bargain was struck. Teresa was triumphant but

careful to continue looking a little disgruntled. The shopkeeper
hid his satisfaction under an expression of resignation.

"That is the way it is in China, Mother," said Teresa, as they
moved off down the street of silks. "Now everybody happy. He
think he have the best of me and I know I have the best of him."

"I see," said Mother, smiling.

She could smile at you like that, thought Teresa, without
making you feel small or look silly. She wasn't laughing at you.
And with Mother, she concluded, it does not matter what you
are—white, black, yellow or green, she treats all the same, the
same—no difference. It would be nice to be one of her Sisters,
she thought. Later she tried it and found out that it was.

Yeungkong, China

Mother was hardly back at the Maryknoll Convent in Kowloon before Father Ford came around to announce that a junk
would leave in two days from Kongmoon for Yeungkong. If they
were to catch it, they would have to leave Hong Kong the following evening on the steamer for Kongmoon, stopping just
outside that city at Pakkai, where the Fathers had a mission
station. From there, they would go by train or, that failing, with
the help of coolie carriers, to Kongmoon. At that point, they
would reach the weak link in their chain of travel. They might
be able to board a junk and they might not. If the junk was
there and if it had not been taken by soldiers, a night or two
and a day or two should bring them to or near Yeungkong. And
after the junk—a sampan for the last few hours. The shifts entailed would have to be accomplished by ten Sisters, Agnes, two
amahs, one catechist, and forty pieces of baggage, with Father
Ford shepherding all. The responsibility for such a caravan
rested lightly on his shoulders and did nothing more than make
him more agile, boyish, and good-tempered than usual.

On the Hong Kong to Kongmoon steamer they found a captain glad to have them because they composed such a quiet and orderly party. He recounted how boats were being pirated and how dangerous the Hong Kong to Kongmoon run was these days, and he advised them against standing in the cabin door outlined against the light: "Only last week a chap was killed that way, you know, shot from the darkness outside."

The sleeping quarters assigned to the women opened on a dark passageway, closed off from the rest of the steamer by an iron gate and guarded by two very tall and fierce-looking Indian Sikhs, their dark eyes watchful under mountainous turbans.

The single sheets on the berths had plainly been used before, and often. Mother philosophically rolled herself in the blanket provided and went to sleep. Agnes took her cue and settled down as comfortably as she could in her upper berth.

The next day was All Souls' Day. The steamer was due at Pakkai at six-thirty but did not anchor until eight. The Sisters were up and stirring early and had time to say the Office of the day before they debarked. A sampan, poled by two women, transferred them from steamer to shore, and surrounded by a gaping, gesticulating crowd of highly diverted Chinese, they made their way to what the Maryknoll Fathers called their procure. There Father Ford would say the three Masses for the dead customary on November 2.

The so-called procure was a two-story building with a duck shop on the first floor. Here the catechist made his home and live ducks were bought and sold, creating plenty of noise and smells as well as business. Upstairs were four small bare rooms. One of these luxuriated in two windows, and in it the Fathers offered Mass whenever they passed through the town. As Father Ford vested, Mother looked around the cheerless place and longed to fix it up. She began to think of many simple things which she could do to make it a more fitting place for the offering of the Holy Sacrifice of the Mass.

She brought her mind back to the makeshift altar and the

slight priest taking his place before it. As he signed himself with the blessed sign of the cross and began his greatest work of the day, next door a small barracks of soldiers were also astir and about their business. They were Russians, lent to train the soldiers of one of South China's many armies. Nobody thought very much about their portentous presence at the time.

After a combination breakfast and dinner, laid out on the planks and trestles which ordinarily served for a missioner's bed, the whole party boarded a crowded and dirty train for a half hour's run to Kongmoon.

At Kongmoon, they found a junk, an ark tethered to a launch, surrounded by sampans—and all alive with Sun Yat-sen's soldiers. Father Ford went ahead to size up the situation and see what could be done. He was gone a long while, what seemed an eternity, Mother admitted to herself. A crowd collected around the gray-clad Sisters as they waited with their backs to an old gray wall, looking as if they would like to fade away into the mud brick. The Chinese pressed as close to them as they could, stretching and jostling to get the best possible view. They studied, discussed, compared, speculated. Had Agnes's brilliant blue eyes been pink, they could have been no stranger to them. Mother, too, proved of special interest because of the color of her eyes, her size, and her affability. She had not yet learned Sister Paul's trick of pretending to sleep and so achieving at least an illusion of privacy.

When Father Ford returned, his eyes were downcast and his face serious. As he came up to Mother, he tried not to look concerned.

"The soldiers have commandeered the junk. I've been talking to the captain, and they agree to move some of the sick men out of the women's quarters—if we are satisfied with that."

Mother realized that even this concession was a triumph. "That will do very well, Father, of course." Her answer carried a wealth of assurance.

From a sampan they all climbed up rickety steps along the side of the junk. On the deck they met slime, vegetable skins, grease, and soldiers. The day was waning now and everywhere men were trying to settle down for the night. Hoisting themselves up one by one out of a black scuttle in the flooring, more soldiers were swinging up tiredly from below deck to find space among their comrades.

When the last had crawled out, Father Ford indicated the hole. "That's it—the way to your accommodations."

Mother let herself down with the others into the noisome darkness. They landed with a thump on a little platform. As they stood, stooping and peering, a flickering lamp of peanut oil sent dim patterns of light and heavy shadows staggering over their quarters, an enclosed space like a large low closet, intended to accommodate five small Chinese. It had a narrow strip of standing room. The rest of the closet was divided in half by a horizontal shelf which thus created two sleeping areas, one above and one below. The one on top was partitioned by six-inch slats into single sections.

Laughing and fumbling, they ate their supper in various ridiculous and uncomfortable positions. Then the *amahs* arranged the baggage in the lower area and stowed themselves away in the remaining space.

Mother looked the Sisters over. "If we are going to fit in at all, we'll have to pair up, a thin with a not-so-thin. Sister Lawrence, dear, you must be the thinnest. I'm afraid you are going to have to share a section with me."

Groaning and giggling, they took off their shoes and crawled into their sections, one sliding in feet first, the other crawling in head first afterwards. No one undressed. No one used any bedding. Air found its way through three small openings, the largest about nine inches square. They could hear the sick and wounded soldiers, separated from them only by the small platform, shifting and grunting with pain and discomfort in quarters like their own.

To give up all thought of comfort and rest induced a certain peace of mind. Mother regaled the Sisters with home news. The Sisters supplied details about their life in Hong Kong and Yeungkong. Agnes contributed from her limitless reserve of fun. They sang the hours away. As the night wore on, the songs dwindled and the conversation petered out, the junk's clumsy waddle, the restless soldiers' voices and movements grew less and less noticeable. The Sisters catnapped, waking with little screams and shudders as rats ran over their bodies and faces and spiders and cockroaches explored their ears.

When the darkness of their lair abated a little and they heard movement and loud talking above, they crawled stiffly up to the deck. Father Ford, rumpled but alert after his night on deck with the soldiers, was glad to find them still hale and hearty. The soldiers made room for them.

The junk was anchored at Ngaimoon. Mother breathed the clean morning air, looked at the glistening water, the bamboo-covered riverbank, the dawn-flushed sky, and thought that she had never seen a fairer place.

The junk lay at anchor through the long lovely morning, the blazing midday hours, the golden afternoon. At sunset it creaked away into the fast-falling dark. The Sisters had to go below again to another night of cramped muscles, sickening odors, rats, roaches, and vermin. They came up the next morning a little more tired, a little less presentable, but hoping to reach Yeungkong that day. At twilight, several hours short of their goal, the junk dropped anchor for another night.

Several cargo lighters rode near at hand, their single bamboo-ribbed sails making them look batlike in the dusk. Father Ford had one hailed across the water. It drew up reluctantly, timid of the dark and the soldiery. Presently the young priest was leaping lightly over baggage and men to tell Mother, "It's all fixed! They'll take us!"

In the small open boat under the clean stars Agnes put her head down and slept. The others lifted grateful faces to the cool night air and gave themselves up to the rhythm of the craft, the rush of smooth water along its side, the quiet and peace that was like a benediction.

By midnight they were beating on the great gates of the walled city of Yeungkong. Delaying, arguing, fearful, the soldiers opened the gates a few cautious inches. Father Ford slipped through.

"You must open the gates wider," he explained in rapid Chinese. "We are fourteen people, and with us there is a very large woman from the beautiful country of the West."

The gates swung slowly open.

Not long after she arrived, during a lull in local military activities, Mother went out with some of the Sisters to visit Sister Gertrude's grave. She had learned the details of Sister Gertrude's death and burial from Sister Magdalen, the Superior in Yeungkong: the long siege of fevered illness diagnosed by the local doctor as malaria, the changed opinion as her condition worsened, the sudden crisis after most of the Sisters had left to make their annual retreat in Hong Kong, and after night had come on, by the glow of the little Chinese lantern, the final short passage from life to death. It was a happy death, a life relinquished into God's hands in the service of a people whom Sister Gertrude loved. Yet in such surroundings there could be no cushioning of the hard physical impact of death, no veiling of its stark material aspect. Worn and white with watching, two lonely Sisters prepared the body for burial which took place the next morning. They told Mother how it was. Thank God for the Mass, the faith, the presence of some Christians in the ocean of paganism that surrounded them, for the consolations of the Church held out by the hands of Maryknoll's priests.

When she wrote to Father Walsh, Mother related some of the circumstances: "The funeral itself must have been very sad . . . the 'casket' was made from a huge tree trunk, the only lining red and yellow paper. There were eight or ten coolie bearers and they either could not or would not carry it on their shoulders down the steep stairs. Instead it was bumped from stair to stair—and open at that. Before they took it into the Church, they stopped outside, set it on the ground, and haggled over the wages they were to get. After the Mass a three-quarters-of-an-hour walk in mud and rain. A real missioner's burial."

Going out to the cemetery in the sunshine, Mother thought and spoke of that other walk in the rain. Having passed several moldering pagan shrines, they reached an area barren of trees or grass which stretched away like a never-ending graveyard, brown, devoid of life and noduled with innumerable shallow graves. The little Christian cemetery could be distinguished from the rest only by the cross that topped each tablet. Among other graves, Sister Gertrude's stood out. It was shallow and mounded like the rest, but the Fathers had had a brick enclosure built around it to keep the earth from washing away. Mother thought gratefully of them when she saw it.

As the Chinese women who accompanied them set about planting the flowers which they had brought from the convent garden, Mother and the Sisters began the rosary. As they said the blessed and familiar words, the place did not seem quite so desolate.

A woman jogging along under a great load of faggots paused, shifted her burden to the ground, and stood watching them from under the shadow of her large mushroom hat. Several little boys herding water buffalo caught sight of them. While the great beasts stood stock-still, sulking and brooding under their wide horns, the little boys stole up softly on bare feet to study these queer-looking women with strange sounds in their mouths. A man minding a flock of geese drew near to enjoy the phenomenon, too.

Mother was glad to have them all there. They took some of the loneliness from the scene. They were the kind of people for whom Sister Gertrude had come to China, the kind for whom she had worked, and in whose service she had died. They would have responded, had they known her, to the warmth of her lovely soul. She must be glad to have her grave where they were at hand.

Mother had brought some crackers and candy with her, and everybody accepted some, the silent woman under the mushroom hat, the faun-like little boys, the pleased and puzzled gooseman and, as they started home, a leper shrinking out of the way for them to pass.

The civil war prolonged Mother's stay at Yeungkong. At this period she wrote home reassuringly, "There is no need to worry, as we are safe." With Father Walsh, she was a little more specific: "We had hoped to leave for Kongmoon yesterday. Instead we watched, from our exceptional lookout on the upper porch, the departure of Sun's men and opened our compound to the frightened natives who came in the early afternoon, begging for shelter . . . today we await the next move."

What this inundation of people and their possessions was like, how it felt to await the new conquerors, to be aware of their progress through the streets and houses of the town, was sketched by Father Taggart in a letter to Father Walsh:

> Another brand of soldiers is in charge, and, so far as we are concerned, one kind is about as good as the other, or as bad, which ever way you want to take it.
>
> The outside division . . . peppered the city for several days, and as far as we could see, it seemed as if the insiders would be able to hold out indefinitely—they had the walls to protect them and were in possession of two cannon. The outsiders captured a hill near the town and the insiders went out and drove them from it; then they returned to the city, picked up all their belongings and left town in such a hurry that we did not know they had gone until the refugees just swamped the mission compound. Fathers

Ford and Paulhus stayed at the mission proper, and I went over to the convent to look after the Sisters and the army of women who were huddled up in their place.

The convent was a duplication of the mission. It was crowded with men and women, with all their belongings from firewood to cats. About ten o'clock, the outsiders got wind of the fact that the insiders had fled, like the hirelings they were, and entered the city. Then it seemed as if hell was let loose. Fires started in about five different parts of the city, guns were banging, people were screaming and, through it all, one could hear the smash, smash of doors as the soldiers got closer on their pilgrimage of loot. The poor souls inside the convent walls were so frightened that one could hear a pin drop. They could not cry out, even if they had wanted to and, strange as it may seem, even their babies were too frightened to cry. . . . The Sisters could see the soldiers making the rounds and carrying off the loot that had not been stored away before the trouble began. Fortunately, it was just stealing they had to look at. The soldiers did not enter the convent. They just passed it by. . . .

Under such conditions no junks at all were leaving Yeung-kong for Kongmoon. Until Father Ford could work out some other way to reach Hong Kong, there was nothing else for Mother to do but settle down. And so she stayed, contentedly, although there was not much for her to do except to share the prayer and life and interests of her Sisters and a little of their work.

She could not speak the language of the people except to say, "May the Lord of Heaven bless you!" but she knew how to make them welcome with her own warm smile and the still halting Chinese of her Sister-interpreters. She could not join with them in their Chinese prayers, but she could and did play the cantankerous portable organ for them in the small parish church. And she managed to make some special dishes for both Fathers and Sisters and to plan little community recreations that would give the Sisters fun and relaxation. She let the orphans and blind girls hang on her and tag after her and cheerfully submitted to the chattering and questioning of the old ladies.

Out in the narrow street when grubby little youngsters took hold of her crucifix or inquiring women fingered her rosary, she was glad for their interest, whatever prompted it, and longed to tell them the story signified by these things. She enjoyed having her way blocked by neighbors who, Christian or not, came out to wave and nod and prittle-prattle about her.

"A big foreigner with lots of laughter on her face."

"And not afraid of the devil. Like the others in that house, she doesn't put the joss sticks down in front of him."

"Ai-yah! Dangerous that . . . but she looks happy."

"Like one having much money."

"And much heart."

"She likes us people of Yeungkong—even if she is an outsider from another province."

"From another province! She comes from far away beyond the river, beyond the sea, so I am told!"

"Ai-yah! There is such a place then!"

The Chinese were drawn to Mother by the same magnet which at home had attracted complaining old Mrs. Kelly, the cook at the Venard; the Protestant farmer who made daily milk deliveries at St. Teresa's and delayed to gossip and observe; Tim the tramp who came and went with the seasons; old Grandma Sinsabaugh, an ancient convert given a home in St. Teresa's that she might live out her last days in the faith in peace.

How the Chinese accepted her, Father Ford tried to communicate to those back home: "Mother Mary Joseph became one of the Chinese family, not a mere friend. She saw China from the inside of kitchens and of the family quarters, cooed in unison with the babies, and smiled her way into the hearts of the womenfolk. She saw family life as we priests cannot see it. . . . The women guiding boats or doing coolie's work would chat with her unreservedly, fully confident that she could divine their thoughts. . . . She gathered the little girls about her and made them fearless in my presence. I always thought it was the foreign face and clothes that frightened them, but I look and dress more Chinese than the Reverend Mother did, and yet they ran to her and lost their bashfulness."

He saw in all this some significance for future mission work: "Her whole trip emphasized the hold our Sisters will have on Chinese women and the utter need of such influence to gain these women's hearts. The Chinese mother, despite her low esteem outside the home, is the real molder of the faith of her children, and an enduring Church is founded on her conversion."

What she meant to her Sisters only they could tell. Mother wrote to Sister Teresa, in charge at the Home Knoll during her absence, "Personally, I can never be thankful enough that I came this year and was here to open the house after Sister Gertrude's death."

She could never quite realize, however, what a benediction just her presence was for the Sisters at that time. They expressed it more by what they were than by what they said. When she was with them, they laughed more often and with more heart. They felt and seemed more truly themselves, renewed, relaxed, and yet at their best, too. She brought with her a sense of well being, an atmosphere of home, and a great faith on which they all rested, as children rest leaning against their father's knee.

While everybody basked in her motherliness, she herself was experiencing at Yeungkong a season of that desolation which comes in one form or another to many missioners. Of what is it compounded? The unfamiliarity of everything?—strange ways, strange tongue, strange sights and sounds? The isolation and divorce from everything accepted and usual? The realization of the absurdity of all natural resources for the task at hand? The insignificance of being a Christian midge in a cosmic paganism? The sharing in some way of Christ's desolation of heart?

Whatever it was and from whatever sources it sprung, Mother

tasted it during those days and remembered it in after years. Sitting on the convent veranda and writing at length to her Sisters at the Home Knoll about Yeungkong and her travels, she referred to it briefly, ". . . the hills, great brown, bare knobs on the earth's surface, while they have a peculiar beauty and fascination as they are outlined against the brilliant blue sky, fill my soul with a sense of desolation: they seem to symbolize the spiritual destitution which they surround."

Years later, talking to her cloistered Sisters, she could still recall it vividly, "I can remember so well the feeling that came over me during my first visit to Yeungkong . . . during the weeks when I would be alone . . . an awful sense of loneliness. . . . The sea of paganism, devil worship, wickedness, that surrounds one eats its way into one's very soul. That is the kind of loneliness that overwhelms our missioners. We know that the only thing that can overcome this loneliness is the Presence of God in the soul, the actual faith that God is with us, the realization of what He is to us."

Yet this experience did not make her love Yeungkong less but rather more. She admitted to Father Walsh when writing to him at this time, "Already I have grown fond of the people here and I wish it might be my portion to stay in this vineyard . . . but God knows what is best for us." On the long journey back to Hong Kong she wrote him again, "It was hard to leave the Sisters in Yeungkong, and I miss them so much now. My thoughts go back to the little group constantly, and I find myself wishing I were back with them."

Father Ford's ingenuity finally achieved a return to Hong Kong. The trip had to be longer, more circuitous, less certain, and perhaps less safe than the trip from Hong Kong down to Yeungkong. It took sampans, sedan chairs, junks, plenty of waiting, and about ten days to make the short journey.

They made the lap of the journey from the island of Hoiling to Pakkai in the dirtiest, most crowded junk that Father Ford had yet encountered. It formed part of a convoy guarded by a sailboat with mounted cannon, rusty enough to have been dredged from the sea. The junk seemed to be carrying a backlog of livestock shipments. The deck was entirely covered with pigs in baskets. Over these, boards had been laid at intervals so that crew and passengers could get about. By day the passengers sat on bags of rice with crated chickens, ducks, geese, and pigs piled high around them. The livestock made known their presence and discontent in manifest ways. At that, the day accommodations excelled the sleeping quarters. By night Mother, Sister Paul, and Agnes went aft and crawled into three little hutches, one on top of the other. These measured three feet in height and six feet in length, and were directly opposite the stoves. Their occupants had a choice of crawling in head first and being coffined alive or scrabbling in feet first and having their heads only a yard away from the communal cooking pots where chickens and ducks were being killed, plucked, boiled, and eaten.

When Mother first stirred in the morning, before reaching out for her basin of brown water, she would ask half in fun and half in earnest, "Now which way did I go in last night, feet first or head first?"

Father Ford was delighted with the way she took everything. Young, slender, already a veteran at travel along the coast and in the interior, he had been somewhat concerned about how she would manage on trips which any Westerner found so difficult. But she proved a better sailor than he, took the dirt and discomfort of travel as a fun-filled adventure.

Since coming to China, Father Ford had tried to picture Mother in a sampan or scrambling up the side of a junk and he had given it up. With her there, actually doing it, he was happy and proud. "She is not so slim as she used to be, but she steadied many a sampan and crossed from bobbing craft to dancing gangplank without a hitch," he bragged.

Only once did she hesitate. The junk taken at Hoiling docked at Pakkai by the simple expedient of drawing as close to shore as possible and then running out two planks from the deck down to the water's edge. They made something just a little less than a forty-five-degree incline and the drop from deck to mud and water was fifteen feet or so.

Father Ford stood studying the arrangement. "Something for a tightrope walker," he observed.

"Do I look like a tightrope walker, Father?" Mother asked. They laughed together but both felt uneasy. "I don't think I can make it," Mother added. She thought of what such a fall at that time and place would mean for all of them. Sister Paul looked anxious.

But when he had gone ahead and demonstrated how it might be done, she followed. And when he moved back up the plank to break her descent, they finished up by tearing down the last few yards together and executing a little impromptu "swing your partners" on the shore. Looking at them, Agnes burst out laughing and, a little breathless, they joined in.

Now and at other times, too, her weight was a burden to Mother that she would have been happy to be without. "How many times during this trip I wish there were only half as much of me as there is!" But she did not let it interfere with what she had to do. Then and always she was too interested in other things and other people to notice anything about herself very much.

All three—Mother, Sister Paul, and Agnes—remembered this ragged trip as a time of laughter and joy. Agnes spent some wondering thoughts on Father Ford. "You know," she concluded "he has no edges."

Shingishu, Korea

After the prolonged stay at Yeungkong and the drawn-out trip to Hong Kong, the days in China sped away. Mother and the

Sisters in Hong Kong had an unforgettable Christmas together, with Mother helping with everything. Their wonder and gratitude that they had been chosen to have a part in the coming of Christ to China were made more poignant on this day when the world celebrated His birth in Bethlehem. She delighted in all the details of the day's celebrations from the decoration of the altar to the fifteen-inch poinsettia which served as a table centerpiece for their Christmas dinner.

She made a brief run to Macao, taking with her all the new arrivals that they might have another and last trip together, a miniature of the happy days on the *Jefferson*. As the little steamer made its way back to Hong Kong through the waning afternoon, Mother talked of what they had seen and learned so far, of the tasks and privileges and trials that lay ahead.

"Don't expect too much of your people. For ourselves, let us ask for nothing. We have not come to be served, but to serve."

January 13, the day of Mother's departure from Hong Kong, came sooner than anyone would have believed possible. She found herself again standing at the rail of an outbound ship and looked down with a wrench of the heart into the faces of the Sisters she was leaving behind. She was, it was true, homeward bound, but in a sense she was leaving home too and found it very hard to go.

She felt that China had taught her much. She knew that she had received from the missioners there a new appreciation of the beauty and heroism of the missionary vocation. She had not been long in China before she wrote to Father Walsh to say:

"Hitherto I have, I realize now, viewed the whole mission life with the exaltation of the enthusiast, and I find myself appreciating, for the first time, what perseverance in a vocation like ours entails. I look at these Sisters here [at Canton], at my own loved ones, at our priests and Brother Albert, with reverence and admiration. You too must have experienced similar sensations on your visits, and can understand what is taking place in my heart and mind and soul these days."

In the north she visited Shanghai, where she was impressed by the gay and yet dignified simplicity of the Franciscan Missionaries of Mary, discovered the Little Sisters of the Poor as delightful as ever, and found her reverence for the Sisters of Charity increasing with her growing knowledge of their spirit and achievements. She went, too, to Hangyang to see "our American Sisters of Loretto" and to bring news of these new missioners back to their Superiors at home.

On this trip she commented, "As such things go, it's not hard —only inconvenient—to get to Hangyang."

She went on to Kaifeng to visit the Sisters of Providence with whom she had traveled out to China and to bring home news of them also. With both these groups she felt a special kinship.

When she reached Peking, she was deeply moved by China's greatest city. "I am glad we saw Peking last. It is like Rome, inasmuch as all other places seem as nothing in comparison with it and one can never, never forget its dignity and beauty."

But the most memorable visit of all these brief stopovers was that to Chusan. She would always remember that little island. It lay five hours' trip by junk off the China mainland east of Shanghai. It was for the well-born Sister Xavier Berkeley, the English Sister of Charity who headed the mission there, a world away from people of her own nationality and background. Into Chusan's pretty harbor only one other visitor had preceded Mother's party. Father Walsh, Superior of Maryknoll, had stopped there on his first visit to the Orient a little over six years ago.

Indelibly impressed on Mother's mind was the walled town at the water's edge, the peaked hills, the mission with its extensive but simple buildings and the people of all ages and kinds who filled them. There was a crèche for the babies, a nursery for the toddlers, dormitories for the blind, the lame, the maimed, and for fine healthy children, too; classrooms, workrooms, dining rooms, a home for old ladies, another for old men, a hospital for women, a hospital for men.

Sister Xavier's welcome to her visitors was characteristically thorough. She met them herself as they came ashore, and when she brought them to the mission gate, it opened upon a long covered portico lined on either side with many children, who seemed like singing chrysanthemums as they bowed and piped their welcome. For them, as well as for the Chinese Sisters who made up her community, Sister Xavier was no foreigner. Her commanding presence, handsome occidental features and blue eyes made no barriers between her and anyone on Chusan. For years anything that needed to be done for anybody had always been taken care of by her and her Sisters. The people looked upon her as a local and beneficent providence.

The miracle of this isolated work, its size, its spirit, its support, made Mother marvel. "Only now have I any idea of how difficult it has been for you to begin and continue all this," she said.

Sister Xavier made a gesture toward the chapel. "If it were not for Him, I could never have done it," she answered simply.

Telling her own Sisters about her Chusan stay, Mother asked them, "Now can you picture, my dear ones, what mission life can mean? Isolation, sacrifice, and joy only in proportion to the closeness of one's union with God and to the spiritual resources within one's self. You're not likely to 'become' spiritual on the missions. If you've made a start at home, however, there is much to make you more so, for you have learned that you must seek all in God and He does not disappoint us."

There was one more place for Mother to go—Korea, "the land of the morning calm," the home of white-clad rural people, the country of tawny little homes of mud and thatch, of overworked fields and naked mountains, burning summers and glacial winters, the land of patience.

The story of the coming of Christianity to Korea has all the wonder of a legend. It was brought into the country by Korean laymen, scholars returning home from Peking, where they had learned of it and accepted it as the gift of God. This bright beginning in the sixteenth century was followed by broken periods of peace and persecution for the new faith. When Mother came to Korea, people still lived who could remember the most recent of the mass martyrdoms that decimated and glorified the Church.

Father Byrne and his few Maryknoll co-workers in Korea were just becoming acquainted with their adopted people and their new country, finding their way—with the help of teachers and long hours of study—through the intricacies of a difficult language, making plans for future mission centers and stations, and beginning to think of having Sisters come to work with the women and the children. It was a good time for Mother to look over the ground and consider the possibilities.

She, Sister Paul, and Agnes made the long railroad trip from Peking, China, to Shingishu in northern Korea by way of the Manchurian cities of Mukden and Antung. At Mukden, Father Byrne, looking himself once more, and Father Morris, already acclimated to the cold, joined them as escorts for the rest of the way, guiding them through the customs inspection and the change of trains at the Korean-Manchurian border.

When they alighted from the train in Shingishu, the cold struck them like a blow. Yet their hearts were warmed to discover themselves surrounded by friends—a number of men and one lone brave woman, all dressed in heavily padded white clothes, bowing and smiling and giving them a welcome—Korean Christians. From the station the priests took them directly to the catechist's house. Some snow had fallen, as fine and light as Yellow River dust. It fumed in shifting spirals over the rutted streets and along the edges of the gray tiled roofs. But the February sun had risen, the sky was already sharpening into a bright blue and the light striking across the cold hills and frozen valleys touched with kind tones the catechist's one-storied, white-washed little home. It even reached inside to brighten its dim candle-lit interior.

Two rooms, innocent of furniture, formed an L. At the doorway which linked them, an altar had been set up. In this "Church of the Holy Spirit," a congregation of about fifty Koreans had gathered to attend Mass, and now knelt or sat back on their heels, the men in one room, the women and children in the other.

The rustle of starched and padded clothing, the odor of warming, kimchi-saturated bodies, the added aroma of lacquer from the gentlemen's horsehair hats, the occasional whimper or whisper of a child, bright as an Easter egg in holiday dress—all these knocked at the door of the senses but served only to direct the heart's awareness to what was taking place.

It was February, 1924. Her mission trip nearly completed, Mother, together with Sister Paul, was about to make her final vows.

Father Byrne heard their confessions in an absurd little room so crowded with two pieces of furniture that he could hardly sit and they could scarcely kneel. When they had taken their places on the straw matting before the altar with Agnes near and the female part of the congregation spread out behind them, Father Byrne came to the altar to vest for Mass. He was girding the cincture around his waist, when he felt a tug at the hem of his long white alb and looked over his shoulder.

Mother asked softly, "Shouldn't you give us an examination, Father?"

He turned. "An examination? Should I? What about?"

"About taking vows."

He was serious, but the corners of his eyes crinkled a little. Their graduated blues glimmered with something other than the dim light sifting into the crowded room.

"What do I ask you?"

"You ask us whether or not we are making our vows of our own free will."

The blue lights were dancing now. "All right, are you making your vows of your own free will?" he asked.

"I am." The answer came strong and clear.

Father Byrne turned to Sister Paul. "Are you making your vows of your own free will?"

As she heard the firm answer, Mother was thinking how fitting and blessed a place they both had for the few words, the simple, single act of will that would bind them until death to the way of life which they had freely chosen.

Father Byrne turned back to the altar, finished vesting, and began Mass. The Koreans took up the swinging cadences of their "twelve prayers." She who loved music so much missed neither singing nor organ. Everything was just as she would have it. Together with the priest she offered Christ to His heavenly Father and with that oblation beyond price renewed the gift of herself. She and Sister Paul received their Lord in Holy Communion. Then Agnes and a number of the congregation followed them to the altar, the Koreans moving forward on silent, unslippered feet, their faces and bodies instinct with reverence.

Right after Mass was finished, Father Byrne turned around from the altar, the stillness in the room intensified, and from where she knelt, Mother's quiet tones carried easily to the farthest ear in the two rooms.

"To the honor of Almighty God, Father, Son, and Holy Ghost, of the Blessed Virgin Mary and of Blessed Dominic, I, Mother Mary Joseph, called in the world Mary Josephine Rogers, make for life the simple vows of poverty, chastity, and obedience according to the Rule of St. Augustine and the Constitutions of the Foreign Mission Sisters of St. Dominic. And I promise in the presence of the representative of our Ordinary, with God's grace, to observe them faithfully, to be obedient to all my Superiors, and according to said Constitutions to devote myself exclusively to the work of foreign missions."

Close to her the sons and daughters of Han, children of the morning calm, by nature religious and philosophic, by necessity grimly preoccupied with their daily subsistence and national survival, picked their wandering thoughts off the price of rice, the dwindling late-winter store of food and fuel, the petty provocations of their ubiquitous conquerors, and set themselves to beg *Tchun Ju,* the Lord of Heaven and Father of us all, to bless these foreign women, Christians like themselves. They could not understand the words that were being said, but they were the descendants, lineal or mystical, of confessors and martyrs, and the significance of what was happening did not escape them.

Half a world away on the hilltop which she loved so well, other Maryknoll Sisters, her own blood sister among them, soon would also be making vows that would bind them until death. To celebrate that ceremony, there would be singing and flowers and homemade decorations and plain but satisfying feasting, and, best of all, the presence of Father Superior.

Mother was mindful of all that, happy for their graces and more than content with her own. The cold, the bare walls, the straw matting, the plain altar, the young Maryknoll Missioner surrounded by his congregation of Koreans, all spoke to her heart.

She tried to share what she experienced with her Sisters at home but had to leave most of it to their understanding hearts. "There was nothing to distract us," she wrote to them, "and everything to remind us of our obligations—poverty—chastity—obedience—foreign missions—sacrifice—restraint—souls."

This first journey to the East, undertaken when Mother Mary Joseph was already forty, proved to be only one of a number which she would make in the years to come. As more young women came to call her Mother and more mission fields opened

up to them and the houses of the congregation increased, her
journeys—spaced about three years apart—lengthened in time
and distance and exacted more of her endurance and self-forget-
fulness.

In 1923–1924 she had just four small mission houses to visit:
two on the west coast of her own country, where the Sisters
worked with the Japanese in Los Angeles and Seattle, and two
in South China. By 1930 there were twenty-three, scattered
widely throughout the world—in the United States, China,
Korea, Manchuria, the Hawaiian Islands and the Philippines.
In 1940 there were forty-nine.

When in March of 1924 Mother recrossed the Pacific to her
homeland, three new works had been planned: two in China,
one in Korea. Of these, two would be realized. She had noted
the need for a Superior to head the whole work in a territory
where more than one convent had been founded and arranged
for Sister Paul to fill the need until she could take the matter
up with her Council. She had measured the American character
in relation to the mission scene and had noted a dangerous flaw
in its generous energy: "It is overactivity and too much unre-
strained zeal that will play havoc with American missioners."
She was confirmed in her conviction of the necessity for the
right motivation and a good strong beginning in selfless living
as a prerequisite for missioners. She had gained much from her
association with Sisters and priests already experienced in missionary life and work, noting the special talent or contribution
or spirit each group and individual had to offer.

As always, she had an eye for the positive. Her attention and
interest turned immediately to what was good in anything or
anybody. As she still looked at sea and sunsets, mountains and
flowers, mornings and snow storms with the awe of a child, she
still looked upon mankind, both in the mass and in the individual, with wonder and reverence. When, later in life, she

remarked, "Next to people I believe I like flowers best," she was paying a compliment to both.

The greatest achievement of this and subsequent visitations was not the planning for new works and missions, the development of policies and methods, the growth of ideas for the formation of missionary Sisters, the improvement of ventures already begun. These were all of value, but the greatest thing that Mother did in visiting her Sisters on the missions then and in later years as well was just being there.

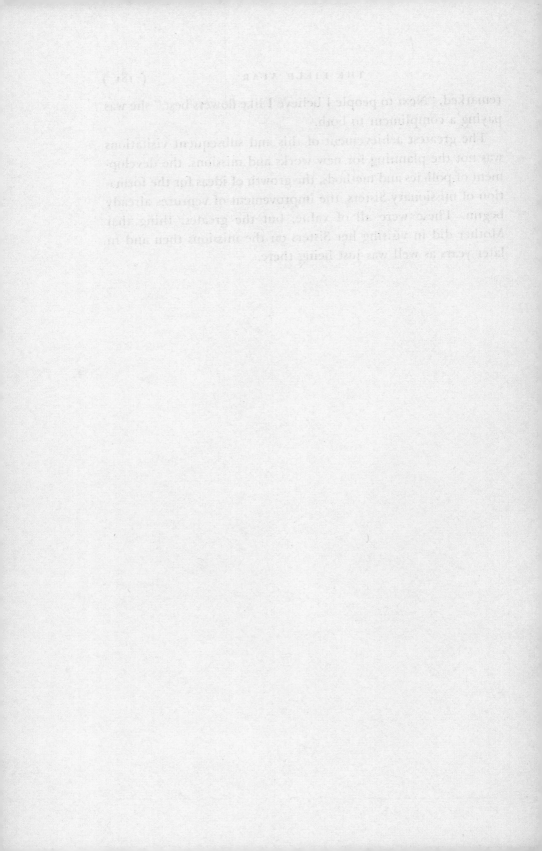

PART III

Who Rules with Love

⸺⊶❈⊷⸺

"She is . . . a superior who rules with love."
—Richard Cardinal Cushing

CHAPTER 7

MOTHER AND DAUGHTERS

As EASTER DREW NEAR, preparations for that great feast and for Mother's homecoming made the days at Maryknoll seem to grow shorter and shorter instead of lengthening out as the burgeoning season demanded.

Right after breakfast, a newly formed special choir hurried over to the squat fieldstone chapel and rehearsed the music for the Easter Mass: "Sisters, that first syllable is pronounced *Kee* not *Kir. Kee-ree-ay*—Kyrie. Try it again. Keep your tone forward. And light. That's good. That's much better. But remember to soften your endings."

In the evenings, after night prayers, an off-Broadway troupe went to the shipping room where during daylight hours *The Field Afar* magazines were wrapped and bagged for mailing, and cleared away the trestle tables to make space for a stage and a play in the making: "Keep your head up and speak more slowly, more deliberately, Sister. Put some life into it. No, no, don't make little wiggly gestures with your fingers and wrists like that. Here, try it this way."

In nooks and corners where things could supposedly be left

out of harm's way and ready to be worked on during free moments, lay other signs of preparation—homemade decorations for the refectory, gold letters for welcome signs, a small hand-painted folder to tell Mother the kind and count of prayers that had been offered for her as part of the celebration. "Has anybody seen the water colors? I thought I left them right here." "Have we enough gold paper to say 'Mother' as well as 'Welcome Home'?"

The postulants who had arrived at Maryknoll since Mother left for the Orient had heard plenty about her. Some had met her earlier. Some had not. They took it all in, as postulants do, some not completely convinced that all this enthusiasm was warranted. The things that most of the Sisters talked about seemed pretty ordinary: Mother sharing Christmas secrets with the different groups, professed Sisters, novices, and postulants, so that each could surprise the other with at least a new Christmas carol or two; Mother shooting off cannon firecrackers on the Fourth of July; Mother with a little group of helpers around her binding books in a great hurry in order to present them to Father Superior on his return from a long mission trip; Mother conducting choir rehearsal, reminding the Sisters how important it was to sing God's praises well—and how much Father Superior liked good music; Mother coaching the play *Fabiola*; Mother, together with Sister Teresa, standing up to entertain them all with a medley of old songs as part of a program for Holy Innocents' Day; Mother sitting at the piano playing while they danced and sang on that happy night when they moved into St. Joseph's; Mother just back from a trip, trying to eat a late supper and answer all the questions of the Sisters who gathered around to hear all about it.

However reasonable a wait-and-see policy might be, by the time the motorcade of two small black cars bumbled into the grounds tooting their horns, the postulants were excited, too, the cool of head and the warm of heart alike. In their belfries, the Father's big bell and the Sister's smaller one were nearly turning turtle trying to outdo each other. Outside their houses, the seminarians and Brothers cheered. Down the hill between St. Joseph's and the fieldstone chapel the Sisters added their soprano echoes.

The postulants had a good look at Mother as she got out of the car and caught glimpses of her as the Sisters surrounded her. They hung back on the fringe of the circle, most of them feeling a little shy and thinking that was probably where they belonged.

Father Superior, who had been among the welcomers at the railroad station, soon moved toward the chapel to vest for Benediction. Presently Mother freed herself from the others and came over to the postulants.

"And here are my Benjamins," she said. "We don't know each other yet, but it won't take long to change that state of affairs."

Once at Maryknoll again, Mother was caught up in the active and demanding life there. In May of 1925 the first General Chapter of the community met to elect the Mother General and her Councilors and to discuss the most important affairs of the congregation. When the community received the Church's approbation in 1920, Archbishop Hayes had appointed Sister Mary Joseph as Superior until the time of this first elective Chapter. If she had ever had any doubts that in doing this he had rightly interpreted the Sisters' wishes, she could certainly no longer question it: as the community's first Mother General, she received every vote except her own for that office. The Cardinal, delighted with this unanimity as well as with such a strong confirmation of his own wisdom, told all the Sisters about it when, as presiding officer of the elections, he announced the results to the community.

Until the summer of 1931 the new Mother General continued to act as local superior as well: that is, she not only looked after the affairs of the whole congregation, but when at home had direct charge of the community there, dealing with each individual Sister and supervising the different works and departments.

Sometimes the Sisters wrote little notes and left them hopefully on the growing pile already on her desk. Usually they carried out their business face to face. Her door was always open. To it came Sisters with bright ideas how to make habits better, dishes wash cleaner, preserves keep longer, laundry turn out whiter, and work shifts move with more dispatch. To it also came Sisters with personal successes and failures, troubles and joys, good news and bad, all to be shared.

Nevertheless, the new Mother General never became so swamped in daily preoccupations that she did not have an eye on the future. During the middle twenties, she was planning for a Motherhouse. The young women who used to come by fives and sixes were now entering by thirties and forties. Soon the last little frame house on the property would hold no more. Some activities and enterprises could not be undertaken for lack of space. And every year or so a young Sister or two would come down with tuberculosis, a fact which pointed up the hazard of their overcrowded quarters.

Yet a building to house several hundred, as the growth of the community indicated should be constructed, would require a vast amount of money, and the Sisters had little. At times the community's expenses outran the sum of their maintenance allowances, and the gifts which they received did not bridge the gap.

Having appealed to her Sisters to economize in every way possible, Mother set herself to increase the income in every way compatible with the life and purpose of her Sisterhood: placing on sale the Sisters' handwork and products of mission workrooms through a Christmas gift shop in New York City and a year-round salesroom at Maryknoll, starting a stamp department to save, collect, and sell stamps, as well as to make greeting cards with them; even initiating an electroplating department for the repair of sacred vessels and a kiln for turning out china and pottery. The Sisters did their own bookbinding and picture-framing, as well as the domestic work for the Fathers and for themselves. Not everything attempted succeeded. In the bulk these efforts helped but did not and would not suffice.

Mother was given an opportunity to appeal to the Catholic Daughters of America for their support, first at several state conventions and finally at the 1925 National Convention in San Francisco. En route there, while changing trains in Chicago, she was in a two-car accident. With a broken wrist she caught her train and traveled as far as Colorado Springs before she could have the bone set. Continuing on, she reached the convention in time, and when she addressed the delegates, lost none of her appeal by having her arm in a sling. The Catholic Daughters pledged themselves generously to give her the support that she asked. However, at best, the results of their action could not approximate what was required even for ecclesiastical permission to begin building.

Then one February day in 1926 as she watched the Sisters plowing through snow drifts to Mass and prayers in one house, to work in another, to meals in another; as she saw their sopping skirts while they stood outside the different houses knocking the snow off their rubbers; as she thought of their crowded dormitories where one could just stand between the beds—and of the beds that had taken over the community room in St. Joseph's, been put up at the end of hallways and at the head of staircases; as she thought of the young girls writing to her by the score to inquire about becoming Maryknoll Sisters—she felt that the time had come to do something more.

With a sense of urgency, she picked up her pen and wrote to Cardinal Dougherty of Philadelphia. Where pastors were willing, might her Sisters stand at the door of the churches of his Archdiocese and receive the offerings of the parishioners? Promptly, and to many surprisingly, Cardinal Dougherty answered yes.

Later, when approached, Archbishop Glennon of St. Louis and Cardinal Hayes of New York gave the same permission. It was boomtime in America. No one in those days—pastors, people, Sisters, businessmen, state politicians or national leaders foresaw that the country's worst depression lay only a few years away.

The Sisters did not expect pastors to swarm out of their rectories to welcome them; they knew what financial burdens many of them carried. They were amazed and heartened by the way in which the priests received them. Occasionally they would meet a pastor who, for one reason or another, was something less than enthusiastic.

One day, having just said their rosary and made a visit to the church with a view to getting heaven on their side, two Sisters went up a rectory steps and one put a hopeful finger on the door bell.

The pastor himself came to the door. The narrow crack which he slowly conceded just allowed them to slide through into the shadowy hallway where all three stood and looked at one another.

Sister Luke, the Daniel Webster of the pair, took a deep breath and began, "We are the Maryknoll Sisters, Father." He did not seem impressed. Seeing that she was expected to say what she had to say there and then, she went on to tell him why they had come, giving a précis of their short history, works, hopes, and present predicament. Since the priest made no comment, she went from opening sentence to conclusion in one sweep.

"That's a very fine speech," he commented. "You must have rehearsed it a long time."

"Thank you, Father. I did. I worked hard on it. I'm glad you like it," said Sister Luke, never anything but forthright.

"Maryknoll Sisters—you say you're Maryknoll Sisters? Never heard of them."

"Do you know Maryknoll? The Catholic Foreign Mission Society of America? Father James Anthony Walsh?"

"Father Walsh? Oh, I know Father Walsh, all right. I visited him once. He had some priests and seminarians living in barns down near Ossining. But there were no Sisters."

Living in barns! thought Sister Luke. Why, only one was a real barn! The others were really lovely old houses.

Aloud she said, "Do you remember some women working in the offices, helping Father Walsh to publish *The Field Afar?*"

"Um-m-m. Yes, vaguely. About a dozen or so, weren't there? Are *they* the Maryknoll Sisters?"

"Yes, Father, they are. Only there are nearly three hundred of us now. Father Walsh has a big fieldstone seminary now and we live in those—um—houses you remember."

"Three hundred! Great Scott!" He looked at them unbelievingly. After a little silence he said, "Well, come in, come in. Sit down there in the parlor. I'll be right down."

He left them, went upstairs. The Sisters looked at each other.

"He doesn't believe us. He thinks we're fakes. Bogus nuns."

"He's gone to call up Father Walsh."

"The police, you mean."

Soon they heard his quick step on the stairs again.

"Well, Sisters, if you have nearly three hundred people living in those barns . . ."

Barns! thought Sister Luke. Then with her usual honesty she said, "Not all of us are living in those houses now, Father. Some of our Sisters are already on the missions."

"So I gathered from your speech," he said, quoting, " 'Some are in China, others in Korea and in the Hawaiian and Philippine Islands.' Even if only a fourth of you are there—that's too many. Can you arrange to come on the second Sunday of next month to take up this collection of yours?"

"The second Sunday? Next month? Oh, of course we can, Father. Certainly."

"All right then, the second Sunday. And here's ten dollars to help with your carfare."

"Oh, thank you, Father. God bless you, Father."

"Now that's a very nice speech. I believe I like the ending of your discourse even better than the beginning." He smiled. "You put such feeling in it. Say it again, please."

At times, the Sisters were almost overcome by the warmth— and originality—of their reception. Two of them arrived at a rectory in upstate New York late one Saturday afternoon to tell the pastor that they were on hand as already arranged. And, please, might they borrow his collection baskets to hold at the door of the parish church the next morning?

The priest rumpled his thinning hair. "You know, Sisters, this is not a wealthy parish or a big parish. And some of the people who are better off than most don't come to Mass on Sunday, more's the pity. I was thinking maybe it wasn't such a good idea for me to have let you come all this way when you'll only get about fifty dollars. Then a few things occurred to me. Come on, I'll drive you over to the convent and tell you about it on the way."

They had not gone far when he drew into the curb before one of the small stores lining the block.

"Now, Sisters, this is Giuseppe's butcher shop. He does a good business, such a good business on Saturday that he's too tired to come to Mass some Sundays. You go in and tell him that I sent you for a donation today because I was afraid that he might not have the pleasure of seeing you at Mass tomorrow. That ought to jolt him. It might even move him to give you a donation today and come to church tomorrow. You never can tell."

The Sisters came back smiling.

"How did you do?"

"All right, Father. Giuseppe gave us a donation. And we told him that when he comes to Mass tomorrow that will remind us to pray for him especially because he was so good to us today."

"Fine. Now for Tony's. He and his Angelina run that handsome fruitstore down the block. And then we'll gather some *fioretti* from Ciccio the florist. Know what *fioretti* are, Sisters?"

That evening after supper at the local convent, the Sister Superior approached the two Maryknollers with a broad smile.

"Father just telephoned. He starts hearing confessions at seven-thirty. He's a very popular confessor. People come from all over to go to him. He wants you Sisters to be in church by seven twenty-five at the latest."

"Us? Tonight?"

"Father says you two Sisters can take turns, one sitting in the back of the church with the basket and the other staying up in front saying her prayers."

"But—what?"

"Well, that's all that Father said. But my guess is that everybody who goes to confession tonight is going to get almsgiving for a penance."

If they did not, a miracle of unanimity developed that evening in the little country church. As the penitents popped out of the curtained confessional and drifted over to kneel, cleansed and grateful, before the tabernacle, each one would then get up and make a beeline to the back of the church and the Sister with the basket.

This ecclesiastical barnstorming gave Mother and the Maryknoll Sisters a deepened appreciation of American Catholics— lay people, priests, Sisters. Whether the Sisters were dressed in gray, black, or brown habit, they all wore the same mantle of charity. They took their mendicant Sisters in overnight, often moving out of their rooms and even sleeping on couches and in armchairs to make room for them; fed them on their best; and, when there was opportunity, invited them to their classrooms to tell the children about missionary life and Maryknoll.

While engaged in the long-range planning demanded for the erection of a Motherhouse, Mother Mary Joseph was building in another and more important way as well. She was building a community: shaping its spirit through conferences, reading, her own accessibility; leading it to greater stability while testing adaptations in community living and in prayer life; looking to the Church, especially in its liturgy, for instruction and guidance in the formation of her Sisters as true Christians, genuine religious, and real missioners. She was making choice, too, among the many fields and works now held out to her Sisters.

She had begun, as early as she could and with the generous help of such communities as the Religious of the Sacred Heart at Manhattanville, the Mount St. Vincent Sisters of Charity, and the Seattle Sisters of Providence, to continue the education of at least some of her Sisters in order to increase their usefulness. In 1926 she was able to open a house near The Catholic University of America until, the Motherhouse being built, a training school for teachers could be initiated there for her Sisters.

Alert to recognize in those around her the capacity to share, and perhaps in time to take over, her increasing responsibilities, Mother gave them the opportunity for experience well adapted to develop their potential, whatever sacrifice this might entail for her.

She looked to Sister Mary Paul for the development and direction of the work in China. When on her visitation to the Orient in 1926-1927, she committed her community to work in the Philippines, she realized that a mission superior of outstanding character was needed for the program projected there. She also saw in this situation a good training ground for a future mother general.

Writing to Father Walsh in January, 1927, from Kowloon, China, after visiting the Philippines, she first outlined the circumstances of the new work to be undertaken and then went on to say:

> From all this, one can easily see the need of a capable superior, one who is an executive, deeply spiritual, and who has the confidence and affection of the Sisters. I can hear you gasp when I mention it, but I would like very much to have Sister Columba launch this new and very important work. She has all the requisites . . . she is needed at Maryknoll and no one can quite fill her place. But I believe there is a greater need here for the moment.
>
> . . .
>
> I believe that the experience would be invaluable for Sister Columba—and that the whole community would benefit by it. She could see Korea and China *en passant* and her knowledge would mean much later. She will always have a high office in the community. I believe that either she or Sister Mary Paul will be my successor.

The following April, Sister Mary Columba, whose buoyant presence and fine mind gave Mother Mary Joseph such support, was on her way to the Philippines.

Besides planned activities, emergencies claimed time and energy. Young and promising Sisters died, and Mother watched long hours and days beside them in their illness. Many young women came to join her Sisterhood, but not a few withdrew, a normal process; yet some who left felt compelled to show that it was not their fault but hers that they had not persevered, and their demonstration varied from enlisting priestly indignation to threatened legal action. Not infrequently those to whom she showed herself most loving and most considerate were the ones who caused her the greatest heartaches.

Within twelve months she had to make a hurried trip to Korea to prevent the collapse of the Sisters' first mission work there and also found herself publicly rebuked in *America*.

This leading Catholic periodical took her sharply to task for her apparently unorthodox views on Catholic education as expressed in a news release covering an extemporaneous speech which Mother gave in December, 1925, to the Newman Club of Teachers College, Columbia, and the College of the City of New York. Her intent was to convince the Catholic students at these secular Universities that they could be, in their present circumstances, both good Catholics and potential missioners. By way of illustration and encouragement she related how her own vocation had developed at Smith College.

Usually wise but never cautious, she had no copy, no notes, of the words in which she attempted to do this and gave her permission to publish the news release after hearing it read over the telephone.

The news release and the resultant *America* editorial caused a small tempest of condemnation and defense with the battle line in confusion. Some Jesuits wrote to express regret, to apologize. Long silent friends rallied around her with strongly expressed support. A flood of advice, sympathy, censure, inquiry, lamentations, and hurrahs inundated her.

One Brooklyn parish bulletin devoted two pages to the "pernicious talk" and Mother, commenting:

"Pious fools sometimes do more harm than wise knaves . . . Lord save us from apologetic Catholics! . . . If the speech of Mother Joseph were laid before the Congregation of the Holy Office, it would be condemned. She would be required to retract her unsound views and apologize for her imprudent address. In the meantime, she should take a course of instruction in Catholic doctrine and do all that she can to administer an antidote to the members of the Newman Club. . . ."

Even leaving aside what she had said, it was contended that "she was out of place there . . . she belongs in her convent. . . . Nuns have their work and their field. Addressing clubs is not in their repertoire."

Mother was grieved to think that she might have brought harm to the cause closest to her heart. Once she had stated her case simply in a single published reply, however, she wasted no time either in controversy or worry.

To Father Walsh, then in the Orient, she wrote, "I did not mind for myself at all, but I did think of you and the Sisters—and especially of our last Council meeting, with your word of warning about doing the unusual thing . . . The Cardinal had given me permission to speak and . . . I had a very good companion in Mother Drexel."

Not everyone was so calm. Father Byrne wrote to Mother from Korea, giving his views and concluding by saying, "Now I am going out to chew on the back fence. It's the only way I can work it off."

What was it like to live with this busy woman who could so easily have allowed her relationships with others to become attenuated under the stress of work and responsibility?

Because of the way her interest and concern could focus so completely on the people before her, it hardly seemed possible that her mind could be filled with concerns other than theirs—things such as blueprints and deeds of land, the initiation of a cloister branch of her Sisterhood, the feasibility of an active Sisterhood adopting the recitation of the Divine Office, the opening of new houses in distant places, the rising cloud of Bolshevism in South China and the imminent danger that this meant for her Sisters in Yeungkong and Loting.

The intricate and many-fibered web of relationships—with Sisters, young and middle-aged, with the sick, with students, with those at home and those abroad; with their families; with the Maryknoll Fathers and Maryknoll's benefactors and friends; with her own family and personal friends, her childhood and girlhood companions, her classmates at Smith College; with chance acquaintances met on the missions and on her travels—all these far-reaching and delicate relationships she seemed to maintain without effort.

And all the while she continued to consult Father Walsh on

all major issues concerning her Sisterhood and its work, kept him in touch with developments, and took every opportunity to express to him in practical ways her gratitude and esteem. No plan or project was thought of without being associated with him and his interests. As the years passed—especially after his death—she was fearful that the Sisters who had not had personal association with him might not appreciate all that he meant to them. At times of joy, on the great feasts of the Church and on Maryknoll anniversaries, she would often speak of him.

"We do not know what the years before us hold. . . . Let us pray tomorrow for one another. . . .

"Particularly, let us remember Father General, to whom we owe so much, who has been a father to us and in the early days a mother as well, watching over us, guiding us, providing for us, and always giving us an example full of inspiration to do great things for God."

Girls who thought they had or might have a vocation to be Maryknoll Sisters came to sit and talk with her sometimes in the little reception room or sometimes, in good weather, on the long porch at Rosary House or on a bench under the trees.

To make a good impression, some came with their hair newly marcelled and wore their highest heels and latest outfits. Others waited for their bob to grow, borrowed something from their mother's wardrobe, and tried to look as conservative as possible. Some came with a sister or friend for support. Some came alone, covering their trail as carefully as if they were about to rob a bank. Some had the blessing and commendation of their pastors; some had not.

"The Maryknoll Sisters, child? And who might they be? Foreign missions, is it? Wouldn't it be more sensible for a skinny little girl like you to join an outfit you know something about? Like the good Sisters right here in your own parish?"

How many weighty problems were disposed of under the shade of the magnificent old maple called "the circle tree."

"I suppose," conjectured Miss Manhattan, "that all the other girls who come to Maryknoll want to be missioners. Well, I don't. I don't care whether I go to the missions or not. I just want to come here because of the spirit of the place, not for any other reason."

"It is enough."

The girl looked her astonishment at having her darling difficulty so lightly disposed of.

"God calls souls in many ways. A young man was once attracted to a religious order when he saw two religious of that order walking along, their cloaks floating in the breeze. God attracts souls in many ways."

Some of these young girls came to see her even as she made her rounds of the mission houses. One of these, a young Nisei Japanese, a child of two cultures, wondered how formal or informal her conduct should be, how much initiative she should take, what she should say and how she should say it.

Sitting like a small mouse in the convent parlor with the monumental Mother General, she was shy and very nearly speechless.

Mother went over to the old-fashioned upright piano and opened it.

"I want to play for the Sisters tonight and I'm beginning to forget the old songs. I wonder if you know some of them? Maybe we could go over them together and they will come back to me."

With her slight sweet soprano leaning confidingly on Mother's deeper tones, little Miss Nisei was soon intoning, "There's a long, long trail a-winding into the land of my dreams."

From singing to talking proved an easy transition. "What is it like at Maryknoll, Mother?" she asked.

"You will love it," Mother answered.

Fathers and mothers did not always part with their daughters enthusiastically. Some, no matter how generous or full of faith, suffered keenly. Mother felt for them deeply. With the vagaries and demands of the less reasonable she was entirely sympathetic. And she could not be provoked by the biting words of the embittered.

More than once, she was asked, "If you think it is such a wonderful idea for my daughter to go to China, why don't you go yourself?"

Sometimes an unwilling parent would try to head off the acceptance of a daughter by a direct appeal to the Mother General.

A father wrote to express his fear that missionary work would prove far too difficult for his little girl.

Mother answered not so much what he had said but what he had in mind. "I can understand and sympathize with your reluctance to part with an only daughter, your most precious possession. What you want is your daughter's happiness. That is what I want, too. If she does not find the peace and happiness she seeks at Maryknoll, I will most certainly advise her to return home."

"You will be all right there," the man told his daughter. "She must be a grand lady."

Mothers have invested much love and patience in getting to know their daughters. Some cannot resist sharing this hard-won insight with others who may need it, especially if it will make life that much sweeter for everyone concerned.

The mother of a young Californian recently accepted preceded her daughter to Maryknoll.

"I thought I'd like to come to see Maryknoll—and you too, of course, Mother Joseph—before my daughter arrives. She is a nice girl, a clever girl, if I do say so myself, but you won't find her at all good at housework—or office work either—or teaching. Things like that. Anything too confining. The out-of-doors, that's what she likes. And meeting people. I myself think that she would make a very good Sister Superior someday but then, of course, I'm her mother."

When the girl herself arrived, Mother Mary Joseph looked at her with even more than her usual interest. Something like mischief sparkled briefly in her eyes. The girl answered her with an inquiring lift of her dark brows and a little deprecatory smile. She knew that her mother had been there ahead of her.

"I couldn't help but wonder what you would be like," Mother said, "after all the things your mother told me that I should and should not ask you to do."

They laughed together, the girl relieved to have her mother's suspected machinations summed up with such concise good humor.

The girls who came to Maryknoll in bevies during the middle and late twenties and into the thirties belonged to the generation that would later be called "lost," the decade that would be tagged variously as "the wastelands," the so-called postwar era. With the First World War they had seen a great fissure open up in the solid security which they and their parents had taken for granted. In the peace that followed, they had not entirely escaped the disillusionment which affected all of their country.

Looking at them, Mother did not see a lost generation or any generation at all. For her, each personality stood out in startling, God-given individuality, gifted with manifold potentialities. Her own part in their lives, she recognized, was small—only to do what lay within her power to help them realize the good things of which they were capable.

She saw in them, too, the precious gifts of Catholic families to the hope and harvest of the Church, to the special love and service of Christ, separated from her own youth by no radical break but by a snippet of time. A certain relaxation in manners, their fantastic enthusiasms and comic clothes, even a thin veneer of the prevailing artificiality, did not hide from her the transfiguring beauty of their aspirations.

For the new postulants she had a special love and understanding. The newcomer to convent life—dressed upon arrival in a modest and uninteresting black dress and a wisp of black veil just like all the other postulants—follows the same schedule as the crowd, lies in a bed identical with all the other beds in the common dormitory, eats the same fare at the same table; moves, wherever she goes, as an indistinguishable member of an undistinguished crowd—and often feels the sharp stab of human insignificance as never before. Stripped of many of the small ways of expressing her individuality and of soothing the human terror of nonentity—she must turn for help to the root business of real character building and the extension of faith into the far reaches of her inner kingdom. Unable to fall back on clothes, hobbies, knickknacks, picturesque speech, and pretty poses for self-expression and reassurance, she feels but may not identify her loss and needs time to recognize and to work with her real self.

Somehow, simply by a kind of recognition, Mother restored one's sense of identity, of value. How many new arrivals whom she came to greet, stopped to talk to, met on her rounds or called over to her, found themselves saying the same thing in a variety of ways.

"Imagine that! She called me by my name right off and remembers all about Dad. . . ."

"To Mother at least I'm a real person, not just another 'little postulant'!"

"I never would have believed it—but she's really glad I came!"

Mother had no idea of "trying" any of her Sisters, young or old. She left that to life and God. She was as careful not to embarrass a postulant as a Cardinal.

Those in charge of the postulants and novices now and then sent them to Mother to tell her of some crowning misdeed. If this was meant to be a penance, it backfired.

"Sister," said the assistant novice mistress, "you have broken the chain on your medal in less than a month after receiving it. I want you to tell Mother that."

"Yes, Sister," said the tall redhead in the badly draped bonnet. She was startled. It seemed to be asking a lot, with Mother so busy, but after all, she told herself, I'm in the convent now and I have to expect to do queer things.

She got a little envelope and put the medal and the broken chain into it. If I were home, I'd call this plain nervy, she thought, but there must be some deep spiritual reason for it that I'll get on to later. She stuffed a note into the envelope to companion the broken chain. It was brief. She wanted to be associated with this odd project as little as possible and wasted no words.

The note read: "Dear Mother Mary Joseph, I have broken my chain. Please fix it. Thank you." She signed her name, somewhat unhappily, and left her prize packet at Mother's place at table.

Several days later she received an envelope addressed to her in Mother's handwriting. Inside it lay the medal on its mended chain. She took it out and examined the chain critically. Who'd have thought it? she asked herself. She really does fix them. And good.

Starting out to become missioners, considering the possibility of martyrdom in the dim, distant, and painless future, eighteen-year-olds have towering ideals but are more prone to expect others to live on their heights than to keep climbing consistently in that direction themselves. All who came to Maryknoll carried in not only the grace of God and good will but also, in varying degrees, physical energy and high spirits, youthful ambition to reform the world and the community rather than self, undirected and oftentimes unintelligent generosity, a feminine desire to please, and a human urge to excel—all wrapped up in one bundle tagged with the attractive label "zealous charity" or "charitable zeal."

Some changes in points of view and patterns of behavior were in order. Mother never felt that these transformations were wrought chiefly through the intervention of other humans; neither did she attempt to avoid her due share in bringing them about. Although her measure was, as she herself stated it, "to see ten faults and to correct one," she was as direct as she was amiable when she spoke of failures and foibles. On the other hand, sometimes she could bring about a change of heart or of conduct without referring to the particular need for it at all.

One community tomboy who was oftener in hot water than out had taken violin lessons before coming to Maryknoll but was far from a virtuoso. Somehow, Mother found a violin for her and encouraged her to practice. Occasionally she would drop in to audition and encourage the struggling artist.

One day, after the novice had gotten herself into a rather outstanding scrape, Mother stopped her and said, "I would like you to play for me today, Sister."

With a sense of doom the novice bent her steps toward the tiny room where she practiced. This is it, she thought. She has had enough. Today I go.

Standing before Mother with her violin tucked under her chubby chin, her thoughts swarming and her pulse and color heightened, she galloped nervously through her meager repertoire.

Mother sat listening, made occasional comments in her usual encouraging way. Apparently she had nothing on her mind except the music, if such it could be called.

Fifteen minutes passed. Twenty. A half hour—an eternity in disguise. The bow had begun to slither like an eel in the novice's perspiring hand. A little cache of dew from her chin had gathered at the edge of the instrument. Ye gods, she thought, why not give me the ax and get it over with! She drew the bow along the strings for a climactic screech.

"That's it. That's all," she said, with her usual tact.

Mother looked at her. The tomboy in the white veil felt herself fading out of focus as a struggling artist and coming into awful clarity as an erring daughter. She waited.

"You are sorry, aren't you?" said Mother and, with a smile and a nod, got up to go.

Not only the Sisters living with Mother at Maryknoll drew on the bounty of her motherliness. Those already abroad, young greenhorns feeling and finding their way through the first years of mission life in China, Korea, the Philippine and Hawaiian Islands, stood in the forefront of her thoughts and prayers. They wrote to her of their joys and successes and of their difficulties, sorrows, fears, and failures as well.

Sitting late into the night at her desk long after others had gone to bed, surrounded everywhere by the evidence of unanswered mail and waiting tasks, Mother wrote to these Sisters with unhurried tranquillity.

The confidence that she had placed in others—their common sense as well as their goodness—shines forth in her letters:

I was very glad to get your letter even though it troubled me to find your dear soul still without the peace I so much long for it to enjoy. . . .

It would seem altogether desirable, a blessing for the mission, for the souls awaiting the word you can give them, and for yourself, if you can find peace and happiness in the present work. Yet your soul is the most precious thing in life to you and its salvation your chief concern. It comes before all other interests. And if you feel that you cannot do this, I shall transfer you, as I promised, to the mission which we shall open in the summer.

You have talents, you have generosity and you can do much for God and souls. I shall not hesitate to change you once you come to a decision as to what seems best for your soul. You know I appreciate your frankness—

. . .

Let me hear from you when you can. In the meantime don't

worry, but face your problem confidently in God's dear Presence and let me know your decision. God bless and love you—

If Mother remained undismayed with the erratic human approach to goodness through mistakes and failures, she was not happy in the presence of anything mean or trifling or callous in dealing with things, with people, with God. Everybody who lived with her knew how she was affected by harshness, discourtesy, and uncharity in any form; what she thought of artificiality and sentimentality as well as a critical outlook; how she reacted to a lack of generosity and a refusal to accept responsibility—whatever promoted unreality, prevented happy family life, and made impossible personal growth and devoted service. If the general instructions she gave for all were not taken to heart, she could be very forthright, however calm and kind, in applying them to a particular individual. Yet she never allowed any sting to remain.

One day, not long after she had pointed out to a young Sister just where her difficulties lay in adjusting to the life and work of the community, they met in a doorway. A young Sister has few ways to show displeasure with her Mother General except through excessive correctness. She therefore stepped aside to let Mother pass with careful overpoliteness.

Almost without seeming to look at the unyielding young face, Mother put her arm around the stiff little figure, drew her forward, and put a good-humored kiss on her cool cheek.

"Oh, you of little faith," she quoted, "why do you doubt?" And walked on.

CHAPTER 8

THE END OF THE BEGINNING

NEGOTIATIONS FOR the old Tompkins property across the road from the Maryknoll Seminary began in 1927. Almost five years later, the Motherhouse was completed and the Sisters moved in. Between time, events were under way in Asia and in Europe that would deeply affect them, their country, and the whole world.

Japanese General Hayashi, using the explosion of a bomb on the South Manchurian railway as an excuse, moved his army from Korea into Manchuria, where the Japanese soon controlled the key rail centers and seaports. A major move in a great expansion plan was on. In China, Communists who had seen the revolutionary attempts of the twenties come to little were taking Russian counsel how to make another and more successful effort. In Germany Adolf Hitler was already beating his ruthless way upward to the Chancellorship.

These happenings, although disturbing, did not have their full impact on the United States, stunned by its own catastrophe, the greatest depression that the nation had ever known. When Herbert Hoover campaigned for the presidency in 1928, he pictured America as "nearer to the final triumph over poverty than ever before." In October of 1929, the nation's economy suddenly crashed. In less than a month stocks declined 40 per cent, and as the new year wore on, banks and factories closed, businesses failed, mills and mines shut down all over the country. Agriculture, long fighting an unequal battle, was soon prostrate.

At Maryknoll, as elsewhere, the sharp pinch was felt. Many who used to give, including the Sisters' own families, could do so no longer. To ask to collect at church doors became impossible, since church-goers were on relief themselves or helping friends and relatives who were.

Loans had been secured, a first and then a second mortgage on the Motherhouse raised. Each time the interest came due on one or the other, it seemed impossible that it could be paid. Sometimes an unexpected gift or legacy received only the day before would make it possible. Bills stacked up. Every time that Mother arranged to talk to the Sisters in a group, Sister John would say to herself, "Now she's going to tell us that we'll all just have to go home to our people."

Looking at Mother's tranquil face, some Sisters could not help but wonder if she were really aware of how serious things were.

"What are we going to do, Mother?" one of them asked her anxiously. "People aren't able to give us anything anymore. They don't have it themselves. And we can't expect those we buy from to extend credit indefinitely. They can't."

Sitting at her desk, Mother looked up at the troubled face. Its distress found no reflection in her own.

"Don't worry, Sister," she said in her most equable tones. "This is God's work. He will take care of it." She took up again the small task that was hers to do just then, but the strength of her conviction reached out to comfort and sustain the other.

In the fall of 1931, Bishop Dunn, who knew so well how the community's finances stood, made a suggestion: people able to attend baseball games must surely have something to give away. Why not have the Sisters collect at Yankee Stadium and the Polo Grounds?

Mother, who never hesitated to ask her Sisters to do difficult things, felt her heart misgive her. To collect at Yankee Stadium would be quite different from accepting offerings at church doors. She did not, however, reject the suggestion and on a brisk fall afternoon Maryknoll Sisters stood outside the Stadium holding baskets and watching the thousands who poured out through the wide gates. Afterwards, when they pooled what they had received, they had exactly $31.86—in nickels and pennies!

Just at the time when circumstances seemed particularly grim, a group of novices were completing their first or canonical year. Since coming into the Motherhouse, they had spent their mornings cleaning up the post-construction mess. They dubbed themselves "The College of Cleaners" and, rounding out the year, held a mock graduation, to which they invited Mother.

She came, bearing a bouquet of new dish mops, and amid laughter and applause, took her place. The college song, composed for the occasion, was sung, and she then conferred the degrees which had been listed for her to award: "To Sister Stella Marie, the degree of D.D.M., Doctor of Dry Mopping; to Sister Miriam Lourdes, the degree of Ph.D., Doctor of Phine Dusting. . . ."

The degrees awarded, at cries for "Speech! Speech!" she launched into an impromptu commencement address in the style familiar to so many in their high school days. She looked around smiling at the laughing faces lifted to her and said, "Although not invited to speak on this occasion, we cannot let it go by, with these young women going out into the world, without telling them that our good wishes follow them. As one of those who have endowed this college, I feel a special interest in it, and there are others too who are glad to be present at this first gradu-

ation. We had no idea when we put our small subsidies into this
university that we would have such remarkable returns. . . .

"We have had a very delightful evening. It is a very good way
to bring an end to your canonical year. In spite of all its fun,
the evening has its serious side. We all realize that." And here
she made one of those transitions so characteristic of her, who
saw life whole in the full circle of its joy and sorrow. "Only today I received a letter from one of the Religious of the Sacred
Heart . . . in which she said, in speaking of the building, 'Whoever builds, suffers.' Certainly it is full of meaning. All of us
who have had any part in the building of the Motherhouse
know there has been suffering along with it. You in your canonical year, all you novices and postulants, who co-operate with us
in meeting the immense debt that hangs over us, all know a certain amount of suffering—joyful suffering, of course—because it
is for God.

"We can apply the same to your canonical year—you have had
a year set apart for the building up of your interior life. . . . You
have made the foundation of your religious life. You have the
rest to keep building, and you are going to suffer more and more
as the years go on."

Coming from her lips, the prediction did not sound dismal.
When she finished speaking by saying, "Always be a novice in
the formation of your spiritual life; it will mean sacrifice, but it
is the easiest way to love and come close to God," the thoughtful
young faces turned to her were still smiling.

The early thirties were not, however, all anxiety and stress:
certainly joy far outweighed sorrow at Maryknoll. Houses and
works in mission countries were multiplying steadily. In Korea,
South China, and Manchuria, novitiates for native Sisters—a
most important work for the future of the Church in those
countries—had been started under the Sisters' direction and
were showing healthy progress. In the Philippine and Hawaiian
Islands, on the west coast of the United States as well as on the

mainland of Asia, works begun earlier were taking deep root. Writing to her Sisters all over the world, Mother expressed something of what this meant to her:

> I think of you all, as I sit at my desk looking on the neighboring countryside and out beyond the hills, and my heart's love goes with my thoughts. . . .
> How good God is to let us love Him in so many different ways, in so many different places.

The Cloistered Branch, long envisioned by Mother as a group set apart for a life of prayer and penance for the missions while at the same time remaining an integral part of the Maryknoll Sisterhood, made a small but stout beginning in the old Tompkins house cresting Maryknoll's highest hill. Mother said it was "simply another means we have taken of expressing our zeal for souls," called it "the core of my heart," and gave to its development careful thought and loving solicitude.

Once the country had weathered the depression, the community's financial situation eased somewhat, although it remained for some time a struggle to make interest payments and nothing on the principal of the debt could be paid.

For Mother one of the greatest joys of these years was Father Walsh's consecration as a bishop. Although others had envisioned the possibility of such an appointment, he had not expected it. He had had, moreover, since the earliest days of his priesthood, an antipathy for honors without responsibility; but on being offered the fullness of the priesthood, he accepted it with honest happiness—as the grace that it was. He realized too that being a bishop would provide him with added opportunities for serving the Church and forwarding her missionary task; and he saw in this action of the Holy Father, Pope Pius XI, not only a commendation of Maryknoll and its work but an appreciation of the role which the Catholics of his country were beginning to play in the mission of the Church.

The day of the ceremony, the feast of St. Peter and St. Paul, 1933, dawned with clouds and showers, but as the bells began to ring in the new day, the sky cleared and the sun came out to throw its golden cloak over the ancient and beautiful city of Rome. The air was clear and the wet streets glistened as several hundred prelates, priests, and layfolk moved toward the Janiculum hill for the ceremony. On her way, Mother thought that even the weather was playing its part to make this twenty-ninth of June a perfect day.

Once inside the lovely and spacious chapel of the new Urban College of *Propaganda Fide,* listening to the glorious polyphonic chant, conscious of the seminarians from all over the world who crowded the balcony, of the representatives of the Church's many-faceted life who moved in the procession, and of the friends of Maryknoll standing about her, Mother knew one of those rare moments when the world seems a very heaven.

Watching Father Walsh move forward in the colorful line of dignitaries, companioned by men of the Church who valued and appreciated him—the consecrator Cardinal Fumasoni-Biondi, the co-consecrators Bishop Dunn and Archbishop Mc-Nicholas, her heart was full. Suddenly she, who in a lifetime conceded few tears either to pain or grief, saw Father Walsh's erect and energetic figure, his grave and alert face, through a haze of tears. Few, if any, knew so well the long traveling through the dark ways of faith which had brought him to this bright eminence. And when, following the singing of the *"Veni Sancte Spiritus"* which he loved so well, he made his prostration and lay clear-minded and petitioning before the altar of God, Mother knew herself to be at one with all that he asked of God.

Home again at Maryknoll, Bishop Walsh greeted his priestly sons and religious daughters with his usual keen-eyed kindliness. To many he seemed stimulated rather than worn out by the events of his consecration. The activities which he resumed belied his years. An editorial in *The Catholic Transcript* of

Hartford, Connecticut, optimistically estimated that he could look forward to "twenty more years of activity." He had, instead, less than three, and much of these would be given to suffering. To those who recognized it, he did not deny that he was tired.

He might well be. Never robust, he had for years channeled all his energies and husbanded his every minute for the task to which he had devoted himself. He alone knew what it had cost him day in and day out to attend faithfully all the common prayers at the Seminary, to supervise the publication of *The Field Afar* magazine, to attend to his heavy correspondence promptly, to be accessible and relaxed with innumerable guests, to travel wherever and whenever his duties took him, to keep in touch with the daily detail of his society and yet to find time and energy to plan ahead for its development, and to be large-minded and great-hearted enough to identify himself with every aspect of the growth of God's kingdom on earth. Now he began to feel the weight of the burdens he had carried so long. His breathing, the very beating of his heart, took on the nature of a task.

In October of 1933, the final enclosure of the first group of cloistered Maryknoll Sisters took place. Bishop Walsh went up the hilltop to the converted farmhouse for the occasion, offered Mass in the small crowded chapel, and gave one of his informal and inimitable talks, glad now to show his approbation of a venture which had once seemed to him of doubtful value.

Among the seven Sisters dedicating themselves irrevocably to the cloistered life of penance and prayer was one whose vocation he had recognized and encouraged years before. Eager to escape the restraints and complexities of wealth, she had been drawn to the Teresians by the simplicity and poverty of their life. Mary-knoll's founder knew how long Sister Mary Magdalen had looked forward to this day during the years spent at old St. Teresa's Lodge, in missionary work in South China, and finally as novice mistress at the center. If the development of this vocation had turned out other than he had expected, he showed himself in this, as in all other things that concerned the Sisters, singularly free of any desire, or even any impulse, to influence things to turn out as he had anticipated.

All the new Bishop's old tasks continued to lay their claims upon him and additional ones seemed to arise weekly because of his new episcopal role. He found it first increasingly difficult and then impossible to meet the demands on his strength. In January of 1935, at his doctor's insistence, he went to Florida in order to avoid, if possible, contracting some pulmonary infection. He was homesick before he set out, returned to Maryknoll in April, and, the day after he arrived, was at the Motherhouse greeting each of the Sisters. Mother had been told and wanted to believe that he had improved. Yet, what was it? She could not say just how—but in some subtle and indefinable way—the well-used body had begun to suggest strongly its human fragility.

Never in any sense an orator but rather a spiritual and thoughtful man who shared his considerations with others in an unstudied and informal way, he spoke with something very near eloquence on the theme of the Resurrection. It was Eastertide.

"Happy indeed are we who have faith in the Resurrection of Jesus Christ. Today we witness the death of deaths. For us death will not be an end, but an experience, and we know that these bodies that are sown in corruption will rise incorruptible. As Christ has risen, so one day we shall rise, and in our risen bodies shall see our Lord. What a glorious anticipation is ours!—eternal union with the Holy Trinity, with our Blessed Mother, the angels, the apostles, martyrs, confessors, virgins, monks, and hermits, with those whom we loved on earth and lost awhile— our parents, brothers, sisters, confreres!

"Surely this is the day that the Lord has made. Let us rejoice and be glad!"

Mother had planned to visit the mission houses in the Orient during 1935. Instead, she decided to send Sister Columba, now her assistant. She did not want to go away with Maryknoll's Founder so ill.

In June of that year Maryknoll received the news that Monsignor Francis X. Ford, then Vicar Apostolic of Kaying, South China, was also to become a bishop. It did not seem so long ago that the dark-eyed young priest had run down the front steps of the old frame Seminary to jump into a rattle-trap car and be whisked away on the first leg of his long journey to China. He had looked so boyish that the same people who regretted that Father Price had received his mission too late in life feared that Father Ford might have come by his too soon. At the ceremonial kiss of peace which was part of the formal leave-taking, he had astounded the younger seminarians by throwing his arms around Father Walsh and kissing him warmly on both cheeks. Seventeen years of missionarying had passed since then.

Where should the newly appointed Bishop-elect be consecrated? Where else but at Maryknoll? And who should be his consecrator? Who else but his Father General, Bishop Walsh? In distant China, Monsignor Ford could not realize what a supreme effort he was asking of his Founder. Everyone wondered if he would be able to do it. He thought so. And it was evident that he wanted very much to do this thing which everyone who loved him saw as a kind of culmination and completion of his full and fast-ebbing life. Better sooner than later, then— yet with time for the necessary preparations. The feast of St. Matthew, September 21, was decided upon.

The Seminary had not yet built its permanent chapel and the lecture room used for that purpose for the past twenty years had no proper sanctuary and was too small. It was decided to hold the ceremony in the Sisters' chapel, not overlarge, but suitable and spacious enough.

With a thick folder under his arm, Father Meaney, the master of ceremonies, would come over from the Seminary to brief the Sister Sacristan, visibly impressed by what had to be readied and remembered.

"Three hundred and twenty-six separate things," she thought, "all in the right place at the right time!"

Sister Pierre, the artist, designed two miters; Sister Perpetua, a master at gold bullion work, embroidered them; Sister Ambrose—the one-time Crawford cut-up—put them together with quick competence. Sister Anna Maria Towle, still fresh-faced and fast-fingered, sat in the midst of swirls of tapestry, of brocades, and ropes of gold braid saying the words that made her happiest, "About the dalmatics, Mother and I thought . . . Mother and I thought that we would make the panels and throws and cushions out of that . . . but for the tabernacle veil Mother and I . . . Mother and I . . ." To be able to say that, to live it, was for Sister Anna Maria the best earth had to offer. And now to be getting ready for Frank Ford's consecration as a bishop! She shook her fine head unbelievingly. She had made his first cassock.

In the bakery, Sister Martha baked two small loaves of bread which, with two little casks of wine, were to be presented as token gifts by the Bishop-Elect at the offertory of the Mass. These were then handed along to the cloister where the Sisters painted them in silver and gold and ornamented them. Other Sisters were busy with dinner souvenirs. And those who could not expend themselves in any other way fell upon the house as though it had never been cleaned before and washed and polished until its windows shone and its long corridors wore the frightening gleam of new ice.

On a day lovely with the lingering beauty of summer and yet touched with the first faint colors of fall, the last vase of roses and lilies was lifted into place around the altar, the last car drove up to the front door, the last prelate was vested and ready in the place appointed him by the master of ceremonies. The sacristan gave a final check, the master of ceremonies, a survey. Everything was ready. Yet even to the end the question remained in many minds, "Will Father General be able to go through with it?"

From her place at the back of the chapel, Mother watched the bishops and archbishops file in, saw the Bishop-Elect in a white cope, accompanied by his co-consecrators, pass by. Then, on a second burst of song, came another figure, walking firmly under the weight of full red pontificals and of his illness.

Writing to her Sisters around the world that evening after the sun had gone down beyond the western hills and the last enthusiastic guest had left, Mother relived the day for them.

> The heart of every Maryknoller was thrilled and filled to overflowing with gratitude that Father was there, so austere and yet so benign—and somehow so fragile. Many of us think he grows to resemble Cardinal Newman.
>
> . . . I do wish that you might have witnessed the scene which was surpassingly touching because of its very nature—a father so wonderfully blessing his son: the father, the living embodiment of the high ideals of the apostolic vocation he has given to his spiritual family—the son, the realization of those ideals—the father's hope fulfilled.
>
> To our surprise and concern—and delight—Father General sang the beautiful Preface. His voice was clear as a bell, strong and steady. After that we had no fears for him. We knew all was well, and the glorious ceremony was too quickly over.

Finishing her account of the day, she could not resist a remark which in its light ironic practicality might have been St. Teresa's own, ". . . the last we saw of him [Bishop Ford] he was surrounded by the ladies, whose admiration we hope will express itself substantially in the future."

The forces which Maryknoll's Father General rallied so wonderfully that day dwindled rapidly in the weeks that followed. By mid-October, when the roadsides around Maryknoll blazed with the red and gold of autumn maples, no one could fail to see how, short of a miracle, his illness must end.

By mid-November he suffered a severe and prolonged hemoptysis. When it was finally checked, Sister Lillian, then on nursing duty, knowing the physical terror induced by such hemorrhaging, said to him, "Don't be anxious, Father. You're going to be all right now."

He answered, with the brevity of one of his office communiqués, "I'm not anxious. I'm ready if, when, and how."

In early December it seemed that the *when* had surely arrived; but each time the Bishop's condition became critical, he made a partial recovery, never fully regaining, however, the ground that he had lost. He was no longer able to say Mass, to recite his office, but he had something else on his mind than the preoccupying endurance of illness. He had not seen his Maryknoll family, all of them, for a long time. Since the Sisters were not so accessible as the priests, seminarians, and Brothers, perhaps it would be good to see them soon.

Before breakfast on December 22, Mother looked down the rows of gray-clad Sisters facing the crucifix at the opposite end of the refectory.

"Sisters," she said. They turned and looked at her expectantly. "Father General has asked to see all the professed Sisters. This morning at ten o'clock the bell will ring for you to go over to the Seminary together. When you reach Father's room, go in one by one, entering by one door and leaving by the other. Kneel and kiss his ring. Don't delay. Don't talk. And don't cry. Because of his weakness, Father does not have the same control over his emotions that he has always had. It is going to be an ordeal, physically, for him, but he wants to see you and no one must do anything that would make this any harder for him. Remember, Sisters, no tears."

And there were no tears—at least in that little room—except for those which shone unshed in the Bishop's own eyes as the Sisters came one by one to kneel and kiss the ring on his pillowed hand. Propped up with his face turned so that he might see them easily, he could not be content with just having them there, but raised his hand to bless each one of the hundred and fifty who came to kneel at his bedside and smile at him as best they could. That evening, against all expectations, Mother could report that he was feeling somewhat better.

Mother went often to see Maryknoll's Founder, to attend Mass when it was said in his room, to do some service, to see that the Sister nurses had everything that they needed for his comfort, if comfort it might be called, or simply to companion him briefly, to pray with and for him. He was as used to her, "the old reliable," as he had dubbed her years ago, as he was to a well-used breviary. As her sick Sisters had good cause to know, she could always slip in and out of a sickroom without causing any flurry or fuss, bringing with her a palpable sense of relief and of confidence.

One afternoon she returned from the Seminary just before the convent supper hour and, with only a few minutes to spare before the bell rang, went to her place at table to sit and wait the coming of the rest of the community. Two postulants were just finishing setting the tables. They saw her come in, looking tired and a little sad. They had some realization of what the death of Maryknoll's Founder would mean to her. Putting down their water pitchers, they went to her.

"Father General, Mother? Is he feeling any better?"

He was feeling anything but better, Mother told them as they stood looking down at her, their young faces full of compassion.

Then suddenly Mother put her head back a little and laughed softly. "But he isn't too sick to check up on me. I know he misses saying his office and so I offered to read a part of it aloud for him. The *Glorias* at the end of the psalms are not printed in the breviary and I just went sailing right along, straight through one psalm into the next, without so much as a pause. Father stood it just as long as he could, and finally said, 'But *where are the Glorias?*' "

The winter wore on. March drew to a close. The trees moved

lithe-limbed in the winds that were the last breath of winter; the dun-colored grass became tinted with olive, and here and there yellow and white crocuses shone out like grounded stars.

April began and Good Friday came, when the Bishop felt "as well as anyone has a right to feel on Good Friday." On Easter Monday, when Mother went to see him, she found him extremely weak.

"I told him," she said, "we were to begin the next morning our novena to Martin de Porres for his recovery. He knew Archbishop McNicholas had asked some fifteen Mothers General to make this novena also, and he seemed pleased. He was always grateful for the smallest kindness shown him. A little later, however, and with effort he managed to say over a considerable period of time, 'If the choice were mine, I'd prefer not to get well. I couldn't imagine myself going back again to the world. . . . In any event,' he continued, 'there are only two courses open to me . . . either to die and be dissolved in Christ [he said this in Latin] or to get well and live in Him. Whatever he wishes will be right!'

"That evening Dr. Sweet, who tended Father so faithfully and grew to love him—and Father was most attached to him—found the right lung completely filled up, and it was evident that the end was not far away. About eight o'clock, Tuesday morning, Father Drought called me and when I saw dear Father General I knew that the 'consummatum est' would soon be said.

"Sister Lillian and Sister Agnes Regina, the nurses, Father Drought and myself were with him. The priests came in, gave him their blessings and passed into the private chapel . . . just beyond his room and recited the prayers for the dying. He was conscious to the end—missing none of the prayers for the dying or the rosary Father Drought said. Very shortly before the last breath came, I repeated the ejaculation, 'Jesus, Mary, Joseph'— and he answered audibly—'I give you my heart and my soul.'"

As Mother came away from the room where Maryknoll's

Founder had just died, Sister de Paul, who had been waiting for her outside, moved forward to take her hand. "I am so sorry, Mother," she said.

Mother returned the pressure of her hand but said, "I do not feel that way about it at all, Sister."

Later she said to the Sisters, "Nothing will ever be quite the same to us again. But we feel, as you must, that Father is very close to us, more loving, more watchful for our interest, more solicitous for our welfare of soul and body than ever before."

In the days that followed, Masses were offered and watches kept by the Founder's body first at the Seminary, then at the Motherhouse, and finally at St. Patrick's Cathedral in New York. This great church was solidly packed for the final Mass offered by Archbishop Mooney and presided over by Cardinal Hayes. Archbishop McNicholas compressed into his sermon much of the affection and admiration which he had had for his dear friend over the years.

Immediately after the funeral Mass, Mother set to work on an article which the Maryknoll Fathers had asked her to write for the May issue of *The Field Afar,* planned as a memorial number for their Father Founder.

As she sat reviewing her thoughts before making a start, a thousand memories crowded in upon her. Which should she choose to express what he was?

Would future Maryknollers remember, for example, his ability to give recognition, to pay a tribute, without overweighting it with words or solemnity? She could hear him saying years ago on one of her feast days—with a smile for the Sisters and a nod in her direction—"I congratulate Mother on having you and you on having Mother." She could recall what seemed like only yesterday but was now more than four years ago, how his little speech on the occasion of Sister Fidelia's last visit to Maryknoll had made the darling old lady sparkle. "This is indeed an occasion. Today you have with you not only your mother and your father but your grandmother as well."

How many would realize, as the picture of the Founder became set over the years, his lightheartedness in disappointments and setbacks? His good humor? One winter evening, having come slogging over to the Novitiate from the Seminary through snow and sleet to give a talk which the novices had requested him to make, he began by saying, with his characteristic twinkle, "It is a compliment to any speaker to find such an audience on such a night!"

Who would hear of his ability to poke fun at himself? Presented by Brother Aloysius with a startling portrait which Brother had painted of him, he chuckled over it and then sent it along for the Sisters to see, noting, "Copies for the missions at $200 each. Come early and avoid the rush." Pressed by a Bishop in Shanghai to interrupt his packed schedule to preach a series of sermons in the Cathedral, he wrote, "Tomorrow I try to convince the Bishop that I cannot preach a Lenten retreat at the Cathedral here. I am the best (and only) native English-speaking preacher available."

Sometimes his humor was coupled with a diffidence which, because of his apostolic outlook and approach, few suspected. Occasionally he had given Mother glimpses of it as in the short note he wrote from Rome just before an audience with Pope Pius XI: "We are due at the Vatican today for an audience—a 'private' one for me and a 'special' one for the community. Picture me trying to interest the Holy Father for a quarter of an hour—edifying him with my poor French."

Who could put a finger on the gift, the quality, most expressive of what he was? His strength or his tolerance and tenderness? His courage or his humility and humor? His fatherliness or his faith?

Where to begin to tell it all? With the cheerful face which he turned on the mammoth disappointments and picayune trials of

Hawthorne? With his delight on finding the site that was to become Maryknoll? With his sober joy at the departure of the first
group of priests for the missions? There were so many pictures
from which she might choose—up to the last, the shrinking body,
the small suffering face and the magnificent endurance of the
past year.

Of all her memories, one of nearly thirty years ago was among
the brightest: the image of a quiet but dynamic priest who rose
to greet her in his small crowded office and to welcome her into
all that his head and heart held for the future. Seeing it once
more—the smile, the keen regard, the outstretched hand—all still
undimmed, she began there, where so much had begun for her.

PART IV

All That Comes

—❦—

"Accept all that comes . . . as from the hand of God."

—James A. Walsh

-->≪ CHAPTER 9 ≫-

THE WAR YEARS

EVENTS both in Europe and in the Far East became increasingly ominous during these years. Hitler's rabid leadership and Japan's expansive program created uneasiness in the United States, but as a whole, however, the people either failed or refused to see in the accumulating crises a revelation of the things to come. With the patent failure of World War I to make the world safe for democracy, the nation had fallen into a disillusioned and isolationist mood. At the end of the twenties and well into the thirties, the people were first stunned by the greatest economic depression their country had ever known and subsequently preoccupied with the struggle to recover from it. In these circumstances, Hitler, with his screaming oratory and Charlie Chaplin mustache, was apt to be considered too fantastic to be taken seriously; Japan was far away, and what she did in Manchuria regrettable but irrelevant.

By the fall of 1939, nevertheless, few in the United States, no matter how disinclined they might be to face it, could ignore the fact that big trouble lay ahead for them as well as for the rest of the world.

Germany had taken over Austria, Czechoslovakia, and Poland and was readying for an attack on Holland, Luxembourg, and Belgium, with a quick conquest of France and an eventual invasion of England in view. Japan, its government purged by assassination of antimilitarist elements, occupied all of Manchuria and invaded China. It had built up a navy which exceeded the combined strength of the navies of the Netherlands, Great Britain, and the United States. Roosevelt was progressively abandoning a neutral stance, which the people of the United States, drawn along by his leadership, gave up more reluctantly.

Well before the end of the decade, the conflict had already broken over the Far East, as the Maryknollers there had cause to know. The increasing pressure of Japanese military and political action against a weak and uncertain China erupted into open warfare on July 7, 1937. On that day a Japanese military contingent on maneuvers clashed with a unit of Chinese soldiers south of Peiping—a so-called incident which lengthened into an eight-year war.

At Maryknoll, where Sisters from all over the Far East had gathered for their Congregation's General Chapter, the news caused dismay rather than surprise. The delegates from Japanese-governed Korea and Manchuria had had first-hand experience of the temper of the expanding Empire and some insight into its ambitions. Yet even those closely in touch with the events in the Orient did not at first recognize the full significance of the conflict.

However, by the first of August, in faraway Kaying, South China, a local wiseacre was already telling the Sisters there, "Buy rice. Buy plenty rice. Maybe no more rice boats reach us from Siam for a long, long time." By the end of August, when the first two Japanese aircraft cruised over their heads, this advice no longer seemed farfetched.

During the first week of November, the Maryknoll Sisters who staffed the women's section of St. Joseph's Hospital outside

Shanghai watched Chinese troops retreat in trucks and on foot past the hospital buildings; on the eighth they saw some soldiers, bone-tired and all on foot, bombed and strafed as they tried to withdraw to the south; they felt the earth shake as nearby villages were totally destroyed from the air; by the twelfth, their ears full of the stillness of complete devastation, they stood at the hospital door to meet a bowing Japanese major who came calling with flowers and a camera; by the twenty-fourth, the hospital staff—German Brothers of Mercy, American Maryknoll Sisters, and Chinese lay personnel—had buried what the swiftly rolling conquest had left behind around the hospital—over six hundred dead, almost all Chinese.

On the twenty-ninth of the same month, far to the south on a small Chinese island known to Christians of the West only because St. Francis Xavier died there, two Maryknoll Sisters were climbing a hill on their way to a small dispensary which they operated. They were the only occidental women on Sancian. Just as they reached the crown of the hill, a band of men came marching up the far side and met them at the top. In that lonely spot between sea and sky, both groups stopped, amazed, and stared at one another—the two Sisters in gray, the small khaki-clad Japanese patrol, carrying a white flag with a red sun upon it.

Stepping forward from among his men, the Japanese officer in charge motioned the Sisters to come on.

"We are not here to harm anyone," he said in English. "We came only to look."

All along the coast of China from north to south, the war was soon racing like wildfire, flaming up the riverways in gunboats and transports, falling out of the skies from widely roving planes. Great cities, key towns, remote villages, all eventually came to cower under the shadow of the planes. Unopposed, they scouted, bombed, and made leisurely returns to assess their own effectiveness.

As early as October, 1937, the Sisters at Kongmoon learned

that the city's river route to the sea was sealed off. By January, 1938, bombing in the Kongmoon area had become a commonplace.

In February, the Sisters at Yeungkong looked up to see a small formation of planes overhead—the first to pass over the city —and before long women were running in to say that four bridges not far away had been demolished and some nearby rice boats destroyed. In June, the city trembled at the knowledge that a fishing village close at hand had been wiped out. In October, five bombs fell in Yeungkong itself, near enough to shake the mission buildings. It was only a beginning. By February of the following year, 1939, air raids had become so frequent that the blind girls at the mission had grown expert in estimating the timing and location of bomb strikes.

The same month Loting was heavily attacked. Three bombs fell on the mission compound. The pastor, Father Kennelly, was struck by shrapnel and lay in the open, bleeding profusely, while Sister Monica Marie crouched beside him and tried to stanch the flow of blood while the air raid went on.

In March, Kongmoon fell after hand-to-hand fighting in the streets. About seven hundred terrified people crowded into the mission compound which Bishop Paschang had readied as well as he could for such a contingency. The mission personnel did what was possible to create tolerable living conditions for the frightened people. The women and children, as was customary, became the Sisters' special care. This sheltering of refugees was the beginning of a pattern that was to extend over years for the Maryknoll Fathers and Sisters in South China.

The uneven contest went on and on, sometimes creeping slowly forward over a period of months, sometimes exploding upon an astounded people in a matter of minutes. Ultimately both Kwangtung and Kwangsi Provinces seemed drenched in destruction. What was at first a stunning catastrophe eventually became an ugly routine. It ate into the nerves none the less for that:

the frequent alarms, sometimes seven to ten in a day; the interrupted work of teaching and healing; the unfinished or omitted
meals; the moonlit nights with ears tuned to the sound of the
alarm and the drone of planes; the shepherding and soothing of
crying babies, frightened children, and young girls; the sheltering of fear-driven, dispossessed families; the running for refuge
in fields, in caves, on riverboats; the crouching under flimsy
tables in flimsy houses deafened by the crescendo of diving
planes and the falling bombs; the facing up to the residual
maimed and dead. Terror itself, and grief, too, became in time
routine.

Around the central fact of warfare itself sprang up its ugly
fellowship: hunger—riceless days for people already existing on
a marginal diet; thievery and banditry—depredations by callous
opportunists and desperate army deserters; epidemics—measles,
polio, cholera, smallpox; growing lists of sick and wounded and
dwindling medical supplies on clinic shelves; increasing isolation because of disrupted mail service, dismantled bridges,
torn-up roads; depressing news—great Canton had fallen, the
Pearl, the West Rivers were in Japanese hands; tormenting
rumors—the Chinese town officials had all fled, the Japanese
were already at the bend in the river; and, last but not least, the
sudden overwhelming panics. Sometimes by night the whole
population of a town silently slipped away. Sometimes by day
some insignificant occurrence touched off widespread consterna-
tion: a thief chased by the owner of a stolen chicken was suddenly joined by ten, twenty, a hundred, a thousand men,
women, and children all crying, "Run! Run! Run!" until the
entire city was emptied into the countryside.

Occasional letters from war-isolated missioners reached Hong
Kong and the United States. Once in a great while, too, over
interminable overland routes or by risky night runs in small
river craft people—priests and Sisters too—squeezed through the
tightening cordon to reach Hong Kong. Sister Mary Paul herself

managed to visit some of the houses in Kwangtung during these years and whatever news reached her at the center house in Hong Kong from the interior she relayed to Mother Mary Joseph. She had little of cheer to tell of the progress of the war, but the Sisters' faith and endurance gave cause for comfort.

Referring with some distress to air raids in the Kaying area in July, 1939, she wrote, "The Sisters' trick is to wrap themselves in *mintois* (quilts) and crawl under the bed—the *mintois* to break the force of any heavy object and the bed to protect them from falling walls. Those houses in Kaying make me ill when I consider them as protection. . . ."

All the news that came to Mother Mary Joseph during this time made her restive to visit the Sisters in the Orient, to know at first hand what they were facing and might yet have to endure, to help and encourage them with all the resources of her mind and heart. She had not been to visit the houses in the Orient since 1930, had intended to start out immediately after the 1937 General Chapter of the Congregation, but first the unwillingness of the State Department to issue a passport for travel in China caused her to wait in hopes of better conditions and then her own illnesses delayed her. It was late spring 1940 before she set out, taking Sister James as her companion on the first such trip that they had made together.

After visiting the Sisters in California, Washington, and the Hawaiian Islands, they arrived in Hong Kong in time for Mother's fifty-eighth birthday on October 27. En route, the SS *Coolidge* had beaten its way through a hundred-and-twenty-mile hurricane and Mother made the Sisters laugh with graphic descriptions of a correct Swiss consul, pursued by all the movable furniture in the ship's lounge, hurtling across the tipping floor to land in her lap.

Before reaching Hong Kong, she had already experienced how different this visitation was to be from the others that she had made. First of all, the whole atmosphere of the world had become strange, full of tension and uncertainty and the sometimes subtle, sometimes blatant shift in values, relationships, and attitudes which war brings.

Everywhere in China, Japan was continuing to have things her own way, although not with the speed with which she had anticipated. This continuing conquest could be felt in contacts both with her own people and with those whom Japan dominated.

In the short time since Mother set out from Maryknoll, Hitler had enjoyed one triumph after another in Europe. The Belgian Army had surrendered, France had fallen, the British Expeditionary Force had been narrowly saved by the magnificent evacuation of Dunkirk. In Russia, Molotov called in German Ambassador Schulenburg to congratulate him on the splendid success of the German forces and then, shielded by the conflict, Stalin turned his attention to the annexation of Lithuania, Latvia, and Estonia.

Lonely but defiant, England fought for the mastery of her own skies and waited through a long summer for the invasion threatened by Hitler. In September the *Luftwaffe* concentrated its full strength on bombing London by night. When Mother reached Hong Kong, she would feel the reverberations of these terrible attacks in the lives of the people there, especially the English. British government officials, military officers, and businessmen had to pin their minds on plans for the defense of Hong Kong, which many of them knew to be futile, while burdened with thoughts of an England they had never known—devastated and in mortal danger.

Another circumstance which made this visitation so different for Mother was the restricted itinerary allowed her. She could not go to Korea or Manchuria. In Japan she had transit privileges, could go ashore only for such time as her ship stayed in port.

At Yokohama, Sister Gemma and Sister Rose Anne spent the day with her and Father Patrick Byrne came to tell her what he could surmise of conditions and prospects. At Kobe, four Sisters came from Kyoto, together with three others who had traveled hurriedly from the continent on receiving word that Mother would not be able to go to see them—Sister Peter from Dairen, Manchuria; Sister Sylvester and Sister Elenita from Korea. Standing in the pelting rain as the ship docked, laughing up at Mother as she stood watching for them on deck, they showed little of the strain of the past months, and Mother was overjoyed to see them looking so well.

It was against regulations for them to board the ship. The precious day would be squandered in travel if they attempted to take Mother and Sister James back with them to Kyoto. Official-dom took pity. The Sisters were allowed aboard. Through the day and into the evening they talked of all that most concerned them: the increasing tension in government circles; the tighten-ing restrictions on travel, mail, and money; the resultant un-certainty as to their status and work; their fears for their people. Together they tried to foresee eventualities and consider how they might be met. Finally the Sisters had to go away in the rain and in the dark carrying carefully with them all that they could remember of that day to share with other Maryknoll Sisters in distant convents in Korea and Manchuria.

At Hong Kong Mother could see how well the Maryknoll Sisters' schools were developing, the increasing numbers of young people whom her Sisters were helping to educate, the additional extracurricular projects which they had undertaken to meet the needs of the times—working in soup kitchens and clinics, distributing food and clothing, training as emergency volunteers. She could sense the way in which they were growing more deeply into the lives of the people.

She experienced, too, how the war was isolating the Sisters in the smaller houses upcountry from the center house and indeed from the whole outside world. Sister Imelda, Sister Albert, and Sister Anna Mary had just completed an incredible twelve-day journey from Kaying through the Japanese lines in order to reach Hong Kong and possible medical help for Sister Anna Mary, seriously ill with cancer.

Other Sisters, without such a critical need, could hardly be encouraged to attempt a similar exploit, although two more did manage to reach Mother before she left the Colony. And there was plainly now no question of Mother traveling to them. Indeed British officials were astonished and far from delighted to find that she had not continued on with the SS *Coolidge*. At a time when they were encouraging foreigners to evacuate, even one alien could not be welcomed.

In the Colony, war was as palpable, and as bitter, as quinine on the tongue. It could be felt in the news and rumors about the fighting between the Chinese and Japanese armies; in the decreasing number of foreigners on the streets and in the shops; in the mock maneuvers and blackout practices; in the unspoken realization that the Japanese could probably take the twin cities whenever they made up their minds to do it; but most of all it could be felt in the thousands of Chinese refugees flooding into the Colony.

Three nights after her arrival, having spent a day of school visiting, Mother stayed up on the convent roof with the other Sisters until late watching a simulated attack on Hong Kong— in the sky, invading planes, sweeping searchlights, and the *phoom-phoom-phoom* of antiaircraft fire; on the ground, mock battles and earth-shaking mortar fire. Those quietly watching on the roof found the show awesome, but some wondered just how much it all signified for the defense of Hong Kong.

The refugees Mother met standing in lines at soup kitchens, found in long queues outside the convent gate, encountered wandering the streets with their children by the hand, their babies and possessions on their back, seeking food, shelter, work.

She saw them, exhausted, sleeping on the bare pavements of the city. When in extremity such as this, some looked up, caught the eye and smiled, Mother was so moved that she could not say just what she felt. It lightened her heart somewhat that her Sisters were able to do a little to alleviate such gross misery.

She undertook to take movies of the waiting crowds at one of the soup kitchens where her Sisters were working. Surely if those at home could see these poor uprooted people, they would do anything to help them. The crowds had no objection to being photographed. On the contrary, of the 1700, most apparently wanted close-ups taken. They were delighted at such attention. They thronged around Mother so that she could hardly move, much less focus a camera.

With her inimitable and gentle courtesy, she kept suggesting in English, "If you would just stand back . . . if you come so close I won't be able to take your picture . . . if you would just step back a little . . ." They understood nothing of what she was saying, but they liked her voice and her expression. They came closer and closer, some smiling into her face, some telling her vociferously what was most on their minds.

On November 20, Sister Imelda and Sister Albert set out from Hong Kong on their return journey to Kaying. Sister Mary Paul, Mother, and Sister Maria Teresa, her fellow-shopper of 1923, drove them to Taipo and saw them aboard the little steamer to Saychung. They, together with Maryknoll's Father Raymund Quinn, were taking a long, circuitous route back to Kaying because it was considered safer.

"We'll be all right, Mother," the Sisters said reassuringly. "This will just take time."

She looked at them with that expression which they knew so well, which seemed to understand all and to say all, and took them in her arms for a final hug and kiss. They knew that partings were never easy for her, and this one, because of the circumstances, had an added poignancy. Again her Sisters were setting out for hardships which she could not spare them and dangers which she could not share.

However, neither she nor they had any inkling then that they had chosen the route along which the main flow of supplies were being moved from the sea to the hard-pressed Chinese soldiery inland. When Father Quinn and the Sisters reached Saychung at dusk, they found the town a vortex of turmoil and urgency. Everything that could float had been requisitioned by the military, and soldiers and coolies trotted back and forth loading sampans until they seemed ready to sink.

After several days of futile negotiations for a sampan, the travelers gave up and took bicycles north to Tamshui. While they were there, the city was bombed. They crouched under the rickety wooden stairs of the Christians' *kungso,* or meeting house, while glass rained from the shattered windows and the dust and debris of the pagan shrine next door burst and billowed around them. A few more days were spent trying to get a sampan and, once again unsuccessful, they pushed on by bicycles to Waichow, another river town. There a party of Presbyterian missioners headed by Dr. Tutel generously offered them space aboard a large sampan which they had been fortunate enough to secure. The Maryknollers could go with them as far as Laolung and then make their way overland to Kaying.

Fifteen minutes after the sampan turtled out of Waichow, twenty-six Japanese planes drilled through the sky and bombed the city. Every time a plane soared up from its dive, a giant arm of smoke and fire reached up after it into the shattered sky.

On the sampan the first exclamations of shock and dismay faltered into silence as the awful circus went on. It was a good time for Li, the sampan owner, to make a point.

"Every morning airplanes come along the river looking for sampan," he said. "Better every morning you leave sampan and walk along riverbank until sun is there." He pointed to the meridian. "Then the planes go and you come back."

And so every morning not long after sun-up the ten passengers climbed the riverbank and began their half day's walk. At the drone of a plane they could take cover wherever they could find it, and the brown-backed sampan would burrow under an overhang of bamboo until the danger flew on. At noon even the weary rowers rested and, hidden under some contrived or natural shelter, everybody had their rice in peace. In the afternoon all passengers stayed aboard and the Sisters managed to pray their divine office. The psalms they said had never seemed more meaningful or more appropriate.

Then one morning as the Sisters stood, shoes and stockings in hand, ready to wade ashore, they realized that although they were the first ready to leave the sampan, it was already past time. The sun stood high over their shoulders. The sampan felt warm under their bare feet. Yet as they slipped over the side of the boat and began to wade ashore they were not really concerned.

Then suddenly they heard it—surprisingly loud and near—a low-flying plane! Almost at once it burst out from behind the riverbank only a few hundred feet above them. As it passed over, they could see the pilot's face turned in their direction. They ran, plowing clumsily through the sand and shallow water as the plane banked and swung back, boring down on them. Its guns blasted into action. Sister Albert dropped into the shallow water and disappeared. Looking back over her shoulder, Sister Imelda saw a narrow seam racing along the water toward the sampan, toward her. She tried to run out of its path and fell headlong. Before she could move, the patter of bullets raced past between her and Sister Albert, lying scarcely a foot apart. The swift shadow of the plane followed. She scrambled to her feet and ran stumbling up the steep bank. Behind her Sister Albert lifted her head for a breath, lay a little longer to make sure, and then got up and ran after her.

A little distance from the top of the bank stood a huddle of

gray mud-brick houses. As the Sisters ran toward the little village, women came out to meet them.

"Ai-yah! Poor foreign devils!" said one.

"Come, sit, dry yourselves," invited another.

"Have you eaten yet?" inquired still another.

Trembling a little, the Sisters sat down on the stools set out
in the sun for them, and one of the women began to squeeze
the water out of their soaked clothing. She crooned over them
as if they were terrified children. "Don't be afraid," she murmured. "Don't mind. You are scared out of your wits, poor
things, and no wonder. But it is all over and nobody the worse.
Nobody the worse."

Another could not help laughing a little. "See! Those white
feet are not practical," she said. "Look at the way they bleed.
But, look, think of it, the blood is no different than ours." She
tested it with her finger tip. "No different. Some hot water
there, daughter-in-law, for the foreign devils' feet."

As the feet were washed, the clothes somewhat dried, tea prof-
fered and accepted, the women unleashed the full tide of their
curiosity.

"Where are you going?" "Where are you coming from?" "And
where are your husband and children?" "No husband?" "No
children?" "You do not marry? How is that?" "Let's see now,
who is this Lord of Heaven?" "Why do you not wear the nice
sa'am and fu as we do?"

Anxious and sympathetic, the Presbyterian women came up
and joined them.

"That was a close call," said one. "We were frightened to
death for you. Until you ran up that bank."

"I was never so scared in all my life," said Sister Imelda
honestly.

"Li had us all stay on the sampan until we were pretty sure
the plane wasn't coming back. Then Father Quinn and Dr.
Tutel let us come first in case you were tidying up."

One of the American women had several pairs of little red socks in her hands. "None of us wear black stockings," she said, smiling. "And we didn't like to go through your things. Would you like to put these on until your own dry out?"

The Sisters held out their hands. "Indeed we would. Thank you."

It was time to go. The Sisters turned to the village women, who crowded around to receive their smiles and thanks and bows. They felt a sudden sharp sorrow at leaving these people who had been so kind to them.

"May the Lord of Heaven bless you!" they said.

As they walked away, the women called after them tentatively, bashfully, "May the Lord of Heaven bless you!"

The Sisters turned back once again to smile and nod. And then, still bleeding a little, the feet in borrowed red socks struck out once more toward Kaying.

After she returned to Hong Kong from the Philippines and before she left for home on December 28, Mother learned that Father Quinn and the two Sisters had reached their mission in Kaying safely.

Before sailing, she cabled the northern missions and once again some of the Sisters came to the port cities to be with her. Sister Rose Benigna from Dairen, Manchuria, met the ship at Shanghai and Sisters Lelia, Celine Marie, and Veronica Marie from Fushun, Manchuria, and Sisters Gabriella, Eugenia, and William from Korea met her at Kobe. On her journey southward Mother had spoken of returning to visit the northern missions in the spring. For the present, that was plainly impossible, and they all knew it. She had already discussed conditions and plans. Now no new light shone into the darkening future. She did not allow the few hours together which were theirs to be given over to forebodings and speculations about war but set herself to make this brief time as memorable a family reunion as possible. When she left them, the Sisters had a vivid and consoling memory of her presence—loving, serene, sustaining.

At Maryknoll once more, Mother had to make, in the months that followed, a hard decision. Should her Sisters in the Far East remain there or not? The United States Government was strongly advising its nationals to leave. The policy of the Church has ever been for pastors to remain with their people unless there are compelling reasons to the contrary. Although certainly not pastors, the Sisters represented in some way the mission of the Church and the love of Christ.

On the other hand, what good could they do if they were interned for months or even years as enemy aliens? There were so many places in the world where they would be free to work and to do some good. Besides, however willing they might be to face whatever their vocation implied, they were just people themselves, human beings who could suffer and be hungry and afraid. And Mother loved them.

In the end, after having at first reduced the staffs of some missions, she followed the general policy of the Church and the particular advice of the Church authorities under whom the Sisters were working. The Sisters stayed.

She watched, and felt, the year of 1941 turn slowly forward like the tightening of a screw. England held out through the long winter and into the spring, fending off the *Luftwaffe* in her skies, eluding the U-boats at sea, protecting her eagle-spread empire as well as she could and battling Germany back and forth across the sands of North Africa. In Japan the military clique watched Germany firm her hold on western Europe and turn, with what seemed unabated energy, to attack her recent ally, Russia.

If military might could create a new order in Europe, some Japanese were thinking, why not in Asia? And was not this the time for Japan to act while Britain, France, and Holland had all become incapable of defending their far eastern holdings? What could prevent Japan from realizing her dream of an Asia for Asians led by the greatest nation of them all?

Deprivation of oil, for one thing. When in July the United States, Great Britain, and Holland put embargoes on shipping oil to Japan, Japan knew that without it her navy could not function, her military enterprise in China would falter, and her home economy would slow down and eventually come to a standstill. Notes were exchanged, talks held, proposals made and rejected, as the tension between the United States and Japan grew.

During that fall, the light in Mother's room stayed on far into the night. Was she worrying? Couldn't she sleep? At last alone after the demands of each full day, she was writing, writing Christmas notes, many Christmas notes to all the Sisters on the missions whom she had not been able to see the year before. It was not a new practice for her, but one which she had never done with more deliberate affection. That Christmas, she had to say, they had to receive some expression of what was in her heart.

By November the question "Will there be war?" began to change into "When will it come?" "Where?" "In the Dutch East Indies?" "In Hong Kong?" "Perhaps even in Manila?" "Or will the curtain simply be rung down on the whole Far East?" President Roosevelt considered Thailand the likely spot. No one suggested Honolulu.

Then suddenly on December 7 the answer to all questions thundered out in the flame and death of Pearl Harbor. On a beautiful Sunday morning, in response to ground-shaking detonations at the harbor and airfield, schoolboys of nearby St. Anthony's parish climbed up into the trees to get a look at what was going on. A wave of low-flying planes swept over their heads. "Jap planes!" they called in astonishment to their disbelieving teacher. "Jap planes, Seesta! Honest! For real! Jap planes!" The war had come to the United States, and the country faced it with the loss of much of her Pacific fleet.

A group of young girls were due to arrive at Maryknoll the next day, December 8, to begin their training to become Maryknoll Sisters. Among them was a Nisei Japanese. En route to Maryknoll she had stopped off to visit friends in Brooklyn. Even as the first stunning news spread through both communities at Maryknoll that Sunday afternoon and Mother waited anxiously for word of her Sisters in Honolulu, she thought of the feelings of this girl and called to welcome and reassure her.

"Is everything all right?"

"Oh, yes, Mother."

"There will probably be some FBI men on hand tomorrow to help welcome you to Maryknoll! It's nothing to worry about, just part of their routine. They called today to check on us."

A few hours after Pearl Harbor, the Japanese attacked the Philippines where, in mission houses on the island of Luzon, there were fifty-three Maryknoll Sisters. By nightfall, both the mountain town of Baguio and the port city of Manila had been bombed and the Sisters staffing St. Paul's Hospital in Manila's old walled city had begun to receive the first casualties from the piers and from the naval base at Cavite.

Meanwhile, as though released by a single cosmic spring, Japanese police and soldiers arrived at the gates and doors of all Maryknoll missions, large and small, throughout Korea and Manchuria. They came to intern or imprison priests, Brothers, and Sisters and, as time permitted and local policy dictated, to interrogate. "Why did you come here? Who are your friends? Do you love your country? Do you pray your country will win the war? What do you think of your guards? Of the Japanese Emperor? If the Emperor ordered what your Church forbids, which would you obey?"

On December 12, following five days of attack, Kowloon, the mainland city of the Crown Colony of Hong Kong, fell to the

Japanese. In lightless rooms behind the locked doors of their school, the Sisters heard in the night the heavy tread of the incoming army, silent and disciplined, on its way to penetrate and possess the city.

The British forces withdrew to the Island of Hong Kong and, bidden to delay the Japanese victory as long as possible, continued to hold out desperately. On Christmas Day, Sister Amata, one of the Maryknoll Sisters serving as volunteer nurses at Queen Mary's Hospital, made her way to a ward crammed with wounded where she was on duty. The days had been filled with the shrieks of air raid sirens, the drilling crescendo of diving planes, the blast of bombs and mortar shells and antiaircraft fire and, more recently, with the sharp chatter of machine guns. Now some change in the terrible cacophony drew her to the window to look out. On a fortified hill across from the hospital a limp white flag was rising slowly. Below the hospital a tired soldier came out carrying another huge white flag, walked to the center of the road and stood there tensely holding it. Other soldiers carried out guns and ammunition and began to stack them on the lawn. It was over. Hong Kong too had fallen.

On the same Christmas Day in Manila, the staff of a hospital hastily organized to receive the war's mounting casualties were assembled for an announcement. The Maryknoll Sisters, who had transferred their personnel there from St. Paul's, stood with the Filipino staff to hear the news: The American forces were withdrawing from Manila.

By six in the evening the American wounded had all been evacuated; by seven the American officer in charge and about twenty of his men gathered in the front hallway taking their reluctant leave of the Filipina nurses, the American Sisters.

"If you want to come with us, Sisters, we will take you."

But the Filipino patients, the Filipina nurses had to remain. The Sisters turned down this final offer.

The men said, "We'll be back in three months." Then they

went out to the doubtful haven of Bataan and Corregidor, the hospital doors were closed and bolted and the long wait began. On January 3 at two o'clock in the morning there came a thunderous knocking and the cry, "Open in the name of the Imperial Army!"

After the shattering news of December 7 and 8, a small spate of reassuring cables reached Maryknoll. "All Maryknollers safe in Hawaii . . . the Philippines . . . Hong Kong and Kowloon." Then as the Japanese armies flowed over Kowloon and Hong Kong, into the Philippines, more widely across China, as the doors of Manchuria, Korea, and Japan were closed to the outside world, the news sources quickly dwindled and dried up. Now and then a drop of information trickled out from the interior of China where the Japanese had not yet penetrated or came to Maryknoll from various places in the Orient through the Vatican, the Red Cross, the State Department. Mother watched hungrily for every report, every rumor.

In general, during this initial period, the missioners behind this wall of silence were treated simply as interned enemy aliens. In most cases, no particular care was given to their comfort or convenience and no particular thought was spent on their harassment. They were not valued prisoners, had no information to give, lacked political and military importance. They occupied space and they consumed food, however poor in quality and meager in quantity. When a way of getting these inconvenient people off their hands presented itself, the Japanese, who had a mammoth food problem to deal with, were not unwilling to let them go.

China's perpetual food shortage had been aggravated by unplanted or unharvested rice crops, the loss of rice imports from southeast Asia, the disruption of transportation, the seizure of food supplies by the Japanese army, and, to cap it all, one of the most terrible Yangtze floods that the country had ever known.

The discrepancy between the population and the food supply of conquered Hong Kong the Japanese solved by decreeing that four hundred thousand Chinese must leave the twin cities. To insure that this be done, the sale of rice was stopped. With a gift of a pint of rice a piece for the journey, ten thousand Chinese set out each day from Kowloon along roads choked with refugees and bandits into a land of deserted fields and phantom villages. Their journeying, their suffering, has remained a saga too vast for any telling.

In April and again in June of that year of 1942, some Maryknoll Sisters were released from internment at Stanley prison—ten to go aboard the exchange ship *Asama Maru* for the first lap of their return to the United States, the rest to make their way in small groups anyhow and everyhow for Kwang Cho Waan via Macao. Like the Chinese, they were all to become refugees, finding a place to stay and services to perform temporarily but moving farther and farther westward with the masses that rolled wretchedly onward ahead of the advancing conquerors.

Aboard the exchange ship *Asama Maru* the Sisters from Hong Kong found among the passengers twenty-one other Maryknoll Sisters from Korea and Manchuria, as well as a number of Maryknoll priests and Brothers. They too were bound for home by way of Lourenço Marques in Portuguese East Africa. There the ship's hundreds of passengers would be exchanged, one for one, with the Japanese nationals arriving from the Occident on the SS *Gripsholm*.

Starkly white and brightly lighted at night, the *Gripsholm* completed its voyage and sailed up the Hudson River on August 25 in a year when a terrible total of 568 allied ships had already been sunk by August 1.

The Sisters on board, looking hungrily for a familiar figure as they docked, found Mother Mary Joseph waiting at the pier to welcome them—with nothing in her face but happiness to have them home with her. During the slow processing of passengers by the Federal Bureau of Investigation, she stayed the entire three days, returning in triumph with the last two Sisters to be released. They drove up at night to a Motherhouse ablaze with lights, spilling laughing Sisters out of its doors and down its steps to welcome them and take them inside to the chapel for a final *Te Deum*.

This air of joyous homecoming puzzled some people. Sometimes they wondered if Mother really understood what was happening, if she realized that all over the Orient the works which had been begun with such labor, which had been carefully and painfully nurtured for years, and which were just coming into beautiful flowering, had all been wiped out in no time at all. She did not seem to be worrying enough when the whole tone and temper of the country had changed.

The distant war being waged so grimly in North Africa, in the South Pacific, in China, and in Europe intruded itself on the mind in a thousand ways—felt as keenly at Maryknoll as elsewhere.

The letters from home bringing news of neighbors, cousins, brothers, and sometimes fathers too, who had volunteered or been called up, the first-hand accounts of people who had been in combat areas—Captain McDonald, an army nurse, and Colonel Carlos Romulo, both of whom were among the last to escape from the Philippines and who could tell what the final days on Bataan and Corregidor had been like; the knowledge that American tankers in flames were going down within sight of the Jersey coast; the nation's general sense of astonishment and dismay at feeling itself everywhere on the defensive, everywhere at a disadvantage; all this together with the loss of so many opportunities to serve beloved people in the Orient just when they seemed to need help as never before, could have created a heavy atmosphere in the big, overcrowded Motherhouse on the hilltop. The limited defense activities, the giving of blood to the Red Cross, the experience of a little rationing —these could hardly suffice as outlets for hearts that longed to alleviate the sufferings of the world and had less opportunity than ever before to do so in this time of crucial need. Here certainly was occasion—and excuse—for some pious gloom.

Yet the girls who came to Maryknoll in the fall of 1942 to start becoming Maryknoll Sisters found the atmosphere anything but murky. And their contacts with Mother were gala events. Those assigned to the air raid shelter outside her room looked forward to the practices. These consisted chiefly in taking a chair and something to do to a place designated as comparatively safe and waiting there for the all-clear signal, which might come in fifteen minutes or an hour. Mother would join the group, smiling and greeting them all, sharing bits of news or some treat and available to anybody who would like some conversational exchange with her. When the all-clear did come, the postulants would go back to their daily round with a heightened sense of well being—they did not know just why.

The next year's crop of postulants experienced the same lift of heart when Mother came to recreate with them, especially when she sat down at the piano and began to play several current song hits which they would never have expected her to know. As she began, she heard the astonished intake of breath behind her. It was worth a little practicing and some expert coaching by one of the Sisters.

"Come on, sing it," she said. "You all know it. Of course you do."

The walls were soon ringing with "Mairzy Doats and Dozy Doats and Liddle Lamzey Divey. . . ."

At Maryknoll, no time was wasted in those post–Pearl Harbor days looking back over the wreckage of past accomplishments. In April of 1942, the Maryknoll Fathers began work in Latin America with a mission in Bolivia. In March of the following year the Maryknoll Sisters followed them there and in the same year started works in Nicaragua and Panama. Once again

Mother went shopping with Sisters to help outfit them for new tasks in new fields—which that year included raincoats for jungle downpours and jodhpurs that could be worn under split-skirt habits for horseback riding through the mountains. And she began to make plans to accept a limited number of works with minority groups in the United States.

The day after D Day, June 6, 1944, when the Allied Forces made their tremendous bid to return to France and the whole United States was given to anxiety, hope, and prayer, she announced the Sisters' overseas assignments for the year. Never unmindful of world conditions and issues, she kept her own responsibilities and her community's commitments in the forefront of consciousness. A motherly intuition, in no wise shrewd and perhaps unconscious, led her to time her announcements and the community's activities wisely, perfectly.

Her usual round—everything from speaking at Communion breakfasts to watching day and night by her dying Sisters—went on as before. Sometimes she was ill and the Sisters knew that she was not well, but usually they did not realize the suffering and inconvenience this caused her. When the healthy are taken suddenly ill, a great deal of concern is shown to them. When the chronically ill have just one more bout with sickness, it is more or less taken for granted. They will manage, they always have, even if the illness is recurring malarial attacks, a heart condition, and an esophageal hernia worsening to the critical stage. At this time, Mother had all these and yet she did manage and people did take it for granted, however unconsciously, that she could and would. And because she did not burden others with her anxiety, few realized how concerned she was for the Sisters still in war zones, especially in the Philippines.

When, after months of terrible combat, the United States Forces took the South Pacific island of Guadalcanal in February, 1943, the initiative of the war passed from the hands of the Japanese to the Americans. After that, with great effort and at great cost, the American forces began island-hopping northwards toward the Philippines and Japan. The change in direction was noticed even by Maryknoll's Father Patrick Byrne, interned and isolated in his Kyoto, Japan, rectory—for he came to realize that all the battles which the Japanese newspapers dubbed attempted American landings and American defeats were bringing the Americans nearer and nearer to Japan.

In the United States and at Maryknoll itself, anxiety for the prisoners interned in the Philippines increased. Those who had found the Japanese armies harsh in victory feared what they would be like when faced with defeat. And once the island of Saipan fell to the Americans in July, 1944, and Japan itself was for the first time open to long-range land-based bomber attacks, the seed of desperation had been sown. When the military leaders of Japan made it clear that the Philippines must be held at all costs, it blossomed into fearful flower. If the Philippines were lost to the Empire, it was said, the war too was lost and, impossible to accept, Japan's great Asian dream, and even perhaps Japan itself.

What would all this mean, Mother asked herself, when brought precisely to bear on the fate of American prisoners in the Philippines? She had no way of knowing.

Except for a few Maryknoll Sisters not restricted either for reasons of nationality or of health, all the others had been interned by Japanese authorities in the big Manila convent and college of the Sisters of the Assumption since January, 1942. In July of 1944, in an atmosphere of haste and secrecy, they were all moved, by covered trucks and by train, to Los Banos Camp, about a two and a half hours' drive south of Manila. They did not know what a fateful month July was proving for Japan. On the eighteenth, Japanese Premier Tojo had to admit the loss of Saipan to a stunned nation, schooled until then to believe in inevitable victory.

Even before July, however, some prescience of defeat affected the Japanese treatment of the people under their domination in the Philippines. Among the Filipinos a vast, amorphous but effective underground existed. The Japanese military police used increased surveillance and ruthless punishment in an effort to stamp it out. Even people who were dedicated only to secretly alleviating the sufferings of the vast number of half-starved, sick, and miserable military men in the prisoner-of-war camps were typed and treated as enemy agents. Sister Trinita Logue, the Regional Superior of the Maryknoll Sisters in the Philippines, was one of these.

In April, first she and then Sister Brigida were suddenly picked up without warning by military police and driven off to Fort Santiago, the dreaded prison in the old walled city where so-called political prisoners were held, interrogated, and tortured.

In the cool of that early July morning when her Sisters were being moved southward toward Los Banos, Sister Trinita too was not asleep. Taken out of the smothering press of stinking prisoners in the tiny humid cell, where she spent her days sitting upright on the stone floor with her face to the wall, she had been led away to be questioned once again.

For interrogated prisoners there was only one escape—the brief, all-too-brief, periods of unconsciousness into which they fell and from which they were drawn again by harsh voices and harsher pain.

Under the water torture it seemed like the depth of the sea in which one struggled—lungs agonizing, belly bursting, muscles writhing in unavailing effort. Sister Trinita would fight her way up, up, up to break the suffocating surface of the sea, to breathe again, to find life once more. At first she would hear someone close by choking and retching—and then, much farther off, it seemed, staccato voices conferring together.

Then—inside her ear? her brain?—came the familiar tones. *"Ano ne! Ano ne!"*

"You will tell us the names. . . ."

Momentarily her mind had a way of shrinking back into the safe shell of unconsciousness, shutting out fear, reality, the pain, the indignities, the relentless, sibilant questioning, "Who? Who? Who?"

But some sharp probe of wisdom or grace reached her even there. Without the aid of words or reasoning, she knew that those whose names she had locked away in her mind beyond speech and even thought would be safer if she who held the key went back on guard again. While she wandered in this near-death, her tongue might slip leash and form a name, any name. And so she returned once more to take up the weary burden of her identity, to recognize the retching and coughing as her own, to realize that she had escaped drowning not in God's good sea but bound down helpless on a prison bench under the play of a garden hose.

Yet she did not need to open her eyes, she did not need to let *them* know that she had returned, that she was accessible again. They would find out soon enough. Meanwhile she could get ready . . . get ready . . . that was her whole life's work now, to husband strength and sanity, to pray for the heart, the grace to meet the questioning. Torture itself was just another form of questioning which asked, "How much can you bear?" "How long can you endure?"

The odor of cigarettes reached her. The tired interrogators had been smoking.

A cigarette lasts such a short time.

"Tell us the name of another person who brought you short-wave news."

Another person! But she hadn't said anything, had she? Care . . . careful now. . . .

"I know no names to give."

"But you confessed that you received short-wave news. Didn't you?"

"I said that at times I heard things."

"What things?"

"They might be news. They might be rumors."

"So—you received short-wave news. You are a spy. Confess it!"

"No. No spy."

"You dare to lie to us! We know that you receive information from the United States and pass it along to Filipino guerrillas."

"If you know, why ask me?"

"Who gave you information?"

"It was common talk."

"Common talk! Common talk! Tell us one name."

"No name to tell you."

"Was it Ramon?"—"No." "José?"—"No." "Concepcion?"—"No." "What is your name?"—"No."

"No! What do you mean 'No'?"

"Besides the names you have already given us, who else is helping you to spy on the Imperial Army?"

"I have told you no names. There are no names."

"José has confessed that you told him about the submarine in the bay."

"Whoever José is, he is mistaken."

"You would not be in prison if you were not a spy, a criminal!"

(What logic! A criminal because in prison—in prison because a criminal.) Her mind hung on, followed after, doggedly, miraculously.

"What is your relationship with the traitor Escoda?"

"I know no traitors."

"You are a friend of Doctora Darby, *ne?*"

"I have heard of her."

" 'The goat has twins.' What does that mean?"

"To me—nothing."

"It was in a letter that we intercepted. Carried by a guerrilla courier. From Baguio. Addressed to you. What does it mean?"

"I never received the letter, but if it says that the goat had twins that is what it means."

"Who would write such nonsense! In wartime who would send word from Baguio to Manila by courier that 'the goat has twins'! Who would be interested in a goat and her twins!"

She almost smiled. "Sisters," she whispered.

"You think we are fools!"

"Show me the letter. Perhaps I can explain."

"Who are your contacts with Cabanatuan?"

"Since the war we Sisters have been interned in Assumption Convent. On April 11 this year I was brought here to prison. I have not been free to contact . . ."

"That is no answer. You sent messages to the American prisoners, *ne?*"

Of course, food is a kind of message. Medicine, too. And clothing. She said nothing.

"When did you stop sending messages?"

"You know that I went to your General and asked him to allow us to send food and medicines to the prisoners but he refused."

"You sent them anyhow, *ne?*"

"How could anyone do that? With Japanese soldiers on guard?"

"Who carried the messages that you sent to the prisoners?"

Her head moved wearily from side to side.

"Name one contact and we will let you go back to the cell and lie down with the other women."

She did not allow herself to think of that relief.

"How much longer can you stand this? We start at midnight. Now it is almost morning. Do you know how many days you have been here?"

"Seventy-eight."

"And some days we question you three, four times, *ne?* And we can do that again tomorrow and the day after and the day after that. And one day you will tell us everything. Tell us now and save yourself all this bad times."

"There is nothing to tell."

"We can put you again in that place where you spent the first night. You remember the man you found down there rotting away in the dark? You will rot away underground too and no one will know it."

The splash of water broke the silence. "Sometimes persons die under the water torture."

Terror. And the urgency to breathe, breathe deeply while she still could. The end of the hose pressed against her chin, the water covered her mouth, assaulted her nostrils.

"Wait," said one of the interrogators. "She said a name."

"It is nothing," said the other. "She says that all the time. Jesus is the name of her god."

Imprisoned and interrogated in the same way, Sister Brigida too kept her silence. Not so robust as Sister Trinita, she became so physically broken that in August the Japanese police, not wishing her to die, had her transferred to the Philippine General Hospital until she should recover sufficiently to be returned to prison. The Filipino doctors there never did—and never would—find her sufficiently recovered and she remained in the hospital until the war's end.

Just as in the Philippines, so in China, too, the changing character of the war brought no immediate relief to the people. However effective the two-pronged American offensive against the perimeter of islands defending Japan, the thrust of the Imperial armies gained momentum in China's southwest during the summer and fall. The obvious objective was to overrun the airfields held and used by the Americans, to capture Chungking, Chiang Kai-shek's war capital, and to knock out Kunming, the base for incoming American supplies flown over the Himalayas and soon, it was hoped, to be the depot for increased material hauled over a completed Burma road.

All through the summer, all through the fall, well into December, thousands and thousands of uprooted Chinese fled before the Japanese advance. On foot in endless disorderly battalions; crowded into carts and the all-too-few dilapidated trucks; clinging like ants to ancient trains—some of which just went on and on until the hastily laid tracks simply petered out— they had gone, it would seem, as far as human resources could take them. Sometimes at temporary bases along their way they would find Maryknollers, priests and Sisters, who gave them what food and medicine they had, tended their sick, their dying, and gave heart to the living. Sometimes the missioners had no choice but to move along with them, doing whatever they could to help those in worse case than themselves and suffering the hardships which none could escape.

Then all at once, as this wave of homeless and helpless people neared, it would seem, the very rim of the world, when nothing apparently stood in the way of the Japanese advance, the thrust of the Japanese army stopped and began to shrink back upon itself. The refugees waiting in box cars and improvised camps along the road, straggling over hills and valleys hundreds of miles from home, found that they did not have to run anymore. Those who had moved with them did not have to run anymore either. Some Maryknoll priests had had to hide in the hills, some Maryknoll Sisters had had to go over the Himalayas into India, but some were still there with the refugees and were, they thought, welded more closely than ever to their beloved people through shared sorrow and travail.

As Mother put together as well as she could the picture puzzle of the distant war and followed the movements of those minute figures—her Sisters—borne along on the tide of homeless millions in China, she was equally alive to the suffering created by war even in the security at home. If her American daughters had been taken for enemy aliens in the Japanese Empire, so were her Japanese daughters apt to be looked upon as enemy aliens in the United States. That summer Mother and Sister Columba, always her second in such enterprises, arranged for and prepared a Japanese dinner for the Japanese Sisters then at Maryknoll. It was an expression of the heart more potent than many words.

She also took the responsibility for having Mr. Kado, an up-rooted California landscape gardener, remain at Maryknoll for the war's duration, working at the craft he loved so well and making a home for himself and his family until he could return to California. For this, he repaid her a thousandfold, building a beautiful replica of the Lourdes shrine in the natural rock near the Motherhouse and transforming the grounds into lasting beauty with rock and shrub arrangements.

That summer she took an active part in the Catholic Rural Conference held at Maryknoll, sent two Sisters to visit Mexico in lay clothing to assess conditions and possible opportunities there, and, in September, welcomed the largest group of recruits ever to enter her community. In October she entered Lahey Clinic in Boston for a series of dilations to relieve an esophageal hernia which had become acute.

Meanwhile, the sixteen hundred internees at Los Banos Camp in the Philippines found conditions there worsening. On arrival, the five hundred religious rounded up in July had been housed like the earlier arrivals in suwali-walled, nipa-roofed barracks. These were surrounded by a bamboo fence topped with eight well-staffed guardhouses. The internees were not interrogated or tortured, they were permitted to have gatherings, to hold religious services, to transform one of their barracks into a chapel. All over fourteen years old contributed a minimum of two work hours a day to the maintenance of the group—collecting wood, making fires, cooking, gardening, while this was still permitted, and making brooms, stools, cleaning up the grounds, burying the dead.

Each had a bed, little privacy, little comfort. At the start, they had enough food to maintain them. As the weeks went on, this was continually scaled down. The internees could almost divine the progress of Japanese reverses from the reduction in rations. American air attacks on Japanese bases in the Philippines began and increased during September. On October 1, with rations already unbelievably light, the midday rice gruel was discontinued.

By Christmas, the internees' plight was desperate. They looked at one another—yellow, dwindling bodies more and more evident in worn-out clothing—and knew that they could not hold out much longer. The children, all mouths and eyes like small unfeathered birds, wrung the heart. The sick increased. Scarcely a day passed without at least one death. The Jesuit scholastics who dug the graves were so weak that they had all they could do to keep from falling flat into the shallow holes over which they labored.

Into this colony of scarecrows a fragile but indomitable figure was suddenly introduced by the Japanese guards on New Year's Day. She had arrived—the only woman—on a crowded Japanese troop train from Manila. Covered with sores, with sunken eyes, unbelievably small—reduced to seventy-eight pounds from her ordinary weight of a hundred and sixty—she was able to walk, to smile, to put up her arms to embrace her Sisters. She knew what date it was, had kept track of the days somehow in the nightmare of her imprisonment. Clear-headed and composed, Sister Trinita was back with her Sisters once more, released at last—she did not know how or why—from Fort Santiago. Perhaps she had just come to die with the rest, but she was glad to be there and they were overjoyed to see her alive. No name had yet escaped her lips.

Just about a week later, American forces, having already taken the island of Leyte, landed on Luzon and began to move toward Manila, where Japanese supplies and manpower were concentrated.

On February 4, Mother told the Sisters at the Motherhouse that radio broadcasts were reporting that Manila had been taken. The Sisters could, if they wished, stay up until midnight to hear more news as it came in. Nothing yet, of course, would probably be heard about the Sisters. Sister Luke, Sister Trinita's blood sister and herself a prisoner of war exchange from Manchuria a year earlier, was among those who huddled around the news-gorged radio which gave them, however, no information about Maryknoll Sisters. On February 16, Bataan was said to have been retaken. On the twenty-first a form letter from relief headquarters in the Philippines arrived to give assurance that liberated internees were receiving the best possible care. And still there was no word of the fifty-three Sisters. Then on February 28, the *Herald Tribune* reported that fifty-two Maryknoll Sisters had been released from camp. On March 13, a letter from Sister Trinita arrived at Maryknoll reporting forty-three Sisters well and safe and together. What did these figures mean?

During this period, Mother celebrated with the Motherhouse community their twenty-fifth jubilee as a religious community, saying "Today we are a strong, vigorous religious body with far-flung missions. We see much of our work built up through years of toil and hardship and at great cost, now apparently in ruin. God alone knows why this is so, as He alone knows why we are now tilling the soil in new mission fields." She gave, as was her custom, the yearly retreat for the first-year novices—six days in which she devoted herself to talking over with them the meaning of their vocation, the nature and work of their religious Sisterhood, the characteristics which their life demanded. Her brother John died and she quietly disappeared for a few days to attend the funeral and be with her family. Only two of the five brothers whom she had loved so well now remained. In her anxiety she did not often refer to the lack of news or the contradictory reports about the Sisters in the Philippines, did not allude to her concern for them. Yet those who knew her well thought that she was at this time as nearly restless as she could become.

By the middle of March, however, letters from individual Sisters began to come in. They brought comforting and thrilling accounts of their wonderful rescue from Los Banos on February 23. Since the beginning of that month, they had hoped and prayed for rescue but had also tried to be ready for death. If they did not starve—and not a few internees had already died and many more were now ill from malnutrition—would the Japanese guards, if forced to withdraw, ever let them all go free? To many it seemed unlikely.

Then suddenly in the early morning of February 23, Filipino guerrillas and American infantry broke from the woods and American paratroopers dropped from the sky in a single perfectly synchronized operation. They fell upon the camp simultaneously, the guards had no time to return their fire, and it was all over in a matter of minutes. Not one life was lost among the hundreds of internees. As the flimsy prison roared into high flames behind them, the soldiers loaded the rescued into amtracks and took them off, under sniper fire, across the blue waters of Laguna de Bay, toward safety and freedom.

Behind lay hunger and harassment, uncertainty and fear. Ahead and all around and fair to see was the beautiful Philippine countryside—the world—which God had made and found good. The Sisters looked at it with new eyes. They could appreciate it as never before. They would serve its people once again. This liberation was like being created afresh, Adam-like, full-grown and wise enough to know one's wealth. Their hearts leaped up to meet whatever lay ahead. The soldiers thought them a game and cheerful lot.

In Manila, Sister Brigida as well as Sister Concepcion and Sister Claver, both Filipinas and therefore not interned, had survived the terrific bombing and shelling and demolitions and house-to-house fighting that had left the beautiful city a smoking shambles.

In those terrible last days, sixteen thousand Japanese had died and had taken with them, in addition to many of their armed foes, unnumbered Filipino noncombatants.

Like two small ghosts among many others, the two Filipina Sisters had moved for days through the smoke-filled, shuddering city. Sometimes they ran, outracing the fires; sometimes they lay sheltered from mortar fire behind a garden wall; sometimes they inched prone across a littered highway under the rake of machine-gun fire; sometimes they found a home not yet destroyed where they gave or received help.

Even after Manila was retaken, small detachments of Japanese held out in the mountains north of the city. Preparatory to landing in Lingayen Gulf, the Americans had bombed Baguio. Two Maryknoll Sisters who had been ill with lung infections, Sister Hyacinth of Brooklyn and Sister Carmencita of the Philippines, had been allowed by the Japanese authorities to remain there in their mountain convent during the war, together with a third, Sister Una, of Irish birth. After the bombings began, these three left Baguio and went to an Igorot village about seven miles away; then when the village itself was bombed, they moved to some nearby caves. Advised that the bombings were to be stepped up in that area, they joined a column of about five hundred refugees who had made up their minds to risk passing through the scattered Japanese units in the mountains in order to reach safety behind the American lines.

Led by native guides sent to them by the United States military, they set out on Easter Sunday. Between then and the following Friday, when they reached Tubao, they traversed a series of mountain ranges, line after line of giant ridges, rugged and dangerous country, making their painful way over rock tumbles, up and down single-track zigzags penciled on the vertiginous heights, through mountain torrents, along volcanic cliffs. Somehow, unbelievably, on the third day of the journey, companioned by her Sisters, surrounded by acquaintances, Sister Hyacinth simply disappeared.

She had dropped out of her place in the column to rest, as many did on the long trek, but when those who had been behind her came up to join those who had been ahead—no one had seen her. And no one ever saw her again. Filipino Gregorio immediately hurried back over the trail and returned hours later without her, went back a second time all the way to the place where she was last seen, and again returned alone. The Sisters waited. The whole column delayed overnight. The next morning Gregorio and a guide went back over the trail again without avail. The five hundred people could wait no longer. The greater the delay, the greater the danger.

A trail branched off near the place where Sister Hyacinth had last been seen. It was hoped that she and some others had taken it and would meet them all where the trails rejoined. Here they waited again fruitlessly and went on once more.

At Tubao, within the American lines, after the main body of the group arrived, others straggled in over several days, but Sister Hyacinth was not among them. Igorot runners, familiar as no one else with their own country, went back and forth over the trails—and brought no news. Over the weeks, the months, the years, every search, every inquiry, yielded no single fact. At last even the torment of rumors died away and the mountains keep their silence even until now.

That May, when she welcomed twenty-one of her Sisters home on temporary leave from the Philippines, there remained for Mother this sorrow and mystery, although at that time she had not yet given up hope. Nevertheless, her happiness was great at having so many for whom she had feared so much home safe again. She planned to have all the fifty-two return in time for leave in the United States, but for the present those who were physically more fit—or thought they were—stayed behind to begin again the works which the war had disrupted. In Manila, St. Mary's Hall had been burnt to the ground and the site of St. Paul's Hospital could not even be located in the mammoth rubble heap that had been the walled city; but elsewhere outside the city denuded school buildings were still standing and the Sisters went back to them, found old friends and new pupils and the willing, helping hands of a courageous and resilient people.

Those who returned to the Motherhouse, although they had already enjoyed two months of good food and kind treatment, still looked like wraiths to Mother. She could read in their thin and colorless faces the deprivations about which they only joked. She knew too that there must be scars and wounds which did not show. She was familiar with the country around Manila. She could imagine what it was like to be penned up for months in a stockade of starving people in a green and beautiful country where bananas and cocoanuts grow without being asked and great dark mango trees laden with fruit line the nearby roads. Even in the early morning to hear the roosters crowing near at hand would be just another reminder that people nearby had chickens and eggs and rice to eat while the starving body cried for food and the mind became obsessed with thoughts of it.

The Sisters told her how they and the other ex-prisoners had astounded the troops at the American camp at Muntinlupa, where they were taken after the rescue. Catching sight of a disposal area near the commissary, some of them ran to it as to a treasure trove. "Tin cans! Tin cans!"

"What do you want with that junk?" the soldiers wanted to know.

Junk! The ex-prisoners were as astonished as the soldiers. Out of such carefully scrounged junk they had made all sorts of necessaries—cups, plates, cooking utensils, stoves, and other priceless conveniences. And they had had to leave these marvels behind them in the burning camp.

"Isn't it all right to take them?"

"Well . . . sure," said the perplexed soldiers. But they were visibly relieved as the days passed and the run on tin cans came to a halt.

What better now for these Sisters so long deprived of sufficient food, so long under strict prison discipline—standing in endless lines for everything, answering roll call, forbidden to do this and that and the other—and under the more punishing necessity of playing down their own nerves and hunger for the sake of others, than to feel that now they were truly home and everything was theirs. And so Mother put aside for them the convent rules of regularity and silence. They were, she told them, welcome to eat what they wanted when they wanted it, to rest when their bodies asked for it, to talk when they had the inclination.

In the weeks that followed she watched with satisfaction how they all began to look more and more like the Sisters whom she remembered. At the end of a month, she felt that they were ready to visit their homes and that their looks would no longer wring the hearts of their families as they had wrung hers.

Summer came and with August the war's end. Even in the sorrow and shambles of its aftermath, a great hope for the future arose in the hearts of Maryknollers. What prospects lay ahead! Buildings might be destroyed, equipment gone, works disrupted, but Mother was conscious of the fact that the Sisters felt more than ever at one with their people. Like them, she believed a new day was dawning and looked forward to meeting it with them.

In South China particularly a climate seemed prepared in which the faith could grow, the Church take native root, the Christian life be embraced and realized as never before. Bishops, priests, Brothers, and Sisters were all sure of it. Maryknoll's

Field Afar was alight with optimism. Maryknoll's Father General, Bishop James E. Walsh, spoke of the days of fulfillment that lay ahead. Bishop Ford began to plan the Kaying cathedral of which he had long dreamed. Everywhere there was a sense of revival and rededication. Maryknollers returned to looted and leveled missions with high hearts.

In the north, of course, there was still some trouble—with the Communists.

--⊰ **CHAPTER 10** ⊱--

AGAIN SEED TIME

I T WAS January 2, 1947. The big chapel at the Motherhouse was
filled with more than its usual complement of Sisters. Delegates to the summer Chapter of 1946 had been re-called and had
returned to Maryknoll. Sitting at the back, Mother could see the
long rows of women who were to her both Sisters and daughters.
They stretched away like a bridge from her to the sanctuary,
like a link between herself and God.

Turned from her toward the altar were the tempered, the
familiar, the especially cherished faces of those who had companioned her from Maryknoll's beginning and the mature, dependable faces of those who carried with her in one degree or
another the burdens of administration. In far greater numbers
were the lively faces of the more recent arrivals, faces on which
life had written as yet only with the clear lines of youth and of
hope. And here and there among the others were faces still
whitened from long months of imprisonment and near-starva-
tion.

"This is the day which the Lord hath made," said Mother,

giving the theme of the meditation which she had chosen for that day. "Let us rejoice and be glad therein."

Her beautifully modulated voice was still capable of reaching the farthest corner of the chapel with ease, and the Sisters felt anew its power to strengthen and uplift them.

" . . . every day in which we die to self and live unto Christ is a day of jubilation for us. Today is such a one."

It was characteristic of her to overlook all the intermediate, the human elements, events, agents, circumstances, and mysteries which had gone into the making of this day and to see only the hand of the good God in its shaping.

The previous July at the General Chapter of her Sisterhood, she had again been chosen as its Mother General. As instructed by Monsignor Joseph Nelson, attending the election as the representative of the Cardinal, the delegates had cast their ballots in the form of a postulation, since the law of the Church limits a Mother General's consecutive terms of office to two. However, since Mother Mary Joseph was their foundress and had already served more terms than that without any question being raised, the delegates expected the postulation to be granted. True, she had had many illnesses and that spring had been so gravely sick that it was thought wise to notify her family; but as soon as she rallied, she was on the march again and had always at her right hand Sister Columba to share her burdens and forward her undertakings. And in recent weeks she had been exceptionally well and her easy grasp of every matter discussed at the Chapter had been striking.

The postulation then had to await ecclesiastical confirmation. The ordinary gesture of acceptance and fealty to a newly elected Mother General was not made. No long gray line formed to go up, kneel, place their hands in those of the newly elected Mother General and kiss her small silver *chi-rho* ring. Weeks and then months passed and no confirmation of the election came. The Chapter delegates, except those from the Far East, went back to their missions. Finally those from the most distant missions set out.

Then on the first Sunday of Advent Mother called the Sisters together to talk to them, speaking first of St. John the Baptist, about whom Maryknoll's Father Founder had always loved to talk at this time of the year. Mother spoke, as Bishop James Anthony used to do, of the special significance of this saint for those with a missionary vocation. "He must increase. I must decrease."

Then she continued in the same normal tones, saying, "Now there is a gift we are each to present to the Christ Child this year. Yesterday the Cardinal sent for me to speak about the postulation. He said he knows it will not be granted . . . and so he advised me very kindly, and with consideration of all our interests, to refuse the election and call an elective chapter. This, of course, I will do, for an opinion of this kind should be law to us, who are subject to authority. . . .

"I was twenty-eight when I came to Maryknoll and now I am sixty-four; that means that for some thirty-six years I have borne —gladly, I assure you—the heavy burden of responsibility. Now God has apparently blessed me with renewed health in order that I may serve you in some new way. I ask you all to do nothing more in this matter but to look upon it as God's will for our community, which He has fostered and cherished so evidently over all these years."

She went on to tell the Sisters what the Cardinal had said was to be her position and title in the community, noticing that by now many were quietly crying but, out of consideration for her, were trying to look as if they were not.

As was her way, she reached out to comfort them. "And so, my very dear Sisters, we ought to face this change with joy in doing God's will, and there should be no sadness in our hearts. I make bold to say, however, that my sacrifice is greater than yours, as I believe my love for you surpasses all possible knowledge that you could have of it. It has been an inexpressible joy to serve you, and I shall be endlessly and boundlessly grateful to you for your love, for your devotion, for your loyalty, and for your self-sacrificing co-operation over the years."

And now, a month later, with the chapter delegates reassembled for the election, she spoke to them and to all the Sisters at the Motherhouse, glancing back at the past only to be grateful for it and to give meaning to the present and direction to the future. "God has yet a great work for us to do. . . . Do we love enough, do we work enough, do we pray enough, do we suffer enough? Maryknoll's future depends on our answer.

"These have been lovely years in which we have worked together, and my heart will always sing its hymn of gratitude to you for your patience, your faithfulness, and your love, and to God for having given us each other in this glorious work for the extension of His kingdom."

Later that morning when Sister Columba had been elected and then asked by the Cardinal's representative if she accepted the election, she stood for a moment facing the delegates without saying anything, her lips trembling and her eyes fastened on Mother Mary Joseph with entreaty, apology, and sorrow.

"Take it, take it," said Mother audibly, urgently. And when the obeisances to the new Mother General were made, she was the first to make hers.

Mother Mary Joseph herself sent out the notices of the election. In a letter following she said, "God has blessed us in our new Mother General—Mother Mary Columba. Knowing Mother Mary Columba's character intimately as I do, I am content to leave you to her loving prayerful solicitude and her wise devoted care. And that says much of my confidence in her, loving you as I do."

From that time on, in the days, the weeks, the months, and the years that followed, she took every occasion to show her satisfaction with the election and her happiness at having

Mother Mary Columba at the head of the congregation. The Sisters had said of her successor, "She knows Mother's mind. She thinks like Mother." Mother herself had much higher praise than that. She said that Sister Columba had been closely associated with Maryknoll's Founder and knew his mind.

Entirely practical, Mother realized that a transfer of authority is accomplished more quickly and more smoothly if the former incumbent is no longer available. Long habit and the ties of affection would be apt to bring Sisters to her for opinions and decisions which should be asked of the new Mother General. She had made up her mind early—to go for a while to one of the Maryknoll Sisters' few houses in the United States—and carried out her decision in spite of persuasion and protest. To those who would have it otherwise she would say, "Yes, I'm going away for a while. I'll be back. But it's better for me to be away for a while. Yes, I know you'll miss me and I'll miss you, too. And I'll be back. This is my home. But for now, it's better for me to go away."

By February 11, she was gone.

For several years the growth of the community had made plain the necessity of expansion either at the Motherhouse or elsewhere. It had been finally decided that a novitiate somewhere else would be the best solution, and a one-time children's hospital about twenty miles southwest of St. Louis was purchased. It had been empty for over a year, the owners were glad to get it off their hands, and the price, as a result, could be managed.

Although the search for such a site had been going on for more than a year, the opening of the new novitiate away from the Motherhouse would be the first major move of the new Mother General as well as a new phase of the community's development. Some of the Sisters were anxious. So far away from the center, would these novices turn out to be real Maryknoll Sisters? Would they have and keep the Maryknoll spirit? Would

not the family ties which Mother Mary Joseph had done so
much to strengthen become relaxed? Of course, the Motherhouse was loaded beyond its capacity already, and if the growth
in numbers increased . . . but still . . .

From the convent in Monrovia, California, where she was
staying, Mother Mary Joseph wrote a circular letter that summer in which she included several paragraphs on the new venture.

"The pitch of interest now centers in the new novitiate plans.
Mother Mary Columba sent us a set of pictures which give us a
fine idea of the new property. We know what tremendous problems are involved and what expense, and we are giving the new
project our prayerful support.

"This step is perhaps the most important in our history,
touching as it does our very life stream. Some Sisters are appre-
hensive about the move, fearing the loss of our unity. I think
this is a needless anxiety. The Religious of the Sacred Heart, the
Sisters of the Assumption, the Sisters of Charity, the Franciscan
Missionaries of Mary, the Little Sisters of the Poor, and many
other communities have novitiates in many parts of the world
and each has kept its spirit. And ours, too, if it is real, will
remain. . . .

"It is for you and for me to preserve this spirit. We alone can
lose it. So we should not fear but rejoice that new branches are
sprouting from which we have a right, as did the Master of the
vineyard, to expect good fruit."

And when the new Novitiate opened, she was there, as she
wanted to be, as everyone wanted to have her. Arriving the day
before the formal opening on October 7, 1947, her heart went
out to it. It spoke to her of the past—another beginning of years
ago—and of the future, in which she would share, but in a
changed and changing way.

She loved it—from the obviously temporary sign that hung at
the entrance and announced that here was "Our Lady of Mary-

knoll Novitiate" to the beautiful but still frowzy grounds and the architectural wonderland of the building itself.

She looked at the large empty rooms and saw not how unready they still were for occupation but how incredibly clean they had been made after long neglect. She went into the chapel and was not concerned to find that it had just been emptied of carpenters, plumbers, and floormen, but was delighted to discover that Maryknoll's Father Early and a group of Maryknoll students had moved in to clean the floors and windows just as the workmen were easing out. It did not bother her that the promised chairs and prie-dieus for the chapel had not arrived. Tomorrow's Mass would be said in this lovely, suitable place on a simple but beautiful altar now waiting for that great event.

She noticed that under the glow of welcome and excitement, Mother Mary Columba and the few Sisters who had been working with her for several weeks on the building looked tired. She knew all about cleaning old buildings, shopping for necessities on limited funds, cooking meals while trying to meet the demanding present and to plan for the onrushing future.

"You have done wonders," she said, "wonders!"

She was brought to her own quarters—two rooms which had once been the hospital supervisor's. These had a lovely view of the Meramec Valley and were completely finished and furnished —a little haven of order and beauty in the great workshop that was the rest of the building. Here was just another message spoken in a language that any woman would understand and a mother could most appreciate, "Here, too, is your home. How glad we are that you have come. How happy we are that you are here with us."

The next morning was one of unmixed happiness. Archbishop Ritter, who had come to offer the first Mass, gave a little talk in which he recalled that October 7 was the anniversary of his arrival in St. Louis and that he looked upon this new house as an anniversary present to him from God. Without being asked, he blessed the building and, together with Monsignor Helmsing and Father Martin of Maryknoll, who had accompanied him, stayed to breakfast with the Sisters. As the two Mothers led the little party to the refectory at a leisurely pace, the Sisters carried the chairs from the chapel to the refectory by an outside route—so that all might sit down at table together.

In the afternoon, visitors were treated to a view of a Novitiate in the making—as the Sisters guided the hundreds who came through the building, they could see and hear plumbers and electricians and carpenters still at work. The ear-splitting rattle of pneumatic drills and the thud of sledge hammers on concrete punctuated conversation. Different phases of development were on display—a small dormitory just begun, two large dormitories half done, and the guest rooms, thanks to the gifts and loans of many kind friends, nearly finished.

The talk given by Bishop Cody before Benediction was no less appreciated because those attending sat on whatever chairs could be rounded up from house and grounds—large chairs and small chairs, lawn chairs and rustic benches, new armchairs and elderly rockers. Seated near Mother at the back of chapel waiting for the ceremony to begin, one little old lady could not have looked more at home in her Father's house as she bobbed back and forth in an old-fashioned rocker and told her beads.

As the celebrant, the deacon and the sub-deacon came out of the sacristy to stand before the altar in the beautiful gold vestments lent by the pastor of the Cathedral—they were a reminder that the whole day was a medley of a thousand kindnesses. The only thing in the chapel that the Sisters could call their own— besides the altar and unenviable motley of chairs—was a single sacred vessel given by Archbishop Cushing of Boston. Everything else had been brought there by willing and generous hands to meet the day's need.

By the middle of the month, Mother Mary Columba had to return to the Motherhouse. Mother Mary Joseph, together with

Sister James, who had come with her, stayed on. The first group of postulants were expected at the month's end. The work went forward. Mother appointed herself refectory reader and occasionally went into the kitchen to prepare a meal with the excuse that she had a recipe that she wanted to try out. She always produced a treat, for she was still an excellent cook. She celebrated her birthday by preparing the breakfast.

Among the tasks remaining to be done, chests of drawers for the new arrivals had to be assembled and then stained. Mother was no apprentice with a paint brush.

"I'll be head of the drawers," she said. She made a long porch her workshop and when any passing Maryknoll Sister arrived to see the new Novitiate and to visit with her, she immediately invited the newcomer to join her union.

As the drawers were put together and stacked around her, she groaned good-naturedly, "Where are they coming from? I feel like I have done hundreds of these things."

"Well, Mother," somebody answered, "maybe you have. There are sixty chests and each has five drawers."

Girls from St. Joseph's High School, St. Louis, came to unpack and wash stacks of dishes, glasses, pitchers, coffeepots. Faithful friends from St. Louis arrived to hem what seemed acres of dormitory curtains. Women and girls from Valley Park's Catholic parish came on the scene the day before the new arrivals were due to make their beds. Even at that, all could not be ready. Among other things, due to difficulties met in converting fixtures for a children's hospital into facilities for adults, there would be normal bathroom accommodations for about sixteen people. The new postulants would have to start their convent life by getting up in staggered shifts.

Mother did not think these inconveniences were entirely regrettable. For many years and in many circumstances, she had watched human nature rise to an occasion. She expected to see it again.

On October 30 and 31, the girls arrived. Seeing them, Mother felt again the wonder and admiration and amusement which raw recruits like these always evoked in her. Most were emotionally worn out by a succession of good-bys, tired from lack of sleep, dazed with their new surroundings. She saw in them the wonderful working of God's grace and the generous response of youthful hearts. On their part they noticed on their way to supper that first night that somebody large and kind called Mother—they weren't sure just who she was or why she was called that—gave them a memorable welcome.

Until their arrival, the weather had been glorious, one day of soft October sunshine after the other, but then it began to rain. It rained much, it rained often. If homesickness has a climate, this was it. Mother invited these new postulants to drop in to see her whenever they were free, and especially if they felt homesick. They did, in threes and fours, sixes and sevens, sometimes in dozens. Sitting on her chairs, window seats and floor, they played her records, read her newspapers, listened to the football games which she turned on for them on the radio, emptied boxes of candy which she had on hand for them, argued with one another, and let her have the benefit of their views on life. But they listened to her, too, and drank her in thirstily, not quite appreciating what she was but knowing that they felt most at home with her and, surprisingly, too, most closely knit to their new life.

When the weather cleared, she had hundreds of bulbs for them to plant. They ranged out over the property with bags of potential narcissus, tulips, crocuses, and lilies, confident that they were going to leave their mark on this place in more ways than one.

Mother was a faithful and appreciative audience at their entertainments, both improvised and prepared. They had no costumes, no stage, no scenery, but they had plenty of ideas and

Mother's blessing on initiative—a magic formula which they invoked whenever they had gone too far in any direction.

From smaller successes, they looked toward bigger things. With Thanksgiving coming up, they suggested that they take charge of the day—preparing and serving meals, decorating the refectory—doing just everything that had to be done without benefit of, or interference from, professed Sisters. Their offer was accepted.

The day before Thanksgiving, Mother was returning from St. Louis along a country road that led to the front gate of the Novitiate. Suddenly the Sister driving her said, "Do you see what I see?"

Mother looked. Down the road ahead of them, coming out of a neighboring farmer's field of autumnal corn stacks, were three stooping girls dressed in black. On their backs each carried as many cornstalks as she could manage and, turning, trotted lightly—both physically and conscience-wise—under the load toward the Novitiate.

"Decorations," said the Sister. "A Thanksgiving surprise. For us. And the farmer."

"Slow down," said Mother. "Don't pass them. We might embarrass them." She laughed. "Let's just park here until they get out of the way."

The Thanksgiving dinner the next day was well cooked, nicely served, and realistically decorated. The *pièce de résistance* was a real corn stack in one corner of the refectory.

"Where in the world do you suppose they got that?" someone wondered.

"I might tell you," said Mother with a smile, but she did not.

One evening after an impromptu show during which a postulant had given a robust imitation of Al Jolson singing "Maa-a-a-my," two others got into an argument over his singing style. One was all for it, one all against. Each had plenty to say and said it over Mother, who sat between them, taking it all in.

"What do you think, Mother?" appealed one, trying to enlist a champion on her side.

"Well," said Mother mildly, "I think it's just a matter of taste, and tastes differ and everybody has a right to his own. For myself, I don't care much for Al Jolson."

The postulant who cared not at all for Al Jolson sprang up and thrust out her hand. "Shake on that, Mother," she said. "Shake."

The dark eyes of Sister Consolata, the mistress of postulants, had become darker. " 'Shake, Mother Foundress, shake,' " she quoted. "Now I have seen everything."

If the Christmas Mass was to be sung, the postulants were going to have to sing it. They worked hard to discipline their croony voices to the Gregorian chant but were plainly at their best with popular songs. Mother came along one day when some were rehearsing around the old piano left behind by the hospital staff.

"What do you think, Mother? How do we sound?"

"Aren't you a little off pitch?" asked Mother.

"Ye gods," said one. "Even Mother can tell we're flat."

Mother made a rueful face. "I like that," she said, "even Mother—"

"Oh, I didn't mean it that way, Mother. What I meant to say is that if you say so, we must be pretty hopeless."

They were beginning to know her.

Christmas came and they did sing the Christmas Mass and Sister James, the community's best organist, accompanied them on the small newly installed electric organ. No one would mistake them for the monks of Solesmes, but for the most part they were on pitch and they began and finished together.

With the new year, the plumbers, still at work under the house and in the house, observed that the girls sure sang a lot better now than they did at first.

By this time, most of the other workmen had finished and

gone, and classes could be held with some regularity. Mother gave the postulants a series of talks in which she told them the story of Maryknoll, detailing in particular the early days, since precious few now remained to tell that part of the tale. One evening she showed them slides of that period, making a running commentary on them. She did not mind when the girls laughed at the quaint-looking people who first inhabited Maryknoll and laughed with them at the evolution through which the Maryknoll habit had passed.

When she left for the Motherhouse in February, these new additions to her Sisterhood were fully aware that she knew them well, that they were dear to her, and that she was convinced great things could be expected of them. She promised to be back with them in May for their reception of the habit. And standing around the car, more moved than they cared to show, they sang her away—on pitch.

During the next few years, Mother was sometimes at the Motherhouse, sometimes at the new Novitiate at Valley Park, and sometimes at Maryknoll convents in California or in the Hawaiian Islands. She continued to give retreats to the Motherhouse novices near the close of their first year of novitiate and began doing the same for those at Valley Park. She was on call too for the professed Sisters and went in the summer of 1948 to Hawaii to give retreats to the Sisters there. From the Regional Superior, Sister Mary de Paul Cogan, who had been especially close to Mother ever since she entered Maryknoll in the early twenties, to the youngest professed Sisters, they were delighted to have her and made use of this opportunity to be with her, to draw her out about Maryknoll's past, present, and future. This she summed up by saying, "I'm getting to be a regular old gossip."

Those who had not had an opportunity to get to know her at the big Motherhouse often made good their loss during these stays in various houses. They found nothing of the "old lady" in their aging Mother Foundress. She did not live in the past, but in today and tomorrow. She was as much at home with the younger Sisters as the older and, as always, made everybody feel completely themselves in her company.

She was sometimes ill, sometimes well. But wherever she was or however she was, she seemed, now that she no longer carried the over-all direction of the community and its works, to concentrate more than ever on the individual. Partly because of this, partly because of illness and perhaps, too, partly because of some reluctance that she did not express, she did not get to some tasks that she was constantly being urged to do—writing of the beginnings of Maryknoll, of Maryknoll's Founders, the story of her own vocation. Evidently, she found this telling less important than the people who absorbed her time in one house or another.

Wherever she might be staying, she was never out of touch with what was happening elsewhere. Mother Mary Columba kept her informed about community affairs and consulted her about many major decisions. The Sisters wrote to her from the missions and she replied in circular letters and personal notes, Sister James helping her with her considerable correspondence.

Very early after the war ended in August, 1945, she had become aware of the ominous situation shaping up in the Far East. The last-minute entry of Russia into the war against Japan; the penetration of Korea by Communists, both Russian and North Korean; the hastily arranged division of that country at the thirty-eighth parallel; the overrunning of Manchuria by Russian troops; all these hinted at greater catastrophes to come. What these events signified was spelled out for her in the lives of those whom she loved. Sometimes she read their stories in letters that reached her months after what had taken place. Sometimes she was told them in conversations several years later. And she did not always learn the way the story ended.

Maryknoll's Sister Agneta Chang belonged to a Korean family

to become illustrious for their services and sufferings both for their country and for their faith. She had remained in her homeland all during the war in charge of a new community of Korean Sisters just coming of age under the direction of the Maryknoll Sisters. Since the interned American Sisters had been returned to the United States in the exchange arrangements of 1942 and 1943, she had had no contact with Maryknoll. After the division of Korea at the thirty-eighth parallel, she found herself in the Russian-administered sector.

In March of 1946 a letter from her finally reached Mother Mary Joseph five months after it had been written. It told the beginning of a story that was to end all too soon.

> Under the Soviet Military administration, we live in a constant terror, especially all women do.
>
> On August 30, a truck drew near to our back door and before we knew it, five of the Russian soldiers were in the house going through every room. Not knowing the language, they made signs, guns and swords pointed to our chests. They were in the house about half an hour. None of us was hurt in any way. However, the purpose of their visit was clearly seen, and in order to avoid the immediate danger, all of us, eighteen in number, left for Peng Yang in secular clothes. But even there it was not safe and finally I had to send all the novices and postulants home temporarily. And the professed Sisters were dispersed among the Christian families. . . .

She went on to recount how later they were able to come back together again and to live hidden behind locked doors, with lights covered at night, listening to the Russians who came to try the doors, go away, and return again and yet again.

One October night in 1950 another Communist vehicle drove up to the house where, ill and in hiding, Sister Agneta had taken refuge. Hard-eyed North Korean Communists tramped into the house and demanded that she come with them at once. No time to dress. No time to take anything with her.

As her stricken friends watched helplessly, she was hustled

out alone and hoisted into a waiting ox cart. They heard her say, "O Lord, have mercy on me!" Then the ox cart creaked away down the rutted road into the dark, into the night. Where it went, no one knew. It took Sister Agneta into oblivion. The terrible silence of her disappearance was soon broken by more terrible rumors: she had been murdered that night, the next day, her body was buried in a mass grave with other victims of Communist hatred.

Mother wrote her own ending to this unfinished story. "Sister Agneta, we are sure, is with God." Beneath this calm statement was a depth of feeling, for Mother felt this death keenly, especially in the light of the lonely appeal in Sister Agneta's last letter: "Mother, how I wish to talk to you directly. . . . I would like to tell you many more things—in fact there is no end . . . but I must stop now and hope God will grant me the opportunity of talking to you directly."

Not only in Korea did the Russian military bring terror when they arrived. Five Maryknoll Sisters—three Japanese, one Korean, and one with German citizenship—were in the port city of Dairen, Manchuria, when the Japanese surrendered on August 14. They were there when the Russians approached the city on August 27. Two hundred and fifty miles to the north, the ancient Manchu capital and modern rail center of Mukden had already fallen. Before the Japanese broadcast fell silent there, it managed to communicate to Dairen what it meant to be in the hands of the victorious Russian soldiery.

As a consequence, on August 27, Dairen was playing dead. Around the circular sweep of Ohiroba Plaza and down every long avenue radiating from it, not a car or a cart, not a man, not a woman, not a child, not even one investigative boy could be seen in any direction. Standing on the roof garden of the proud Yamato Hotel and looking over the city, you would have thought it deserted. But it was tenanted. It was alive. You had only to listen and you could hear the drumming of its heart, the drumming of its fear, along its every artery, every vein, every capillary. All over the city hidden people were hammering, hammering, hammering, boarding up shops, nailing down windows, barring doors, trying to seal themselves up against the violence to come. The whole of Dairen pulsed with the sound.

The war years with their increasing and weakening privations were poor preparation for this climactic terror. Like most of the people, the Sisters had been hungry most of the time. They were cold in the harsh winters as the fuel supply gave out, enervated in the brief hot summers, and sick by turns. Sister Sabina had begun to hemorrhage from the lungs, Sister Rose Ann was sometimes bedridden with a crippling arthritis. Nevertheless, for nearly four years, the five of them had managed to keep the school running and to continue part of the work of the other two Dairen missions which had been left unstaffed.

Sometimes when the convent could not even be maintained at zero, a minimal standard, and the food supply was particularly low, Sister Marie Elise would remind herself that Mother Mary Joseph had never made heavy weather over suffering herself and that she was happy when her Sisters took hardships light-heartedly too. Just the same, she was glad that Mother could not know how distractingly hungry they were.

Occasionally she even had little mental conversations with Mother, not entirely unlike the ones that she was continually engaged in with the Mother of God.

"We are busy," she would say, "and that's good, Mother. Having so many others to think about is the best thing in the world for us. So don't worry. Blessed Mother will take care of us. She always does."

With the others, she had longed for peace, prayed for peace and now, as she waited with her four Sisters through the long August night, she had many things to say to Blessed Mother about the kind of peace that had come to Manchuria.

At last, as the darkness waned, the Sisters heard what thou-

sands of hidden people like themselves awaited and dreaded—
the distant metallic thunder of the Russian tanks headed for
the center of the city along the broad avenue of Yamagata-dori.
The sound grew and swelled until it finally burst into a violent
and prolonged crescendo as the tanks began to pass the inter-
section less than a block away. Outside in the street, no human
voice rang out in exultation or despair. There was no other
sound except that robot thunder. Only later did the shouting
and screaming and shooting begin.

With full daylight the Chinese *boy* of all work was the first
to dare the streets. Only a fortnight before he had been bubbling with joy and malice after the Emperor of Japan had made
his surrender broadcast.

"The Emperor surrenders!" he had exclaimed to Korean Sister Margaret. "Good! Now we kill all the Japanese!"

Not convinced that the Japanese broadcast from Mukden had
given a true picture of his allies, he went out into the city to
have a look at them. When he came back, his eyes were blazing
with fear and rage.

"Nobody go out! Nobody!" he cried. "They are dogs. Dogs!
Dogs! Dogs!"

Almost at once a trickle of women started to arrive at the
convent. Knowing that the United States and Russia were allies,
they hoped that the convent, as the property of an American
society, might be left alone. Some came by day dressed in men's
clothes with cigarettes dangling from the corner of their mouths.
Some hurried in at dusk. Even the few who had a husband or
father still at home were as unprotected as the others. Against
several pistol-carrying soldiers, what could one unarmed man
do except die?

In the nights that followed, about thirty women would bed
down on the convent floor while the Sisters took turns on watch.
Among these women were two lovely young Mohammedan girls
for whom the Russians were searching high and low. Whatever

the cause, whether the unusual comings and goings were noticed, whether the two Mohammedan girls were traced as far as the convent after they had been passed along to a safer refuge, whether a new policy began to trickle down from the higher military echelons—the Sisters never knew; but just when conditions started to turn a shade less terrible for other people, they worsened for them.

As autumn came they had reopened the school at Nanzan, about a half hour's walk from the convent on Chitose Cho. Daily an escort of fifteen or twenty big boys—Japanese, Chinese, and White Russians—accompanied the Sister-teachers and the older girl students to and from school. Once at school, all seemed comparatively safe. Occasionally Sister Sabina and Sister Marie Elise were harassed by Russian officers who came seeking big boys to work for them or who wanted to know if all those girls who claimed students' exemptions from serving in the soldiers' canteen were really still in high school. Weren't they past high school age? Yes, but they were taking a business course; their names were registered; they were at class right now studying bookkeeping with an excellent male instructor.

Back at the convent at the end of a long day, the Sisters knew little ease. Days might pass, weeks even, when no soldier rang the doorbell or tried to break in through the windows, but no one could tell when the next attempt might be made. Someone was always on watch at night. No one undressed. Many times the Sisters did not go to bed at all, but spent the long hours locked up in the dark church, stretched out cold and sleepless on the floor of the sacristy or kneeling and sitting before the Blessed Sacrament, pouring out their anxious hearts to their Lord.

The front door was never opened before first looking out to see who stood waiting there; but one day a woman of the household thought that she recognized a familiar outline—one of Sisters' unofficial bodyguards. She opened the door. A Russian officer walked in. He was drunk. He could speak neither English nor Japanese, but he was well able to walk and to gesture with his pistol.

He herded the three women whom he found on the first floor to the stairs and motioned them to go up. At that moment Sister Marie Elise came to the stairhead. Looking down, she saw the terrible little procession coming toward her, the women starting up numbly with white stricken faces, the soldier behind them with his pistol in his hand.

The only possible help lay behind and beyond him—out the front door or by telephone. She had to try. She started down the steps. The women drew aside a little. The soldier blocked the way. She shook her head. Angry, unintelligible words burst from his lips. They looked at one another.

Seeing that she did not give way, the officer lifted his pistol and wagged it at her. She had no reason to think the gesture a bluff. She had seen other women die on the streets for as little resistance.

All the same, I have to try, she told herself. She felt a sudden lift of heart. I never dreamed it would be so easy to die. I've always been such a coward. She started to take another step forward and the officer steadied his pistol on her.

Suddenly above her, a soft voice called down, "Sister! Sister Marie Elise!"

She turned. Standing at the head of the stairs, gentle Japanese Sister Sabina bent toward her and said in unruffled accents, "Do not die yet, please. Two gentlemen are up here in the library to inquire about enrolling their children in the school. Bring the officer this way."

Not understanding, the officer interpreted the soft tones as compliance, slipped his pistol into its holster, and followed the little parade up the steps after Sister Marie Elise. Everybody trooped after her into the first room at the top of the stairs. The surprised Russian found himself in a small library faced by two indignant men, one a Czechoslovakian, the other a Chinese.

He explained to them that he had lost his way and come into the wrong house. He could not make these stupid women understand. He found that the men also misunderstood him. He went away furious, silent, and nearly sober.

When the two men had also left, Sister Sabina and Sister Marie Elise turned to each other.

"He was in such a rage. He'll be back."

"This mentality I do not understand," said Sister Sabina, who had always known how to win the Japanese military to act their punctilious best. "But I think yes, he will be back."

In time, the multiplying harassments and threats, the restrictions and confiscations that made their work impossible—and yes, the coming back—drove the Sisters to leave. They managed to reach Shanghai, and there they hid until they could board an outbound ship. Already in Shanghai, too, they felt the hand of Communism closing in upon reactionaries and imperialists like themselves.

The sensation of being hunted followed Sister Marie Elise back to the United States and was not obliterated when on a station platform in Los Angeles a man whom she had never seen before came up to her and asked, "Do you speak Russian?" Frightened, as only an escapee can be, she answered, "No, no, I don't speak Russian." Only then she realized that he had addressed her in Russian.

She never saw him again and she was soon at home with her Maryknoll family. In that atmosphere the fearful shadows of the past years began to fade, especially when at last she had the comfort of telling Mother face to face what it was like when peace came to Dairen.

Having covered Manchuria, a large area of North China, and half of Korea, the Red tide continued to spread, saturating

North China and beginning to roll southward. It had crashed in upon the north in a wave of violence which was later tempered for a period simply for expediency's sake. In the south, for the most part, it would rise like a flooding backwater, subtly, slowly, but with equal power to destroy, to annihilate.

Beginning in 1948, the Maryknoll Sisters' center house in Kowloon was like a barometer of Communist progress in China. As the take-over in the north progressed, well-dressed refugees came to tell the Sisters of their disrupted and uncertain lives—families of Chinese nationalists in military and government service, European businessmen with Chinese wives and Eurasian children from threatened centers like Peking, Shanghai, Nanking. Then, too, from villages and remote country places, as well as from the cities, came foreign missioners, sometimes a lone priest, sometimes communities of men and of women; groups of Chinese clerics, monks, whole novitiates of young Chinese religious; and, as time went on, a multiplying stream of professional personnel from schools, hospitals, and other institutions.

However, throughout the forties, missioners, both veterans and neophytes, men and women, continued to go to their posts in the interior of South China. Travel in country China had never been easy. Now it had a few more complications. In areas where the issue had not been settled between the Nationalists and the Communists, there were troop movements and occasional battles: in twentieth-century South China, war was nothing new. In areas where the Communists had taken over but were not yet ready to show their hand, they set up a network of baggage inspections and custom duties: but *squeeze* was nothing new either. The Chinese people and the people who loved them and lived with them had learned to put up with inconveniences such as these.

As late as October of 1950, a year after the establishment of the Chinese People's Republic, with its capital at Peking, and

ten months after the last of Chiang Kai-shek's Nationalist troops
had withdrawn to Formosa, Bishop Ford was asking for more
missioners for his Kaying area. He wanted an immediate increase of five Maryknoll Sisters and, in the near future, an additional six.

Yet by the end of the same month, the pattern of his future
fate was being roughly sketched in the life of his colleague,
Maryknoll's Bishop Patrick Byrne, the Apostolic Delegate to
Korea.

Taken captive in Seoul by invading North Koreans in July,
Bishop Byrne was about to begin the culmination of his sufferings as their prisoner with a death march through the rugged
mountains of North Korea. With hundreds of other prisoners,
he was moved from one remote spot to another out of reach of
possible rescue by counterattacking American troops.

Toward the end of that forced flight, soldiers and civilians,
young American G.I.'s and South Korean R.O.K.'s, old French
priests and nuns, seasoned missioners in their prime like Columban Monsignor Quinlan, men and women of many nations
caught up in the Communist net for one reason or another—
pushed their slow way for a hundred miles along rutted mountain roads through lashing wind and snow. In thin and ragged
clothing, ill and dying with dysentery, beriberi, influenza and
pneumonia, they sometimes lay in the open on the bare ground
at night, sometimes were herded into barracks where they were
so closely packed that those who died in the dark continued to
stand among the living until the next morning.

Behind them this tragic procession left their dead: those who
succumbed to disease and cold and those who were shot because,
exhausted, they fell out of line. Bishop Byrne died of pneumonia
on the earthen floor of an open, unheated shack. He had his own
view of what was happening to him and managed to express it
to those who companioned him and were heavy of heart because
they could do nothing to alleviate his suffering.

"Next to grace of the priesthood, I look on it as the greatest privilege of my life to have been able to suffer with you for Christ."

It was many months before those at Maryknoll learned what had happened to him. Only in December of 1952 were Masses of requiem offered there for his soul.

In June of 1950, Sister Imelda had written to the Mother-house from Kowloon that Kweilin and Wuchow and Kaying all seemed peaceful, but that in Hingning some sentiment against the Church had become evident. That same month, in Toishan, officials of the new government had begun to bear down on Sacred Heart Hospital. The Maryknoll Sister Supervisor, Sister Dominic Marie, was told she must buy war bonds to the amount of $2500 in Hong Kong currency. When she bought only a fraction of that amount because she could not afford to purchase more, the hospital was suddenly surrounded by police, she was taken to the police station, questioned and lectured, and then released. In less than two weeks she was again threatened with punishment, this time for her failure to pay business taxes—although the hospital treated patients free of charge—and with failure to provide someone to clean the public streets. Maryknoll's Bishop Paschang, subject to increasing co-ercion himself, advised her not to do either, saying laughingly that she might end up by having to clean the streets herself.

That summer and fall, wherever Maryknollers—priests and Sisters both—had mission houses in Kwangsi and Kwangtung provinces, they felt the tightening pressure of government control and the hardening of official enmity. Inspections of mission compounds, schools, hospitals, clinics, rectories, convents, and personal baggage multiplied and were conducted with diminishing courtesy. Greater and greater demands were made on institutions for standards that could not be met, for taxes that could not be paid. Travel permits had to be secured for the most ordinary trips. Prohibitions increased. New regulations were put into effect without notice, and those who failed to observe them were sometimes threatened, sometimes fined, sometimes briefly jailed.

December was to be an important month all over South China. The Communists were now a year in the saddle and unopposed by any organized resistance. The ordinary people had been reassured by the orderly take-over and stimulated by an impressive show of power and purpose. They had been saturated with months of propaganda. The mammoth October 1 celebrations of the first anniversary of the Communist regime served as demonstrations of mass solidarity and helped to create the desired climate for the Communists' next giant step. The time was now ripe to weed out everything alien to their purposes—foreign influences, bourgeois tastes and standards, religious beliefs, practices, and allegiance.

Late in November the Kongmoon convent was overrun by Communists. The night before, at the rectory, Brother Albert was arrested and taken away. The Communist police told Sister Patricia, the Superior, that mission employees had reported on both Brother Albert and her. They were wicked. They were oppressors of the poor. They were both to be beheaded.

On December 2, soldiers arrived at the Novitiate for Chinese girls at Laofuheo, where there were two Maryknoll Sisters in charge. The soldiers went through the house, examining everything. As they pawed over Sister Marcelline's personal things, they dropped some bullets among them and then, with shouts of indignation, discovered them. They demanded that Sister Marcelline turn over the gun that obviously must go with the bullets. When she was unable to produce a gun, she and Sister Paul Therese were arrested and, together with them, the mission pastor, Maryknoll's Father Bogaard, and eight of the mission employees. Under guard, through the long afternoon and into the night, they were all marched twenty-four miles to prison at Laolung. Thus was the mission at Laofuheo canceled out.

At Wuchow, the same technique was used to discover that Sister Rosalia was in possession of opium. The other Sisters were kept under house arrest, but she was taken off alone to prison. This singling out of one person as a scapegoat and a possible tool was repeated elsewhere. The more prominent the person, the more beloved by the people, the greater was their potential to weaken the influence of the Church and to warn the Chinese what it meant to be an enemy of the new regime.

As Christmas neared, few priests and Sisters were not either under house arrest or in prison. On the twenty-third, Communist police took over Bishop Ford's house in Kaying. There he was isolated and interrogated for hours, for days. His files were ransacked in an effort to find material that would serve to label him as a foreign agent. At the same time, all the Sisters at the Kaying mission except one were placed under house arrest in their own convent. Sister Joan Marie had done secretarial work for the Bishop. She might prove useful in the process of discrediting him. She was locked up alone in a little shed on the grounds.

Word of these widespread and continuing arrests began to reach Kowloon and then the Motherhouse. Sometimes the news came immediately in cryptic telegrams, such as "Kettl same Albert Moira"—Sister Moira saying that Sister Rosalia as well as Brother Albert had been arrested. Sometimes it came by word of mouth weeks or months after the arrests had taken place. News of what had happened to Bishop Ford and Sister Joan Marie in December reached Kowloon only in the middle of February, 1951.

Sometimes, surprisingly, a written message came through, guardedly relating a few facts. A letter from Sister Ignatia, then at Ng Fa, was a revelation of what she was able to do for the sorely pressed Sisters at neighboring Hingning even when she herself was under house arrest.

"Sister Paulita is sick and very thin . . . am planning to send vitamin pills and food . . . also have asked a reliable Catholic to come for some Bread for them. It is hard to trust this Nourishment to a carrier, so we must wait for a Christopher. . . ."

The dismaying news continued to come in for months, but even in December, Mother Mary Joseph had already learned enough to know that her Sisters were to have much to endure. In one of the few statements which she ever made about her own feelings concerning their dangers and sufferings, she said at this time, "I thought that when we went through the last dreadful siege of internment for our Sisters in the Philippines, in China, in Manchuria, wherever they were, that my heart could never bleed again as it did during those months, even years, of anxiety. And yet today we find ourselves even more cruelly upset, more tortured, by the thought of what is happening to our dear ones."

Once in prison, the Sisters experienced in varying degrees the techniques by which the Communists undertake to change the mind and bend the will of the nonconformist.

Dirt and discomfort; unmitigated heat and cold; physical weakness induced by undernourishment and loss of sleep and the lethargy and confusion of mind that result; a complete and continuous lack of privacy; the constant pressure of conforming cellmates bribed with the promise of lesser punishment if they bring others to conform; hours of loud and repetitious mass indoctrination; sessions of public criticism and self-criticism; private interrogations by day and by night; demands for written confessions; insistence that every autobiographical fact, every opinon, every emotion, every mental reservation, be revealed; reiterated accusations of bad faith, of guilt; all these were employed on the so-called reactionary. The Sister was a foreigner, she was bourgeois, she was religious: her influence with the people had to be canceled out. She had to be made an object of contempt and hatred and, if possible, ideologically remolded as well.

The process of cleansing the mind, as the Communists called it, she resisted with all the resources provided by her faith and her own personality—courage, patience and prayer, the grace of God, and the knowledge that her endurance was part of the Church's treasure and of the world's salvation.

Sometimes, at the extreme of bodily exhaustion and mental fatigue, no longer able to reason or to pray except in one-word exclamations, she defended herself by using the Communists' own technique of mindless repetition.

"I am right . . . you are wrong. . . . I am right . . . you are wrong. . . . I am right . . . right . . . right . . ."

It was on this ultimate outpost of human will that Sister Rosalia took her stand and held out through months of unrelenting pressure.

Even in prison the Sisters sometimes found an opportunity to do something for others and helped to care for the babies of women prisoners, to amuse and teach their small children, and to comfort and cheer, as well as they could, women who had lost everything.

The gift and habit of laughter came to their rescue, too. One threesome, deprived of their habits and dressed in Chinese *sa'am* and *fu,* looked at one another, laughed, and agreed that it was just as well that they were on slim rations.

The Chinese village women who shared the prison cell with Sister Colombiere were fascinated by her complexion, fair and with still a faint touch of rose, but they were completely captivated by her teeth. They were beautiful—they were detachable—and, therefore, more practical and convenient than any teeth they had ever seen before.

Sister Colombiere chuckled. "Do you mean to say that you have never learned to take yours out?" she asked. "Why, it's very simple. You just get hold of them so and give them a little special twist and out they come." She demonstrated.

The women did their best to imitate her, but no matter how hard they tried, they could not get the knack of it.

"You're not really trying," said Sister Colombiere, encouraging them. They never managed to succeed. Whether they got the joke or not, they did not let on. A little fun was too scarce and precious a commodity to be wasted.

"House arrest" sounds less rigorous than imprisonment, but it can be made equally punishing, as some of the priests and Sisters were made to learn. Complete isolation alternating with sudden, wholesale invasions of privacy by police, soldiers, and young Communist zealots, the necessity to feed and clothe themselves with all their provisions locked up and their funds frozen, the feeling of growing alienation from townspeople, China, the world: these were part of a skillfully planned pattern. That it was crudely administered only added to its effectiveness.

By the spring of 1951 no Maryknoll priest or Sister moved freely in the two provinces. Some were in prison or under house arrest; others had been sentenced and expelled; some, advised by their Bishops to do so, had asked for exit visas and were on their way out. Not only were they no longer of any use to the Chinese: they had become a hazard to them. The next stage of the Communists' program, the nationalization of the Church, was under way. Fewer and fewer Chinese dared to speak to a foreign priest or Sister, to smile at them, to recognize them. In time, it became dangerous even to look at a foreigner with compassion or interest.

Mother Mary Columba was away from the Motherhouse that year visiting the Maryknoll Sisters throughout the world who could be reached. Meanwhile, at Maryknoll, Mother Mary Joseph was not simply waiting dejectedly for the bad news that continued to come in. She was active, involved in all that concerned the Sisters and the work of the community. With the Mother General away, she was particularly in demand by the many visitors who came to Maryknoll for one reason or another —"old girls" from schools around the world, government officials and educators from Latin America, prelates from many countries. From the requests of these Bishops, she could be assured that there would be no dearth of opportunities for Maryknoll Sisters in any foreseeable future. As the door to China was closing, others were opening in the Marshall Islands and in South and Central America. There were new opportunities, too, in places where missions were already established—Africa, the Philippines, Japan.

Recently, when she felt the need or was advised to do so, Mother periodically made use of a wheel chair to cover the long distances in the big Motherhouse. That way she could be with the rest of the household at prayers and at meals and was more easily available to people who wanted to see her—whether guests in the front parlors or Sisters sick in the infirmary.

Sister Cabrini was appointed her chauffeur. She had been one of the first group of postulants at the Valley Park Novitiate and knew Mother well. She was delighted to have a chance to be with her again. However, she reported for her new duty apologetically, saying, "Mother, I am the world's worst for the job. Since earliest childhood I've never seemed to be able to guide any moving vehicle—doll buggy, tricycle, or anything else."

"Oh, fate," said Mother, laughing. "We'll manage. You push and I'll guide."

They sailed through the long ambulatory, made a smart left turn into the back of the chapel, resumed speed, and crashed into the holy water font. It rocked back and forth and splashed Mother with holy water.

She blessed herself with some and remarked, "Stopping for holy water was to have come in the second lesson."

Thereafter when her chauffeur would appear at her door with

the wheel chair and look at her with an apologetic expression, Mother would greet her with a cheerful, "The chariot of Elias and the driver thereof!"

The wheel chair was not sufficient concession to the disabilities which plagued her—the high blood pressure and fibrillating heart, the nagging diabetes.

In late March of the same year Sister Carol, then infirmarian at the Motherhouse, wrote to Mother Mary Columba, who was at that time in the Hawaiian Islands:

> I want to tell you about Mother Mary Joseph. She isn't feeling very well for the past week. On Monday, when I gave her the insulin after Mass, I got the impression she wasn't her dear old self. She was very quiet with that "far-away" sense about her. She didn't mention that she wasn't feeling well, so I didn't press the point. However, she went to the city that day for some good reason or other. In the evening . . . I made the pretense of reporting on Sister Aloysius [ill with pneumonia] then I asked her how she was feeling. She said that she had a very peculiar feeling all day and one that she had never had before. She wasn't dizzy, but had the sensation of unbalance, couldn't articulate as she wished to and couldn't think straight. This of course alarmed me because my first thought was cerebral spasm with the possibility of a stroke. I told her I would like to call Dr. D'Esopo in the morning and have him check her. She agreed readily. . . .
>
> She looks more rested today and hasn't the previous symptoms. I think we caught it in time and perhaps prevented a stroke by increasing the medicine and making her rest. . . .
>
> We are anxious to get some good news on Sister Rosalia. . . . I know Mother has been very worried about the Sisters and the present situation in China. She tries not to show it but it is there just the same. I think it has been a big factor in this present condition.

For a while there was little news that would lighten the heart, but a trickle of released missioners began to come over the border into Hong Kong that spring. Subsequently, through the summer and fall and into the winter, South China emptied itself of missioners. Even with this tragic ending to many bright hopes, to know that the Sisters were alive, that they were free, was reason to be glad.

As the months went on, those who came across the border showed increasing signs of what they had borne. Of the first to arrive, Sister Imelda had written, "They are solid as rocks."

Then she and the other Sisters who met the refugees as they reached Kowloon had other things to say.

"She was so thin that I would not have known her."

"She looked years older, bent, and needing a cane."

"Our hearts sank when we saw them, but it is amazing what a bath, a good supper, and a Maryknoll outfit will do for a person. By bedtime, after listening to some of their funny stories, we began to think that they looked ten years younger than when they arrived."

"We did not ask them too many questions, but learned enough."

Some needed to talk. Some wanted to say nothing.

As the number of Maryknollers expelled from South China grew, Mother became increasingly aware of those few who remained behind—especially Bishop Ford and Sister Joan Marie. She could appreciate the importance which the Communists would attach to breaking the influence of a man who had loved the Chinese unto folly, as Christ had loved mankind. While her Sisters at Maryknoll were concerned for her in the spring of 1951, she was thinking especially of these two, praying for them, waiting and hoping to hear some scrap of encouraging news about them.

It was well that she did not learn just then how they were faring. Those who remained in China stayed only to suffer that much longer, that much more.

For Bishop Ford and for Sister Joan Marie, too, because of her association with him through keeping the mission books and doing his typing, their rejection by the people had to be made not only punishing, but public and dramatic.

After months of harassment, they were condemned at a public trial in Kaying on April 14, 1951. They then set out under guard for imprisonment in distant Canton. Weeks of propaganda had preceded them. Giant demonstrations were arranged en route to testify to the mass condemnation of these two spies, these imperialists, these enemies of the people.

In Kaying itself the demonstration lacked robustness. People did not seem to put their hearts into it. Bishop Ford had lived there a long time. Many Chinese knew him, his serene and level look, his slow but ready smile, his skill with their language, his use of the best of their manners and customs, his open door and open heart.

On the other hand in Hingning, which had early responded with some readiness to Communist propaganda, he was a stranger, his only introduction the printed vilification and vocal rabble-rousing that had gone before him.

As the bus carrying the two prisoners and their guards drew into the outskirts of Hingning and stopped, a deep murmur, a pervasive hum, filled the ear. It sounded like the throb of some great engine, the roar of some huge furnace. It was the voice of the crowds already clogging the streets, already alerted and waiting for them to be paraded through the city.

In Sister Joan Marie's home town of New York a parade meant sights that shone, sounds that danced, feelings that took wing. It meant the huge colorful caterpillar of the circus with painted wagons, soft-stepping elephants and swivel-headed clowns. It meant columns of Hibernians stepping out along Fifth Avenue on a windy March 17. It meant a whooping, waving, whistling welcome to some returned hero, some darling notable, who rode bareheaded sitting on top of an open car drowned in ticker tape and cheers.

How different were the parades of South China that year.

They had been standardized. They came in two kinds, both fashioned by experts. First of all, there were parades designed as mighty demonstrations of loyalty and conformity to the new order. Through these marching, singing, swinging, and apparently identical thousands, a man learned how comfortable, how safe, how intoxicating it is to be one of the herd, submerged and hidden in the whole. Secondly, there were the parades contrived as communal acts of rejection, the stark and simple processing of a scapegoat. Through these exhibits, a man was taught how unutterably lonely and desolate and untenable is the position of one set aside from the herd—the deviationist, the nonconformist.

In Hingning, the guards got off the bus and conferred with some rock-faced officials waiting with final instructions. Some boys, too impatient to wait with the rest of the city, gathered around the bus, gesticulating and screaming at the two prisoners inside.

A guard gestured to the foreigners. Everything was ready. It was time for the parading of the scapegoat. No one offered to help Bishop Ford. Earlier, at Kaying, one of the soldiers, a fresh-faced boy, had leaned over and caught up his bundle—a few clothes, a few books wrapped in a quilt.

"Put that down," said an older man. "He carries his own pack."

Now Sister Joan Marie asked, "Let me take it? My hands are free. How can the Bishop carry it with his hands tied behind him?"

"He carries his. You carry yours."

The Bishop leaned forward slightly. The single rope that encircled his neck went down his back and bound his wrists, tightened, jerking up his head. Somebody hoisted the pack to his back. His bound hands moved up to give it support and he straightened a little and followed the guards off the bus.

Picking up her own bundle, Sister Joan Marie got out after

him. The guards fell into line on either side of them and the little procession set its face toward the police station. The aroused city moved forward to meet it. A great wave of shouting and screaming broke over the small column as it advanced into the crowd. The prisoners, their guards, seemed to submerge into an ocean of pushing bodies, thrusting faces, clenched fists, and open mouths. Paper banners of denunciation shook in the wind of hatred, and a few stones, a little filth flew, the first drops of the torrent to come.

The guards, who had once seemed so threatening, now became transformed into the prisoners' sole security against the inhuman menace of the mob. The chanted slogans, the screamed stereotyped insults, left them unscathed; but as the middle school boys pressed upon them like small furies, striking out with bamboo poles and hurling stones, garbage and excrement, the guards first grumbled and shouted with anger and then began to look afraid. They would not dare to fire on people taking part in an official demonstration. In such hysteria, who in the mob would care whether a few guards got killed or not?

The Bishop's tired arms gave a little, the pack slipped lower on his back and the rope tightened around his neck, pulling his head back and leaving his face defenseless. He walked on somehow, as steadily as he could, taking the blows as they came. A boy reached out and thrust a bamboo pole between his legs. He fell heavily then, unable to brake his fall or to get up alone. The guards got him to his feet, put his pack upon him once more, and the crumpled procession pushed forward. Howling men and boys broke through the line to strike the Bishop and to wrench away Sister Joan Marie's veil, beating guards and guarded indiscriminately.

Then, within sight of the police station, the soldiers were suddenly gone. With battered faces, filth-covered uniforms, and the wisdom of survival, they were gone, to live and guard another day.

Now it was time for the Bishop to run, for the scapegoat to be chased, to show himself a comedian and a coward as well as a villain. The clogged street opened up a little to give him room to perform, to be seen. He did not run but moved ahead at the same dogged patient pace and Sister Joan Marie followed him, shielded somewhat by his slight body. They had not far to go, but it was a nightmare distance, and they reached the door of the police station like spent swimmers crawling ashore. The breakers of wrath and hatred broke over their backs to the last.

Police officials came forward to claim them. One more parade had been completed. Others still awaited them at Waichow, at Chung Muk Tau. And finally there was Canton ahead.

Bishop Ford could scarcely speak. "They don't know what they are doing," he managed to say. "They are only following orders."

The words had a familiar ring.

There might be many happenings, known or feared, to sadden the heart in the years of the Communist take-over in China, but life was by no means all grief for Maryknollers or for Mother. To Maryknoll's big family came continued opportunities for heartening accomplishment in other areas and many joys, too, to share with one another.

One of these was Mother's return to her old alma mater. In June of 1950 she was invited to go to Smith College on the forty-fifth anniversary of her graduation to receive an honorary degree. She had been invited ten years earlier but could not at that time accept the invitation. Now she was happy to be able to say yes. Meanwhile, first Regis and then Trinity College had accorded her like honors, which she had received with simple gratitude as a tribute to the movement and work which she represented and as evidence of the goodness of those who gave them.

Telling the Sisters about the ceremony at Regis College in

June, 1945, she said of the degree given her, "It was as much yours as mine, and everyone felt it was the Maryknoll Sisterhood that was being honored—not an individual. It made me very happy."

She was happy, too, to accept the degree of Doctor of Humane Letters from Smith, and for many reasons: to meet again associates of her college years, with many of whom she had maintained not only friendship but communication; to have the College itself express in this way its appreciation of spiritual and Christian values; and, on her part, by accepting the degree, to acknowledge the providential role which Smith had played in the genesis of her own vocation. Whether this vocation had developed in an ordinary and understandable way was for Mother beside the point. It was a case of undeniable fact: the influence and inspiration of Protestant students and teachers at Smith had led her to Father Walsh, and Father Walsh had led her to Maryknoll. The affection and gratitude which she felt for her old College was bound up with that.

When during the still familiar pageantry of June Week the citation was read and Mother moved forward to receive the degree, many of her old friends were there to congratulate her. Among them was Miss Elizabeth Deering Hanscom. Her small body still active, her fine mind still incisive, she watched with bright blue eyes as the gold and white hood was laid over Mollie Rogers' arm. She was more than content with the part that she had played in the shaping of this day and all that it signified.

CHAPTER 11

AS ONE LAMP

IN THE LETTER which he composed to the Maryknoll Sisters just before he died, Maryknoll's Founder said, "It is a comforting thought that Mother Mary Joseph is being spared for your guidance and inspiration. May God keep her strong for many years to come!"

His prayer seemed to be answered. Although in the ensuing years Mother was more than once gravely ill, she made good recoveries and did not herself speak of dying until in December, 1950, when she made an oblique reference to it.

Expressing her gratitude to the Sisters for what they had done for her at Christmastime, she said, "May I thank you now for your gracious loveliness to me, your prayers, your gifts, your devotedness, all of which I cherish dearly. And may I in this New Year be allowed to love you, pray for you, and serve you yet a little while."

Many of the beloved companions who had once surrounded her were no longer at her side. Sister Philomena had gone striding ahead into eternity with giant steps of suffering. Sister Theophane was no more at hand ready to smile her twinkling smile and give timely support to the bruised reed and a gentle breath of encouragement to the smoking flax. If Sister Anna Maria was still saying "Mother and I," it was in heaven, where she might well already be planning what she and Mother would do together when Mother finally arrived. Many other old friends and companions, members of her family too, were gone.

But many too still remained, and among them, Harriet. The girl whose heart had gone out to Mollie Rogers at sight when they met as freshmen at Smith came back to her occasionally over the years through letters and in person. Warmhearted and much wounded, she was driven at times to some of those stratagems devised by the human heart to defend its deepest self— poses, fads, withdrawals.

In a letter written to Mother in 1930, she was able to say, even if she had to put it lightly, some of the feelings that she had been unable to express at all when she was younger.

Dear Mollie:
    I went back to Hamp for the reunion. It was my first return in a quarter of a century. I just made myself go back. I didn't want to go worth a cent. I had four such unhappy years at Smith that it never seemed possible I would willingly return.
    You will probably wonder why I say that you are responsible for my return. Well, you are, Old Dear. As I look back on those first days in Hamp, yours is the first face that I remember. You were such a comfortable person, such an understanding friend. On one of our walks down Elm Street, I yelled at the sight of some caterpillars. . . . You stopped short on the sidewalk and turning said to me, "Harriet, you should put your hand in a nest of caterpillars and let them crawl over your hand until you have broken yourself of this fear." . . . I gasped at the thought and I have never physically had the courage to touch a caterpillar, but I have taken your advice in a good many instances and spiritually flung myself into a nest of beasties. . . . My trip back to Northampton was an excursion of this sort. . . .
    Well, I had a glorious time and my one regret is that I did not see you. . . .

When I was twenty-eight I joined the Episcopal Church and at one time, Mollie, I seriously considered entering a Sisterhood. I was so tired of the storm and stress of the world (this being a mixed blood in America is not always a bed of roses). . . .

My love to you, dear, and if there is ever a chance of seeing you, please let me know.

Affectionately yours,
Harriet.

Nearly twenty-five years later, they were still communicating with each other. Mother wanted Harriet, who had been ill, to know the secret of her own peace and to share it with her to the full.

In January of 1954, she wrote to her old friend by hand, not an easy task for her anymore.

Dear Harriet—

I am wondering how you are and what you are doing. It is good to know that you will be youself again and no need to worry.

It is two years now since I was stricken. I had a very great grace at that time. I was in the car when the stroke came. Very unusual —it came gradually and as I felt my tongue sort of rolling up I said to the Sister beside me—"I think I am having a stroke." And at the same time I said to Our Lord, "I don't know what is happening to me but I not only accept it as Thy will—I wish to embrace it, no matter what it is." And ever since I have tried to love what He has sent me. It has made a very heavy cross light to carry and the days sweet instead of full of bitterness as they might have been. So sometimes when you are praying, thank Him for me, please.

I am improving all the time, came back from the hospital just before Christmas.

When you have a chance, write me about yourself.

Enclosed is the Pope's prayer for the Marian year. May Our Lady bless you!

Sister James sends greetings with mine. Love to you and your companions. God bless you.

Mollie

In the period between March 23, 1952, when she suffered a cerebral thrombosis and this handwritten letter of January, 1954, Mother had gone through a period of invalidism.

Paralyzed on her left side, her rich voice reduced to a broken, struggling whisper, she was completely bed-ridden at first. This illness, in itself critical, was complicated and made more painful by all her old complaints. Whether she would be able to make even a partial recovery was for some time in doubt.

In the first weeks, when she was almost entirely helpless and barely able to make herself understood, her tears came readily whenever the Sisters were allowed to slip in to see her briefly. She was astonished at herself. This was something new. The Sisters had never seen her weep before. She did not want them to be saddened or depressed by seeing her weep now.

"Tears don't mean a thing," she would whisper. "Am just an old softie."

In a note written for her feast day in April, the first note that she managed to sign by hand, she took pains to reassure everybody on this point.

"I had hoped to be able to greet you all, but that is out of the question, as I have no control over my emotions, and you might interpret my tears of joy as unhappiness! (I never thought I'd get the 'gift of tears'!) I am very content and am being most wonderfully taken care of by our nurses.

"I can never find words in which to thank you for all you have done for me by way of prayers and other offerings during these days of my illness. You have all been remembered and I hope some special graces will come to you."

As she regained some strength, she set herself to the long task of rehabilitation, determined to walk again, to recover as much motion and usefulness as possible. She was ready to follow the exacting routine and often exhausting exercises which this demanded. There was nothing grim about her determination, however, and whether she was in her room at the Motherhouse or at the hospital, an atmosphere of good cheer, of normality, of optimism, surrounded her. Sometimes it seemed as if she and her nurses were simply holidaying together.

During an earlier illness when the Sisters were anxious about her, she had written to them to tell them quite frankly of her condition, concluding by saying, "I thought you would like to know about the 'hair shirts' Our Lord sends to one who is not given to much penance of her own choosing, but prays for the grace to lovingly and cheerfully embrace those God sends."

That attitude was more marked than ever now, so much so as to have become a kind of second nature.

Some of the younger Sister-nurses assigned to take care of her went to the task convinced that they had a real privilege but a nerve-racking responsibility as well.

However changed Mother might be physically, her outgoing, motherly nature was just the same, and she put her nurses at ease without seeming to try. She was not only one of the best patients that they had ever had but one of the most interesting.

The first time one nurse was on duty in the early days of Mother's illness when any recovery still remained problematical, Mother asked her just one question all day.

"How do you make glass?"

"Glass?" echoed the nurse. "That's a good question. Are you going to make some, Mother?"

They both laughed.

"No," said Mother, "I'm not, but I just can't remember how it's done."

The Vicar for Religious, Monsignor Joseph Nelson, gave permission for her to have Mass said in her room. There was space for half a dozen others and little notes went out to the Sisters in turn inviting them to fill these places. When possible, the notes would coincide with their feasts or some other special occasion—such as their arrival home from the missions or their imminent departure. After Mass, each would go to her bedside for a greeting, a kiss. She would ask for their families by name, be aware of anything that particularly concerned them and refer to it. Sometimes, when their families were visiting, they too were invited to come.

A few Sisters had brothers who were priests and these were sometimes the celebrants of the Mass.

One Sister who had just returned on decennial leave from the Far East, had a priest brother who had grown up and been ordained while she was away. She was so overcome by the occasion that when she went to greet Mother after her brother's Mass she could only say, "Oh, Mother—" and struggle to hold back the tears.

Mother patted her hand. "Don't mind," she said. "I know just how you feel. That's the way I'm going to be when my nephew Gerry comes to say his first Mass."

In her illness, she kept the same apparently effortless courage that she had always had. No one expected her to be conservative, but even at that she would sometimes astonish people with what she would undertake.

For Christmas of 1952, the Sisters at the Motherhouse had made a new outdoor crib. Mother had seen some of the figures before they were placed and had heard a great deal about it, just where it was and how it looked when set up.

All this gave her an idea which she tried out half-jokingly on Mr. Potter, the engineer. At this time she had not yet managed to stand even with assistance and there was no possibility of getting her into a car.

"I'd like to see that crib," she said. "Do you think you and Joe could get me—in my wheel chair—into the truck and drive me there?"

It was January and very cold. The truck was open.

Mr. Potter digested the idea. "Well, sure," he agreed.

Once up the improvised board ramp and into the truck, Mother looked out of her blankets to say, "Now that we are out, we might just as well continue up the hill and see the Sisters at the Cloister."

They went. She was a sensation. The outing was a huge success. It was also a trial-run for later and longer excursions. When she had improved enough to be helped in and out of a car, she went as far as the Venard Convent in Pennsylvania and the new Novitiate at Topsfield, Massachusetts.

When she was at St. Vincent's Hospital for a rehabilitation program during November and part of December in 1954, the whole staff enjoyed working with her. She was always eager to begin the day, ready to try whatever was suggested, unafraid and trustful, unfailingly good-tempered.

One day she was on the elevator with her nurse and another Maryknoll Sister in training at St. Vincent's at the time. A very well-dressed woman got on and, looking at the three of them, said, "Oh, you're Maryknoll Sisters."

They admitted it.

"I used to know your order years and years ago," she went on. "Whatever happened to that great big—oh, she was a *very* big woman—who started the whole thing?"

A small silence fell. Mother did not let it lengthen. She could never bear to have anyone embarrassed.

She pointed to herself, smiling. "I'm it," she said. "Guilty on all counts."

During this rehabilitation program she had to be weighed daily. She could not, of course, stand on an ordinary scale and her nurse used to take her in her wheel chair to the kitchen commissary, where she would be weighed on the meat scale, one of the kitchen personnel assisting in the job. Mother and her nurse used to laugh together over the ignoble implications in this procedure.

Then one day Mother said, "Don't we pass the morgue on the way to the kitchen?"

"The morgue? Yes, I believe we do."

"I've always wanted to see the inside of a morgue," said Mother, "and never have. Let's go in."

They went in.

"There's the scale," said Mother. "All you have to do is roll the wheel chair on it. Then you can weigh it separately when I get back to bed. That will be much easier for you than helping that man get me on and off the other one."

"You're really the smartest Mother in the world," said her nurse in affectionate bewilderment. How did she know about that scale? she asked herself. And think of her planning to use it!

"Oh, no, I'm not," said Mother, laughing. "I was reading about the city morgue in my detective story last night. That's how the thought came to me."

At the hospital, Mother was just as aware of those around her as she was at home. She noticed that a priest who was also a wheel-chair patient looked shabby.

"He may not have any people still living," she said. "You must go out and buy him some shirts and pajamas."

A young religious hospitalized in a room near Mother's came to call on her. She stayed only about ten minutes, but when she left, Mother said, "I think Sister must be a community problem. We must be good to her." And she found ways to show her little attentions.

While Mother was at St. Vincent's, Sister Mary de Paul Cogan, who had been closely associated with her since the early twenties and who had always had a special place in her affections, died at the Motherhouse.

When told of this, Mother said nothing but sat silently for some time. Then she asked that arrangements be made for her to return to the Motherhouse for the funeral and took up again the book which she had been reading.

That evening Sister Rose Assunta ventured to express her sympathy. Mother had been with almost all her Sisters when they died. And yet, she had to be absent from the side of one who must have wanted her very much.

Mother said only, "Yes, she wanted me to be there and, had I known, I would have been. But I was where God wanted me and it doesn't matter now."

Because of her deep faith, losses such as these were not all sorrow. When the news reached her in September of 1952 that Sister Joan Marie had finally been released from prison in China but had brought with her the news of Bishop Ford's death, a rush of memories, of compassion and affection, of pride and sorrow and yet a certain joy filled Mother's mind and heart. Throughout her illness, all imprisoned missioners—but particularly these two—had been remembered in her sufferings, during the long wakeful nights and in the unnumbered rosaries which she said both alone and with Sister James.

Remembering Maryknoll's first seminarian with his boyish smile, the agile buoyant young missioner whom she had seen in all kinds of situations in South China, the handsome prelate who had been consecrated by Bishop James Anthony in the Motherhouse chapel, she found it hard to imagine the figure that Sister Joan Marie had glimpsed through a crack in a prison wall months after they had both been jailed in Canton. With hair and beard like cotton wool, emaciated and tottering, he had been unable to walk without the supporting arm of another prisoner. Yet, even in that extremity, his attitude and expression had conveyed an impression of peace. That indeed was recognizable.

In a letter to her Sisters dictated at this time, Mother referred first to the joy that all experienced at the news of Sister Joan Marie's release and then went on to speak at some length of Bishop Ford.

The sad news of Bishop Ford's passion and death dimmed our spirits, although we rejoiced that God had given him the necessary grace to go to the bitter end. It is appalling to think of his sufferings, but those of us who knew him well could easily picture how gladly he bore them all for Christ. I find myself going back to the early days: that first group of students had much manual labor to do, and were often asked to help us. But even outside of that, Bishop Ford was always on hand—on laundry days especially he would come over to help us; he helped us hang out clothes in wintry weather when the work was real suffering. And so it was with everything—we could always count on him.

In his work in China to which he gave himself so completely, he was like a Father to our Sisters. They co-operated perfectly, doing the work of the direct apostolate in which he directed them, gave them conferences and instructions, and fitted them for this type of mission activity. He and I had very much in common, and before this last trouble came for China, we found that we were in perfect accord about novitiates for the native Sisters. I hope we are still going to carry out his ideas when peace comes again to China.

She ended this letter by saying, "The picture of Maryknoll-in-Heaven—isn't it a lovely one? It is not hard to die when one thinks of the family awaiting us."

In the face of her own poise and tranquillity, death and suffering seemed to lose much of their threat. Indeed many came to think that she and sorrow were strangers. She was not unaware of this.

One day during her illness, when she had recovered enough to sit in her chair and a nurse was straightening up her room, she said reflectively as though thinking aloud, "I don't know why everybody thinks I have had such an easy time all my life. I haven't."

Those who knew her well could have told her why people had come to that conclusion. It was difficult to learn that Mother had any troubles, especially those in which others were involved. All her life she had shielded people who brought her hardship and grief—not only those who loved her yet failed her in one way or another but also those who opposed or rejected her either in forthright or covert fashion.

It was an old habit with her. At Smith her classmates had become conscious of it during the year that she roomed with a girl who was, they thought, odd.

"How do you stand her?"

"You know she's queer, Mollie."

"She's different," Mollie would concede. "We're not all alike."

Through the years, the heaviest crosses that others laid upon her shoulders she shared with no one unless for one reason or another she had to do so. At one time she became so concerned over a problem that others had created for themselves and for her that she traveled to Cincinnati to consult Archbishop McNicholas about it. Sister Columba, then her Vicaress and always admitted so frankly into her confidence, accompanied her. Yet she could only draw inferences as to what Mother had gone so far to discuss with one in whom she placed great confidence.

A decade or so after this, the letter of someone who had done not a little to have Mother's fitness for office called into question was brought to her. It was an authentic but not a creditable revelation of the writer's character. By its nature, it would show how little trust could be put in the judgment of such a person. She might find it useful to have.

Mother took the letter into her hand. Her face saddened. She looked up and shook her head.

"I could never do that," she said and tore up the letter quietly and dropped the pieces in her waste basket.

If age, if the failures and cross-purposes of human beings, could not dry up the deep well of Mother's heart, neither could illness accomplish it. As soon as she was well enough, she let it be known that every Sister who arrived at the Motherhouse from another house or who left it for some mission was expected and welcome to come to see her. To her room, too, were invited the large groups of entering postulants. To most invalids such numbers of coltish young recruits would have been physically overwhelming, but Mother delighted to see all this new life pouring into her household to carry on its work and prayer. She was eager to be back with the community at prayers, at meals.

Her gratitude and affection overflowed on others as much as ever in whatever means and opportunities were still available to her. These might be only a look, a greeting, an invitation to come to see her, a small gift, one of her little notes.

To the novice who prepared her trays, she sent a feast day remembrance and a little note that read, "I pray the day will be a singularly happy one for you. I am most grateful for the lovely trays you prepare—I can appreciate the work and time involved. God bless and thank you for me!"

To Mr. Potter, who for many years had been the dependable engineer at the Motherhouse and had recently been a strong and ready arm to support her in her daily attempts to walk again, she sent a picnic case with a note to express what his faithful co-operation meant to her.

> This is for you. It comes as a token of the gratitude that is mine for all that you are to us, and for all that you do each and every day to insure our comfort and protection. I feel safe knowing that you are around—this has always been so; and seeing you "on the job" gives me the warm feeling that "All's Well!"
>
> . . . I am especially grateful for your kindness, and for all the thoughtful things you have done for me during this illness—we have come to depend upon your service as part of our very existence!

Spring had never seemed more beautiful at Maryknoll than in 1955. When the weather was good, Mother was out as much as possible. Wheeled here and there in her chair, she missed nothing. She had a way of putting out her good hand in a gesture that seemed to encompass and pay tribute to all nature— violets, daffodils, budding maples, evergreens, sky. "Perfectly beautiful!" she would say. "Lovely!"

She would sit watching the Sisters gardening, whether they planted or weeded. She was particularly interested in a section then being developed called "Sarto Garden" in honor of Pius X. To this she contributed a number of plants, including dozens of petunias, remarking, "They require so little attention and contribute so much—like the right kind of people."

As the summer wore on, those around her noticed that she seemed increasingly tired. And she had a new symptom which made them fearful. They, as well as she, had become used to many of the old ones which could have been frightening—the high blood pressure, the fibrillating heart, the difficulty that she often had in retaining food. But now at times she seemed preoccupied and almost uninterested in what was going on around her. This was unlike her. On several occasions she herself was aware that she had not been attentive.

In late August a Sister from another house came to see her and sat beside her in the Motherhouse court. The day was oppressively hot and the nurses had taken Mother there because it was the coolest spot that they could find. Mother greeted the Sister and then seemed to forget that she was there. Presently the Sister got up, said good-by to Mother, and went away. She was hardly gone when Mother sent her nurse after her to bring her back. She asked her then about herself, about her family, trying to make up for her apparent lack of interest.

On the third of October, she went to the Cloister and spent almost a half day there with the Sisters at Maryknoll's "coronal," as she liked to call it. That evening Lily Windsor came to sing at the Motherhouse. Mother was fond of Lily and enjoyed both her humor and her beautiful voice. She stayed for the whole program.

The next day, she took her regular period of adoration in the chapel from twelve-thirty to one-thirty in the afternoon. Gentle Sister John, one of the dwindling group who had been professed with Mother in 1921, wanted to see her. Learning this, Mother had the nurse take her to the infirmary, where Sister John was ill. They talked about Maryknoll's early days, about its growth, about the decree of praise which the Sisterhood had received from the Holy See the preceding December. They recalled together some of the joys, and some of the heartaches, too, that they had shared.

Back in her own room and encouraged to take a nap, Mother found it hard to settle down, wanted to change her position frequently.

In the evening, however, she seemed quite herself and received a brief visit from Cardinal Gracias of Bombay, India, together with Bishop Lane, then Father General of the Maryknoll Fathers, Monsignor Jeffers, and Father McCarthy.

Thursday morning she said that she had had the best night in many nights and was soon up in her favorite chair, reading her mail and the newspapers. That evening she was taken suddenly very ill. The next day she was no better, and during the following night alarming symptoms developed.

Very early Saturday morning arrangements were made to take her to St. Vincent's Hospital by ambulance. Before she left, Father David I. Walsh came over from the Seminary to anoint her and to give her a small portion of the Sacred Host.

She was very calm. "What time is it?" she wanted to know.

"It's nearly time for Prime. The Sisters will soon be praying for you."

"Good," she said.

When the men came to carry her to the ambulance, Mother did not want them to think that they had to be excessively careful with her.

"These Sisters," she said, smiling at the nurses, "move me around like a sack of potatoes."

On the way to the hospital she said to one of the Sisters with her in the ambulance, "Give them a tip. And more than enough for a cup of coffee."

Arriving at the hospital, she remembered that Sister Kevin, a

Maryknoll Sister, was there after having had some minor surgery.

"I'd like to go to see Sister Kevin," she said.

"Later, Mother, when you feel better."

During the morning it was decided that surgery should be attempted. With it, Mother might have a chance. She was taken to the operating room. To those awaiting word, time dragged, but in all too short a while Mother Mary Columba was called to come to the operating room. Standing outside, she needed only to see the faces of those who came out to know that there was no hope. The surgeon, Dr. Rousselot, expressed his sorrow and regret. There was generalized peritonitis, probably due to a mesenteric clot, although that could not be absolutely determined because of an almost completely gangrenous condition.

"I do not believe that she will last twelve hours, and I think it will run down faster than that."

When Mother Mary Columba was admitted into the operating room, she found Bishop Rada of Ecuador, a patient at the hospital, Father Gilson, S.J., and another priest already there. They were just finishing prayers for Mother, including the Apostolic Blessing.

Mother was fully conscious, having had block anesthesia. Mother Mary Columba went to her and put her hand on the arm that was tied to the intravenous board.

Mother looked up at her. "I'm fine. Everything will be all right."

After about an hour in the recovery room, she was taken back to her room. Both before and after the operation, young Dr. East, who assisted Dr. Rousselot, remarked that her subjective and even her objective symptoms did not seem reconcilable with her condition. She was alert, smiling, alive to the people around her, greeting them, thinking of their needs.

She made no reference to her own condition or her own feelings. It had been necessary to insert a Wangensteen tube in one nostril and a tube for oxygen supply in the other. Once in a while she would raise her free right hand to indicate that she would like to have these removed, but as soon as the nurse would say "Just a while longer, Mother," she would lower it.

As the day wore on, Mother Mary Columba said to her, "We are going to sing the *Salve* now, Mother."

How many times Mother herself had sung that softly by the bedside of a dying Maryknoll Sister. No one knew better than she what that sweet song of last appeal to Our Lady, "our life, our sweetness, and our hope," signified.

"Good," she said.

Saturday evening and Sunday morning a number of visitors came and went, Bishop Lane, Monsignor Nelson, Maryknoll Fathers and Sisters, Mother's own relatives. They did not disturb Mother. She had always been used to a big family, first at home and later at Maryknoll. As long as she was able, they all had the benefit of a word or two of greeting, her look, her smile.

Mother Mary Columba remained close to her bedside. Sister James was near at hand, saying one rosary after another. She and her Mollie had been much together since Mother's retirement from office. This close association would not make the imminent parting any easier. Not sure that Sister James, who was deaf, could hear her, Mother said to Mother Mary Columba, "Tell Sister James everything is going to be all right."

By Sunday afternoon, she found it hard to speak and when Doctor Sverdlik, the director of rehabilitation therapy, whom Mother admired and liked, came to take her hand, she made a great effort to say something to him and finally managed a halting, indistinct "How are you?"

He patted her hand and said, "I am fine, Mother. Don't try to talk. It's 'how are *you?*' Be quiet now and try to rest."

When Father Cotta, the Motherhouse chaplain, her friend and confessor and informal photographer for many years, arrived, he could hardly believe that she who had always admired his pictures and laughed at his jokes could be unconscious of his presence.

"She doesn't know that I am here," he said sorrowfully. "She doesn't know."

She did not turn anymore to look with recognition at those who came and went. She did not speak again.

It did not matter. What was left for her to say to those to whom her mind and heart had always been open, to whom she had spoken not only in words but in a thousand, thousand tellings which only love could devise?

To her Sisters, her Maryknoll daughters, she had already dispensed whatever of her inner treasure could be shared. She had shaped a way of life for them. They knew what she expected of them, prayed for them. They had entered into their inheritance during her lifetime. Whatever she had was theirs—from those quotations which she had loved and made her own, such as "Where there is love, there is no labor . . ." to her ideal of a Maryknoll Sister developed in full at their request. She had made them a family, more through her own capacity as their Mother than through any instruction. She had shared with them the beloved burden of her responsibilities as well as the recognition that sometimes came to her, and she had more than once reminded them that it was together that they had done something for God.

Only a short time ago, she had said it again. "People always say, 'Mother has done this. Mother has done that.' I could have done nothing without all of your co-operation. Maryknoll is a continuous project. If some of you have not a conspicuous place, it does not mean that you are not the actual builders."

She died shortly after five o'clock on Sunday, October 9, 1955, but as long as there is one Maryknoll Sister left in the world with a heart to love and a will to serve, her life will not be wholly at an end.

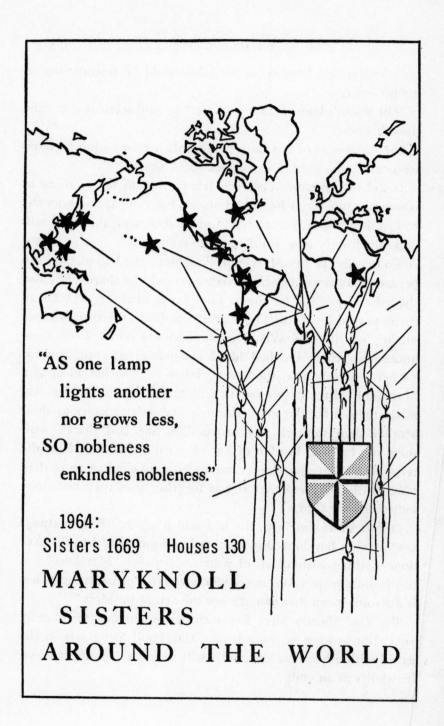

"AS one lamp
lights another
nor grows less,
SO nobleness
enkindles nobleness."

1964:
Sisters 1669   Houses 130
MARYKNOLL
SISTERS
AROUND THE WORLD

INDEX